The End of Tolerance

The End of Tolerance

Racism in 21st-Century Britain

ARUN KUNDNANI

Pluto Press

LONDON • ANN ARBOR, MI

First published 2007 by Pluto Press
345 Archway Road, London N6 5AA
and 839 Greene Street, Ann Arbor, MI 48106

www.plutobooks.com

British Library Cataloguing in Publication Data
A catalogue record for this book is available from the British Library

Hardback
ISBN-13   978 0 7453 2646 7
ISBN-10   0 7453 2646 3

Paperback
ISBN-13   978 0 7453 2645 0
ISBN-10   0 7453 2645 5

Library of Congress Cataloging in Publication Data applied for

10   9   8   7   6   5   4   3   2   1

Designed and produced for Pluto Press by
Chase Publishing Services Ltd, Fortescue, Sidmouth, EX10 9QG, England
Typeset from disk by Stanford DTP Services, Northampton
Printed and bound in the European Union by
CPI Antony Rowe Ltd, Chippenham and Eastbourne

Contents

Acknowledgements

This book would have been unimaginable without the unique political and intellectual environment that has been carved out and sustained at the Institute of Race Relations (IRR). Over the last decade, I have been fortunate enough to benefit from this 'surrogate university' and the political vision of its founder, A. Sivanandan. Most of the ideas for the book began life in articles written for the IRR's publications *Race & Class* and *IRR News*, and my colleagues there – including Harmit Athwal, Jenny Bourne, Liz Fekete, Hazel Waters and Rosie Wild – have contributed in immeasurable ways to every page of this book; I owe them a further debt of gratitude for allowing me time off to finish it.

A large number of other people have helped me to develop the ideas in the book, through discussions, talks or through reading sections of the text. Particular thanks are owed to Lee Bridges, David Edgar, Suresh Grover, Arzu Merali, Herman Ouseley, Colin Prescod, Jeremy Seabrook, Ghayasuddin Siddiqui, Frances Webber and Salma Yaqoob. Others who have contributed in important ways include Monica Hingorani, Dashty Jamal, Naina Patel and Deeder Zaman. The assistance I received while undertaking research in Bradford, Hull and Oldham is greatly appreciated. Those who accommodated me, sometimes literally, in those places are the real authors of this book. I would also like to thank all those involved in the Civil Rights Caravan of 2000, which provided the initial impetus for this project, and my editor at Pluto Press, David Castle.

My greatest debt is to Tanuka, without whose support, expertise, intellect and love this book would never have been written.

I would like to dedicate this book to my parents, whose sacrifices made it possible.

Foreword

A. Sivanandan

Racism is not an isolate. It is imbricated in the socio-economic structure and political culture of a society. And if it once functioned as a rationale for slavery, it today serves as a justification for imperialism. But the imperialism of industrial capital differs from the imperialism of information capital. Hence any analysis of twenty-first-century racism needs to be situated within the parameters of globalism and globalisation. Globalism, the latest stage of imperialism, holds western civilisation and values as superior to all others, and insists on visiting them on the rest of the world, by force if necessary. Globalisation, the process that underpins and advances that project, engenders a monolithic economic system which immiserates and displaces Third World populations and throws them up on the shores of Europe.

Against this background, the war on terror, following on from September 11th and July 7th, has created a populist anti-Muslim, anti-asylum culture, based on the politics of fear – which in turn has led to the erosion of civil liberties and the ushering in of a new state racism. And it is state racism, as Arun Kundnani argues, which through its laws, administrative edicts and judicial decisions fosters institutional racism and shapes popular racism.

But nowhere has such analyses been forthcoming: the academics, caught up in yesterday's mantras, are unable or loath to speak truth to power; the think-tanks speak to the New Labour agenda and the activist Left is still idealistically looking for a borderless world.

The End of Tolerance not only shows how the global fall-out has determined Britain's migration and asylum policy but how, more immediately, the war on terror, in demonising multiculturalism, seeks to put an end to Britain's proud record of integration and ally it instead to Europe's assimilationist policies in a descent into nativism. On another level, *The End of Tolerance* relates global forces and intellectual currents to personal experiences (by way of interviews) and their impact on families and communities. On all these levels – of analysis and narrative, of the empirical and the theoretical, the personal and the political – Kundnani follows in the grand tradition of the Institute of Race Relations' corpus of work that began with the pioneering study 'Race, Class and the State' in 1976. All future works on racism will have to begin where Kundnani has left off.

A. Sivanandan

Introduction

It is the moment of the boomerang ... it comes back on us, it strikes us, and we do not realize any more than we did the other times that it's we who have launched it. – Jean-Paul Sartre[1]

Officials at the United Nations speak of 'problems without passports'. European thinktanks write of 'identity and security' issues. Media commentators warn of the 'dark side of globalisation'. Under all these headings, what is being referred to is a cluster of issues to do with immigration, integration and terrorism that have, since the end of the Cold War, come to dominate the political landscape of the West, from Europe to the US to Australia. In all these countries, political leaders, policymakers and pundits ask themselves how 'abusive' asylum seekers and migrants can best be deterred; how minorities, particularly Muslims, whom they regard as being at odds with Western societies, can be integrated; and how Islamic terrorism, 'extremism' and 'radicalisation' can be prevented. These issues – commonly grouped together, albeit with differing emphases in different national contexts – are the new spectres haunting the West. The argument of this book is that what has united these various issues and brought them to the fore at the present time is their being symptoms of a deeper shift in global political geography: the fact that the great wells of human despair, rooted in poverty and powerlessness, can no longer be contained within national boundaries. The failure of Western societies to come to terms with this fact, and recognise in it an unintended consequence of the very brand of 'globalisation' that their governments have promoted is what lies behind the anxiety and fear that surrounds those the West defines as 'aliens', whether migrants, asylum seekers or 'Muslim extremists'. It is the moment of the boomerang.

The world can no longer be imagined, as it was half a century ago, divided into neatly separated nations, each a separate ship on the sea of humanity. According to the old model of national sovereignty, a state claimed responsibility for its own national ship but had no obligations to assist those on other vessels; nor were states generally entitled to intervene across the clear blue water that separated one nation from another. National sovereignty placed a wall of mutual non-obligation between 'us' and 'them'. Following the formal independence of the Third World from colonial rule, the poor and powerless of Africa and Asia looked to their own states to uplift them and rarely took their anger across national boundaries. But since the end of the Cold War, under the auspices of 'globalisation' and the 'war on terror', multinational corporations have assumed unfettered power over most of the world's national economies and Western governments have arrogated to themselves the right to openly intervene anywhere in the world. Globalisation spells the end of national sovereignty and, in its present guise, gives rise to a 'global' sovereignty in the hands of a few. But the more that the world becomes interconnected, the more glaring the contradiction that only certain interests have a say in its direction. The upshot is an inevitable resistance to the structures of power that are concentrated in the hands of Western states and corporations. Although that resistance takes many forms, ultimately it implies a demand for global citizenship.

Nowhere are these contradictions greater than in the Middle East, where millions are held in poverty by authoritarian regimes, which owe their continued existence to a willingness to acquiesce in the demands of US foreign policy. As 9/11 demonstrated, anger at such regimes no longer stops at national borders but reaches all the way to New York and Washington. Yet, in trying to make sense of global terrorism, Western governments do not comprehend their own role in creating a world of fundamental inequality and injustice; instead they must systematically deny that terrorism is a symptom of these facts. Terrorism is cast simply as an expression of a fanatical Islamic value system that is culturally at odds with the West. The idea of a cultural rather than a political antagonism, rooted in a 'clash of civilisations', as Samuel Huntington famously labelled it, provides a convenient explanation for why the end of the Cold War did not lead to Francis Fukuyama's much-vaunted 'end of history'.[2] A new global drama is invoked in which the West and 'Islamic extremism' are the only two characters and the only story-line is the inevitability of a violent conflict between two distinct value systems. On the one side is 'Islamic extremism' and its supposed envy and hatred of Western wealth and freedom. On the other side, the 'liberating forces' of the United States, Britain and their allies. There is no middle ground or overlap between the two. 'Terrorism' originates from the Islamic world with the West and its history contributing nothing to this process. The converse is true of freedom and democracy. Obviously, the full complexity of different societies and their relationships are trampled in the staging of this ideology. As Edward Said wrote in the 1990s:

[M]uch of what one reads and sees in the media about Islam represents the aggression as coming from Islam because that is what 'Islam' is. Local and concrete circumstances are thus obliterated. In other words, covering Islam is a one-sided activity that obscures what 'we' [Westerners] *do*, and highlights instead what Muslims and Arabs by their very flawed nature *are*.[3]

A similar approach is followed in trying to make sense of forced migration. The epic social upheavals associated with 'globalisation' have led to millions of people in Africa, Asia and the Middle East being forced to leave their homes as their existing livelihoods collapsed around them, or as a result of the warfare, ethnic conflict and political repression that were symptoms of a state's inability to manage a nation's 'integration' into the global market. These migrations have been exacerbated by the state terrorism, regime change and sponsored warfare that have been orchestrated, first in the name of the Cold War and, later, in the 'war on terror'. The 1951 Geneva Convention on Refugees had already implied the existence of a 'global' right of foreign nationals to claim asylum in any signatory state in order to escape persecution. By the 1980s, asylum seekers from Africa and Asia were beginning to exercise this right in Europe, and the struggle for personal security no longer restricted itself to the boundaries of one's own nation-state or refugee camps in neighbouring countries. Yet, when these migrants and asylum seekers wash up on the shores of Europe, they are demonised as a threat to the global economic hierarchy that divides 'our' wealth from 'their' poverty. In place of an understanding of what causes forced migration comes a farrago of aggressively promoted stereotypes that merely reflect the West's own anxieties. The media-manufactured stories of 'bogus asylum seekers', the comic-book stereotypes of foreign scroungers, 'illegals' and terrorists, and the fear that the West is being overrun by the 'Third World', therefore go hand in hand with a deadly silence on the West's actual role in Africa, Asia and the Middle East, and the ongoing devastation which that role inflicts. Indeed, the persistence of these stereotypes depends on hiding from view the reality of what asylum seekers are fleeing from. The system looks everywhere for explanations except within its own tangled and complex responsibilities. Of necessity, it turns to the demonisation of the 'alien' peoples whose shadows it fears. Poverty, violence and dependency are seen as what asylum seekers necessarily *are* rather than as symptoms of the crimes done to their countries. The intricate history of the West's exploitative ties to the rest of the world is erased by an army of commentators, pundits and so-called experts who construct the scaffold on which a myopic view of the non-Western world is constructed. The media then build on this framework, creating a wall of untruths between the West and the rest. In this entire edifice, there is no understanding of the underlying causes of disease, famine, corruption, 'tribalism', 'failed states' and terrorism in the 'developing world', for causes are redundant if these phenomena are represented as the defining characteristics of those places and those peoples, their 'heart of darkness', as if they carried a barbarism gene. All of which points to the fact that racisms are no longer domestically driven but take their impetus from the attempt to legitimise a deeply divided global order. They are the necessary products of an empire in denial. The inexorable logic of globalisation is a choice between global citizenship and global racism. It is the conflict between the two that will define the political struggles of the 21st century.

Of course, the exact path that each nation takes in its adoption of these new stigmatising discourses varies, but all converge on the same fears and insecurities. The United States government, for example, has recently stepped up attempts to criminalise Latin American migrant workers, emulating the anti-immigration campaigns that have become common in European countries since the end of the Cold War, despite the US's very different history as a country of immigration. With the paramilitary Minutemen who hunt down Latino migrants along the Mexican border, the US has its own variation on Europe's violent far-Right anti-immigrant groupings. In Europe itself, it has been through the icon of the 'asylum seeker', representing an image of impoverished immigrants coming to scrounge off European welfare states, that a new racism initially galvanised itself in the 1990s. 'Asylum seekers' (a phrase that has come to refer, in general, to the new underclass of unwanted foreigners) have come to form a convenient screen onto which can be projected fears and tensions thrown up by a changing global order. 'Asylum seekers' were transformed from a group claiming humanitarian protection into 'economic migrants', supposedly coming to benefit from European welfare states. A series of tough deterrence measures were introduced which, based as they were on myths about asylum-seeking, inevitably failed to solve the problem and instead turned the asylum issue into a national crisis in each EU country. Then asylum seekers became no more than illegal immigrants, threatening national sovereignty by crossing borders in vast numbers. Governments responded by tightening border controls, which, in turn, fuelled the rise of a criminal network of traffickers and made the problem look worse still. Finally, 9/11 made every asylum seeker into a potential terrorist and led to a fear that Europe was threatened by an alien culture that brought division and unrest. In Britain and the Netherlands, countries that, to varying degrees, had officially accepted cultural diversity, 'multiculturalism' came under attack as having fostered a dangerous separatism. In the name of 'integration', they now demanded that minorities, Muslims in particular, subsume themselves to a prescribed set of national values. In France and Germany, countries that had no history of multiculturalism of their own, any signs of cultural difference expressed by Muslim communities were interpreted as acts of anti-Western aggression and met by a series of state measures aimed at assimilation. Hence, France's ban on 'oversized religious symbols' in state schools was transparently directed at Islamic headscarves, while Muslims were singled out by the German state of Baden-Württemberg to undergo specially designed interviews to test potential citizens on their support for Germany's 'fundamental principles and values'.[4]

The subject of this book is the particular path that Britain has taken, over the last fifteen years, towards the consolidation of new anti-Muslim and anti-immigrant racisms. The significance of Britain as a case study lies not only in its unique history of anti-racist politics but also in the fact that the British state has gone further than any other in Europe in reconfiguring its structures around free market principles and dispensing with older notions of the welfare state. In addition, its role, since 9/11, as a leading partner in the neoconservative 'war on terror' means that the British state now sits squarely on the fault-line of a global conflict between the dispossessed and the centres of political, military and economic power. The roots of the new stigmatising discourses in Britain can be traced to the mythology surrounding asylum seekers that emerged in the 1990s. Newspapers and politicians blamed asylum seekers for the spread of TB, AIDS and SARS; for failing schools and hospitals; for falling house prices and for rising house prices; for low wages, rising crime, prostitution and road accidents. They were even to blame for the dwindling number of fish in Britain's rivers, the declining number of swans and the disappearance of donkeys.[5] In the short number of years they had been in Britain, they had not only achieved all this but also held on to a reputation for laziness. If asylum seekers did not already exist, they would have been invented. For, asylum seekers were not the problem but the solution: for a Conservative Party that wanted a short cut to popularity or for a Labour government that wanted to prove that it was still in tune with the raw instincts of the people; for newspapers that wanted an easy front-page story; for local authorities that wanted someone to blame for a shortage of council housing; for an economy that wanted cheap and docile workers. Thus, 'asylum seekers' came to be seen as responsible for the erosion of the welfare state, even though there would not be a welfare state without the immigrant workers who staffed it. The perceived loss of national sovereignty came to be regarded as somehow the fault of 'asylum seekers', even though they too were victims of 'globalisation'. And 'asylum seekers' were taken to be culturally inferior, having nothing to contribute to the world of political or cultural value.

The template of demonisation that had already been established in Britain against asylum seekers was transposed on to Muslims after 9/11. The riots in Oldham, Burnley and Bradford in the summer of 2001 had highlighted how the interaction of industrial decline with institutional racism in housing and employment created segregated communities in some areas. Yet, as soon as Britain had woken up to the fact that a generation had grown up living 'parallel lives',[6] this whole history was forgotten and, instead, it was Muslims who were blamed for refusing to mix. The problem of segregation was misdiagnosed as resulting from an 'excess' of cultural diversity. A new emphasis on Muslims having to declare their allegiance to 'core British values' in the name of 'integration' marked a decisive break with old thinking. Ever since Margaret Thatcher's comment in 1978, that the British people were worried that 'this country might be rather swamped by people with a different culture', those on the right of British politics have seen cultural diversity as a threat to national cohesion and security.[7] But from 2001 onwards, it was from the Left and from liberals that attacks on multiculturalism came most forcefully, seeing in it the cause of segregation in Britain. First, it was home secretary David Blunkett who blamed a supposed over-tolerance of cultural diversity for allowing Asians to 'self-segregate' in northern towns.[8] By 2004, there was a raft of liberal commentators, including Polly Toynbee of the *Guardian*, David Goodhart of *Prospect* and Trevor Phillips, chair of the Commission for Racial Equality, who had joined the voices arguing that multiculturalism allowed extremism to fester in British society and that a new emphasis on the integration of minorities was required.[9] Muslims were singled out as needing 'integration': it was their cultural difference that needed limits placed on it; it was they who had to subsume their cultural heritage within 'Britishness'; it was they who had to declare their allegiance to (ill-defined) British values. In so doing, an idea that Muslims are inherently at odds with modern values, into which they need to be forcibly integrated, was reinforced – exactly the same notion that runs through the 'war on terror' as conceived by Blair and Bush. But it is entirely dishonest to pretend this is a demand for 'integration', when what is really being called for is assimilation.

This bogus 'integrationism' was centred on New Labour and its fellow travellers but it soon became a new consensus across Britain's political elites – one that will undoubtedly survive the end of the Blair era. Much of the liberal Left shares in the damaging mythology that some kind of 'national story' of Britishness has to be created in order to promote 'community cohesion' and manage what are seen as cultural conflicts that emanate inevitably from a diverse society. In Gordon Brown's speech to the Fabian Society in January 2006, the active development by the state of a new sense of Britishness was made a centrepiece of Brown's politics.[10] Similarly, David Cameron's Conservative Party wants to promote a greater emphasis on pride in British history, identity and values and move away from multiculturalism.[11] The lynchpin of this new politics is the demand for a recharging of the batteries of national belonging, for the state to once again connect with the nation, for a return to a clear sense of 'them' and 'us' in the face of a world in which sovereignty has been increasingly globalised. But the state has so far chosen to bind itself to the people through fear rather than hope; through national security rather than social security; through the politics of a phoney Britishness rather than a genuine universalism. The result is a worsening climate of racism and division and an end to liberal tolerance of ethnic and religious diversity.[12]

At the same time as 'community cohesion' and 'integration' policies signalled the death of multiculturalism, 'managed migration' policies broke with earlier policies of zero immigration. 'Managed migration' meant carefully regulating the supply of migration into the country to produce, where necessary, a pool of disposable and easily exploitable migrant workers and, at the same time, to recruit skilled workers from abroad in those fields where shortages exist. It represents a new *modus operandi* of border controls that reduces immigration policy to market value and ranks potential migrants on their perceived assimilability to 'British values', while rejecting any claims based on rights, thereby rendering asylum seekers as valueless and rightless. Moreover, 'managed migration' policies demand a vast expansion in the powers of the state in order to regulate flows of migration and police access to services and jobs according to categories of entitlement. It is primarily in order to assist policies of managed migration that ID cards, and their associated systems of electronic surveillance, are being introduced in Britain.

From 2001 onwards, 'managed migration' together with 'community cohesion' formed a new model of race relations that replaced an old consensus forged in the late 1960s, of strong immigration controls aimed at ensuring zero immigration coupled with anti-discrimination legislation to integrate 'ethnic minorities'. It was in the 2002 White Paper *Secure Borders, Safe Haven: integration with diversity in modern Britain* that the new model received its clearest description.[13] In its foreword, David Blunkett outlined its core message: the tensions that flow from migration are best dealt with if there is 'confidence, security and trust' in 'our sense of belonging and identity'.[14] In order to create this secure national identity, it is necessary to have a sense of the shared values that make up Britishness; citizenship tests and oaths of allegiance would be introduced for those becoming British citizens in order to affirm these values. While these 'cohesion' measures were one half of the model, reassuring the public that its national identity remained secure, the other half sought to prop up public confidence in the proper management of the nation's borders. But the fear of perceived 'overseas' threats has not been diminished. Instead, it has been used to justify ever tighter border controls, internment without trial, new grounds for deportation and expulsion, restrictions on freedom of speech and virtual house arrests. The 'war on terror' has mirrored the 'war on asylum' in its systematic refusal to engage with the actual nature of what it claims to be fighting and, in its place, pursue a path of demonisation and actions that perversely aggravate the original 'threat' still further. In both cases, too, the whole process is wrapped up in a self-serving mythology that shields the state from criticism. What is emerging is a state that fuses absolute powers and absolute fear, in order to create absolute conformity – or so it is hoped. It is the model of the state as a Leviathan, Thomas Hobbes's seventeenth-century vision of a monstrous body that 'hath the use of so much Power and Strength conferred on him, that by terror thereof, he is inabled to conforme the wills of them all, to Peace at home, and mutuall ayd against their enemies abroad'.[15]

Of course it is true that society needs a set of core values to unite around. But those values are not specific to Britishness. Rather, they are universal values of human and democratic rights that all communities share. Ironically, it is those values that are most under attack in the 'war on terror' and the 'war on asylum'. Given the state's current undermining of the core values of human rights, it is little wonder that it prefers to look elsewhere for common denominators to bind society. Moreover, the government's refusal to heed the warnings of the anti-war movement on Iraq has been a huge factor in alienating young Muslims (and non-Muslims) from British institutions and the democratic process. What this indicates is that it is the methodology of the 'war on terror' that has been the largest factor in eroding a true sense of cohesion in British society today. It is here that the 'honest debates' on multiculturalism, national identity and immigration must begin. In such a process, there remains the possibility of understanding the real roots of terror and forced migration and the possibility of creating an open sense of British citizenship, in which all who live in Britain can participate equally.

1
Echoes of Empire

One thousand wogs [equals] fifty frogs [equals] one Briton. One European is worth twenty-eight Chinese, or perhaps 2 Welsh miners worth one thousand Pakistanis. – BBC journalists' formula for the newsworthiness of disasters, early 1970s[1]

Racism is conventionally thought of as a matter of individual prejudices and the ways that these are expressed in word and deed. On this view, racism describes any kind of hostility or offensiveness on the basis of race, culture, nationality, religion or other kinds of belonging. It is closely related to parochialism or xenophobia and is often seen as a part of human nature or national culture, perhaps the regrettable but necessary correlate of patriotism. It is also this view of racism that focuses attention on the need for cultural sensitivity and awareness, the need for everyone to be equipped with a working knowledge of other cultures and sufficient respect to avoid causing offence. This is not necessarily a false account of racism but it obscures a larger truth. For racism is also about society as a whole and the relations between different societies, their structures and their processes and the power relationships they embody – the ways in which some groups of people profit from the systematic exclusion and subordination of other groups, which, in turn, result in some groups living lives that are harder, shorter and less free. This alternative, structural view of racism is important because it directs us to racist laws, conventions, practices, institutions and ways of thinking, not just individual acts and attitudes. It is a view of racism that also calls our attention to the machinery of states in sustaining racist practices. Crucially, it puts racism into history, asking us to consider how particular forms of racism come to exist and who profits from them. It also sets the experiences of different groups of victims of racism against the common social structures that have excluded them and asks how those structures have interacted with other forms of oppression, such as those of class or gender. In taking racism to be an aspect of society as a whole, it moves beyond questions of whether one region or class of society is more or less racist than another. Finally, it abandons attempts to account for different racisms in terms of different 'national characters' and instead explains the shifting character of racism in different contexts in terms of the political struggle against racism, its progress or lack thereof. It is only the structural view that can fully explain the changing nature of racism in Britain and guide the fight for racial justice.

The modern idea of racial identity appears to have its origins among the Portuguese of the sixteenth century, who sought to legitimise their early development of the Atlantic slave trade and the plantation economies of the 'New World'.[2] By the end of the seventeenth century, England had surpassed the Portuguese in the supply of slaves, primarily to the Caribbean. The more that slave-traders and sugar-planters faced criticism and rebellion, the more they turned to the idea of Africans as a subhuman category of being in order to provide quasi-intellectual cover for the violent transportation of slaves from Africa to the Americas.[3] It was the need to insulate the lucrative slave trade from moral condemnation that prompted the first attempts to create a systematic ideology of racism and solidified the fateful association of African features with inferiority. The raw material for this systematisation was a prior legacy of unorganised racial beliefs, superstitions and fears directed at Africans, such as the association of blackness with monsters and the devil and the idea of Africans as closer to the animal world. Before the intervention of the slave trade ideologists, the perception of Africans had been less rigidly defined. To Elizabethans, it was not the African as such but the 'Blackamoor', with connotations of an Islamic threat, that conjured racial fears. Although Islam was a multiracial civilisation, it was reduced in the European mind to the 'Moors' and associated with Africans.[4] In the suspicion of the 'moor', race and religion were intertwined in a way that would recur in later centuries. The Islamic world of the 'East' was demonised as a monstrous realm, needing to be captured by Christendom and transformed according to a God-given mandate. Not for the last time, the East was allotted a role within a Western drama not of its own choosing.[5]

AN 'IMPERIAL RACE'

England's eighteenth-century domination of the slave trade carried with it the beginnings of the mass diffusion of the modern concept of racism. The racism produced by the Caribbean sugar plantations was recycled to legitimise the expansion of British colonialism in

India at the beginning of the nineteenth century. Racist ideology became central to the growing tentacles of British capitalism and its imperial project. It was over the hundred-year period of high imperialism from the mid-nineteenth century through to the mid-twentieth that racism was popularised to the British public and a racial view of the world came to be widely adopted. As the historian Marika Sherwood has written:

from the mid-nineteenth century ... the building of an empire and the containment of labour troubles at home ... required the institutionalising of an earlier myth of the superior Englishman, now with a civilising mission. It required also the derogation of everyone else to an immutable racial hierarchy whose bottom rung was occupied by Africans.[6]

Thus 'a new national ideology of beneficent imperialism' was propagated by an army of

writers, philosophers, economists, scientists and politicians, the churches and their missionaries, empire societies, children's and women's organisations ... the purveyors of popular culture, including magazines and the formal education system.[7]

At first, this was an entirely middle-class ideology in which 'lower classes' were also conceived in terms of race: the working classes were imagined as 'literally racially distinct from the middle and upper classes';[8] the Irish, too, were interpreted as literally 'dark'. Notions of the 'racial health' of populations became a mounting obsession and gave racism a pseudo-scientific veneer, in which physical differences were taken to be signs of differing aptitudes for civilisation. The influential nineteenth-century anthropologist John Beddoes compiled an index of 'nigresence', cataloguing the inhabitants of the British Isles by their racial features. His conclusion was that 'nigresence' was increasing in the lower classes owing to the presence of Irish immigrants, whom he described as 'Africanoid'.[9]

But from the late nineteenth century, racial categories were brought 'into ever closer proximity to working-class lives'.[10] The drawing of the working class into a new national ideology proved necessary to mobilise Britain as 'an imperial race' and the sentiment of white superiority that was previously centred on the elite became available to the masses.[11] Empire dictated a shift away from concentrating on the differences between racial/class subgroups of the population of Britain. Instead, Britannia was construed as racially homogeneous and rigidly distinct from its colonial subject 'races' and alien immigrants.

Humanity was imagined as a hierarchy, with the 'lesser breeds' as 'backward', child-like, incapable of self-rule or historical progress and as therefore requiring colonial tutelage – the 'white man's burden' of empire-building. One consequence of this was that, by the 1900s, the socialist-inspired class consciousness of earlier decades had given way to demands for social reform that were increasingly linked with the national interest in imperialism. An expanding empire abroad was posed as the necessary economic base for the avoidance of class conflict at home, and the guarantor of 'the working man's prosperity'. In the famous words of Cecil Rhodes, speaking in 1895 after witnessing an angry meeting of the East End unemployed,

in order to save the 40 million inhabitants of the United Kingdom from a bloody civil war, we colonial statesmen must acquire new lands to settle the surplus population, to provide new markets for the goods produced in the factories and mines.[12]

In this spirit, reforms to education and health policy, which anticipated the creation of the welfare state, were pitched by groups such as the Fabian Society in terms of the need to breed 'an imperial race', fit and able enough to take its place in the forward march of empire. Sidney Webb, writing in 1907, worried that England was threatened by 'race deterioration, if not race suicide'. Since the 'least patriotic' 25 per cent of the citizens were producing 50 per cent of the next generation, there was a threat of 'this country gradually falling to the Irish and the Jews'.[13] The government, argued Webb, must intervene in 'the production of healthy, moral and intelligent citizens'. This was a period when Darwin's theory of evolution had been taken up by the 'science' of eugenics, which had been founded by Sir Francis Galton in the mid-nineteenth century. Eugenicists held the view that the 'lesser breeds' were destined for extinction in the name of natural progress. It was necessary, therefore, for the 'civilised races' to isolate themselves from these subhumans, and it was permissible for societies equipped with this 'science' to assist the natural process of their 'inevitable' extinction. Thus the wiping out of entire populations was made intellectually respectable.

In these ways, the empire came to provide the British public with a grand lens through which to view events in Africa and Asia. But, it was a lens that blocked out the actual experiences of the people living under British rule, thus enabling the demonisation of those same people when they settled in Britain – in ways that parallel today's hostility to migrants fleeing the upheaval unleashed by global capitalism. Take, for example, the Chinese, who began to settle in the UK towards the end of the nineteenth century. They were depicted as a sinister threat to British civilisation with their secret societies and loose morals. These prejudices took on a harder edge after the end of the First World War, when newspapers began a campaign of scapegoating against the Chinese of London and Liverpool, portraying their communities as hotbeds of opium addiction where white women were regularly seduced and corrupted. A whole industry of films and novels portrayed the sexual and narcotic dangers of the 'yellow peril'.[14] The government responded to these fears with the introduction of the Alien Restriction (Amendment) Act 1919, which extended into peacetime the emergency wartime powers to prevent immigration to Britain,[15] and the Dangerous Drugs Act of 1920, which prompted a campaign of police raids on Chinese areas. What was systematically ignored was the actual history of opium smuggling, a history that heavily implicated Britain's own exploitation of China. That history began in the early nineteenth century, when Britain depended on imports of porcelain, silk and tea from a Chinese economy that was, in many ways, more advanced than, and did not require exports from, Britain's. British capitalists thus faced the problem of a long-standing trade deficit with China that they were desperate to overcome. A solution was found in growing large quantities of opium in colonised Bengal and then exporting these to China, in spite of the official Chinese state ban on the drug. The result was spiralling levels of addiction in China, as the largest drug-smuggling operation in world history led to Britain's acquiring the huge trading surpluses that were necessary to underpin the rise of the City of London as the centre of the world economy.[16] When the Chinese authorities attempted to stop the trade, the British state sent in gunboats to defend its tax revenue, beginning the first 'Opium War' of 1839.[17] Ironically, the unfavourable terms of trade thereafter imposed on China by British guns led to economic hardship in China, resulting in the beginnings of emigration and the emergence in Britain of Chinese communities. By this time, though, the stigma of opium abuse had attached itself to the supposedly degenerate Chinese character, rather than to British colonial practice.[18] With such twists and turns does empire discharge its 'white man's burden'.

Thousands of episodes such as this left deep marks on the texture of English/British culture, producing a selective collective memory, a repertoire of mutually supporting racisms – based on culture, religion, fantasy, science or history – built up over time, to be drawn on and mobilised in different situations. It was not that racism constituted the essential foundation of Englishness; that was no more true than the claim that liberty, equality and fairness were the underlying forces of national history. But a recurring feature of that history was the way in which racism was given new life and old ideas were transformed, in step with changing circumstances. Thus, in the nineteenth century, as the British Empire faced the challenge of an Islamic-oriented resistance to colonialism in India and Africa, the idea of a specifically Muslim fanaticism was at hand to 'explain' these disturbances. Though mobilised as part of a Victorian imperial project, the concept of Islamic fanaticism had medieval roots and would continue to have force in the twenty-first century. While some periods favoured the revival of old forms of racism, at other times racisms were discredited and defeated. In the second half of the twentieth century, scientific racism underwent this fate to a large degree.

Yet the end of the British Empire in the second half of the twentieth century did not bring the end of racism. Rather it offered the pretext for its transformation. Like a ship rebuilding itself at sea, racism could survive the damage inflicted on its structures at various historical moments, even exploiting such moments of crisis as opportunities for renovation. Such processes are usually ignored in conventional accounts, which prefer to ascribe racial ideas only a superficial role in British history. But race is a socially constructed concept that is both wider in its range and more profoundly rooted in the history of the nation than is commonly supposed. Moreover, the restriction of the concept of racism to 'colour' difference has concealed the full range of ways in which racism has operated in Britain, including against Jews, Gypsies and the Irish. The standard view, in which Victorian imperialism introduced colour-based racism to British society while the end of empire left behind a residue of racial attitudes that have been progressively eradicated, is mistaken. The history of racism began earlier and, as we shall see, the end of the British Empire provided the conditions for a reincarnation of racism, as it was reborn in the form of a white cultural nationalism. Those who had been made into colonial subjects as Britain expanded its imperial rule over multiple 'races' were now to be excluded from the white nationality that Britain sought in a context of contracting sovereignty.

NATIONAL SOVEREIGNTY

It was in the name of national sovereignty that anti-colonialists had fought the British Empire. If there was one idea that defined the new world that was to be built on the ruins of the Second World War, it was the idea of national sovereignty. The war itself had been started, ostensibly, to defend the sovereignty of Poland from Nazi invasion. At the end of the war, the world was imagined as divided up into sovereign nation-states. 'Sovereignty' referred to the right of each of these states to manage its own 'internal' affairs as it saw fit. No other state had the right to intervene in sovereign territory. That most of the world remained in the grip of European colonialism was regarded as a temporary phenomenon, which would disappear as soon as the nations of Africa, Asia and the Caribbean were 'mature' enough to take over the management of their own affairs. It was this framework of national sovereignty that was seen as the best way of ensuring peace and progress. Nations were to choose their own ideological path, either through elections, revolution or uprising. But ideology would not be forced on a nation through outside military intervention. To prevent that from happening, the United Nations would establish a system of 'collective security' in which the aggression of any nation would be rebuffed by the 'international community'. Of course, these principles were constantly violated in the following decades, and the formal equality of nations posited by the United Nations was contradicted by the vast differences in military and economic power (hence decision-making at the UN was split between the General Assembly where all were equal but powerless and the select Security Council where real power resided). But the fact that the principles of universal sovereignty were the standards by which states were judged remained important. The Cold War game was defined by the rules of national sovereignty – even when these rules were broken. The US war in Korea, for example, could only be justified on the grounds that it was to free the Koreans from foreign intervention. It was not justified, as it would be today in a different era, by the notion that the North Korean government was a 'rogue state'.

The rules of this game also provided the pretext for nationalist struggles against European colonialism, following the Second World War. In what was now referred to as the Third World, Europe's ideals of national sovereignty fed into national liberation movements. If European countries deserved sovereignty from foreign intervention, why not India, Ghana and Jamaica? These arguments were all the more pressing given the sacrifices that these nations had themselves made in the war effort. The middle-class elites who led these liberation movements understood themselves to be fighting on behalf of a *nation* – a coherent and unified mass of people with a shared interest in anti-colonial struggle. The nation-states that freed themselves from European rule in the ensuing decades were seen as expressing the will of the people, and it was this that gave them their immediate legitimacy – even if the national elites became disconnected from the needs of the masses; even if the new nation's borders were often entirely arbitrary, having been drawn up in the backrooms of Europe; even if the peoples congregated within them for the convenience of colonial rulers did not think of themselves as a single unit.

The universalist principle that every people should have their own nation was taken to mean the converse too: only through their own nation-state did a people gain official recognition within the international community. In this way, the fate of the people was bound up with the fate of 'its' nation-state. When a representative of a newly liberated nation took his seat at the UN General Assembly (and it was usually a man), it was as if the entire mass of his people were joining him there. In reality, of course, the UN was an assembly of national leaders not of peoples. But this contradiction was resolved through what was effectively a pact between nation-states and the 'world community', as represented by the UN. The state would take on the responsibility of sovereign protector of its people and their welfare. In return, the state was granted autonomy within its borders by the rest of the world. The paradox of the framework of national sovereignty was that it could imply both universalism and compartmentalism. National sovereignty proclaimed the universal rights of all peoples even as it drew borders between them.

Not only was nationhood essential to finding one's 'space' in humanity, it was also required as a vehicle for economic and social development. In the poorer countries, the nation-state offered itself as the only way to lift its people out of poverty and colonial underdevelopment. In Europe, development was linked to the ability of the nation-state to provide welfare. The experience of capitalist industrialisation had unleashed a massive upheaval across Europe over the previous hundred years. Karl Polanyi, the Austrian economist who 'sought asylum' in Britain in the 1930s, described in *The Great Transformation* how the creation of 'self-regulating markets' in land, labour and the supply of money led to the violent tearing apart of existing social bonds that eventually culminated in the rise of fascism and world war.[19] But by throwing labour into the nexus of a 'self-regulating market', industrial capitalism also provided a basis on which the force of so-called free markets could be challenged, through labour organising itself into unions and threatening to withdraw from its contract. The power of organised labour was used to counter not only the economic power of the capitalist class but also its control of the nation-state. The working class won for itself first political rights and then greater influence over the nation-state. As its power rose in the first half of the twentieth century, the nation-state in the richer countries settled into a new social contract between the forces of capital and labour, based on the welfare state. The Prometheus that had been unbound by the industrial revolution would be stayed by social provisions: free education, free healthcare, a social safety-net for the unemployed and so on. The very nation-states that had plunged Europe into conflict, therefore, also offered a way of balancing the arbitrary judgements of market forces and reducing social upheaval.

The welfare state system was not just about providing access to services. It also transformed the notion of citizenship, expanding the relationship between the people and the state. To the civil and political rights, which had themselves been forged in earlier political struggles between the capitalist and labouring classes, were added 'social rights' – entitlements to welfare.[20] The authority of the state increasingly rested on its ability to actively promote the well-being of the entire population both through the welfare state itself and a measure of economic planning that the state commanded through its weight on the economy. However, there was a potential tension between the ethos of universalism and inclusion that the welfare state embodied and the compartmentalism of nationality that usually determined entitlement. While welfare provision was proclaimed as 'free for all', it rested nevertheless on membership of the nation that provided it. Was access to the welfare state to be based on national belonging, service and contribution, or was it a universal right? This issue was initially regarded as marginal but in fact went right to the heart of what the welfare state stood for. The tension was reflected, for example, in the early debates about access to the National Health Service in Britain, which were caught between the principle of universal access for all residents and the narrower need to promote the 'racial health' of the nation – as pioneers such as Sidney Webb had understood it. While Aneurin Bevan's National Health Service Act of 1946 had made healthcare available to anyone present in the UK irrespective of their nationality, later measures would rescind this commitment.[21]

The responsibilities that a nation-state had to its own citizens might be quite high – particularly in those countries that introduced a welfare state – but the responsibilities a nation-state had to individuals of other nations were minimal (the formal availability of the NHS to foreign nationals in the UK was exceptional). There was a vast gap between what the state owed to a citizen and what it owed to a foreigner. We were sailing on our national 'ship' and they were sailing on theirs – between us was clear blue water. We owed them nothing and likewise they were supposedly free from our interference. The borders of a nation thus defined the limits of its sovereignty but also of its accountability and its responsibility. Of course, this picture was complicated, in Britain's case at least, by the facts of monarchy and empire. Without the wealth and labour-power generated out of colonialism, the 'British' welfare state would not have been possible. But, in formal terms, the colonies were not foreign nations. In order to give a semblance of respectability to the political structures of imperial authority, the empire had defined the populations under its charge as legally subjects of the monarch. In this respect, they were no different from the population of Britain itself. There were no citizens as such, only subjects of the king, and, technically, colonial populations were his subjects too, rather than foreign nationals. British nationality had thus been expanded to cover a multiracial empire. It was this legal notion of British nationality that facilitated settlement in Britain from India, Pakistan and the Caribbean in the 1940s and 1950s. The 1948 Nationality Act confirmed that citizens of Commonwealth nations were to be British subjects – partly to allow for the immigration of colonial workers to meet demand for labour in the UK and partly to sustain Britain's 'links' with the empire after independence.[22]

A NEW CONSENSUS

On a legal level, the empire had made British subjecthood multiracial, even as, on a popular level, Britishness was bound to white superiority. With the end of the British Empire, it was this multiracial notion of British nationality that became the prime target of a new racial campaign by Enoch Powell, Conservative MP for Wolverhampton from 1950. There was, he argued, a contradiction between the legal version of nationality and the version of nationality felt by the people, in which being white was a prerequisite to being British. Thus, Powell's two-part programme: the amendment of the legal definition of citizenship so that race and nation were once more aligned; and the repatriation of the non-white population of Britain to correct this earlier 'error'. Together these would complete the 'unfinished business' of empire and reorganise the nation around a concept of white identity that was no less racist than the imperial notion of racial hierarchy it displaced. As Tom Nairn has written, when it became clear in the 1950s that the death knell had been sounded for the British Empire, it took Powell 'some years to recover from the blow'.[23] He sensed that a notion of 'England's destiny' had been lost and spent a decade brooding on how this national identity might be redefined. His first solution was a disavowal of the empire itself, claiming that it had never existed at all: it had merely been a mirage. But that did not satisfy Powell's deep longing for an answer to the national identity question – 'what sort of people do we think we are?'[24] – to which empire had offered a ready reply. Powell's eventual, grim insight was that the *racial* identity that empire had fostered could be recast without reference to empire itself and its associated hierarchy. Whereas the empire had required a picture of the British people as racially homogeneous in order to delineate an 'imperial race' at the centre of an aggressive project of expansion on foreign lands, Powell's new vision was of a white cultural identity engaged in defending itself against threats that had landed on British soil itself. Immigrants from Asia and the Caribbean were thus invoked as convenient foils against which this new national identity could be built. In his most famous speech of 20 April 1968, Powell not only prophesied an inevitable violent clash of races in Britain's cities, the 'rivers of blood', but also popularised a new language of white victimhood, quoting an 'ordinary man' as saying: 'In this country in fifteen or twenty years time the black man will have the whip hand over the white man.' The idea that 'coloured immigrants' were a mortal threat to the British nation had circulated on the fascist fringe for some time and was already implied by the drift of public discourse on immigration over the previous five years. As a member of the shadow cabinet, Powell put his own stamp of authority on such sentiments. He introduced that perennial theme of British racism that has reverberated through newspaper columns up to the present day: the notion that a British majority has been abandoned by a 'liberal elite', which is in thrall to empty cosmopolitan ideals and which knows nothing of the true sentiment of national belonging. White identity is thereby doubly endangered – by immigrant invaders and 'soft touch' politicians.

By the time of Powell's 'rivers of blood' speech, the lines of racial conflict had already shifted from the colonies to the metropole. It was to be questions of immigration and 'integration' that would be the new locus of 'race relations' and, in this, Britain's experience was unique. Other north European countries had recruited immigrant workers through the 1960s (either by exploiting colonial ties or through guest-worker schemes with southern Europe) and then begun to introduce controls in 1973 as economic recession set in. Britain, on the other hand, began a post-war tightening of controls much earlier, in 1962, the immediate prompt being social conflict (the anti-black riots in Notting Hill and Nottingham in 1958).[25] It was not that a 'liberal elite' had allowed non-white immigration and then been forced to respond to a 'racist backlash' against it. Rather, successive post-war governments had always been suspicious of immigration from India, Pakistan and the Caribbean, reluctantly tolerating it in the interests of maintaining the pretence of imperial and Commonwealth unity and to provide labour for post-war reconstruction. But administrative devices were gradually adopted to turn what were then still officially not immigrants at all but British colonial subjects into first 'immigrants' and then 'coloureds'.[26]

In fact, the first half of Powell's programme – the ending of a multiracial notion of nationhood – had already been under way since the 1962 Commonwealth Immigrants Act, albeit through immigration law rather than nationality law *per se*. The awkward dilemma for legislators was how to draw up an immigration policy that made a racist distinction between different Commonwealth citizens on the basis of colour, without it seeming explicitly racist; restricting immigration from the (white) 'old' Commonwealth countries of Canada, Australia, etc. was neither politically feasible nor desirable. Hence, immigration legislation in the 1960s was marked by convoluted attempts to divide between 'Old Commonwealth' immigrants and 'New Commonwealth' immigrants from India, Pakistan and the Caribbean, who had to be barred. Eventually, the 1971 Immigration Act found in the concept of 'patriality' a less clumsy but more odious way of achieving the same outcome: the right to settle in Britain from the Commonwealth was granted if you could trace your ancestry back to Britain in the two preceding generations. It was a polite way of allowing whites in and keeping 'coloureds' out. For the rest of the century, there was to be a consensus (and little debate) on the fundamentals of Britain's immigration policy. The aim was zero 'primary' immigration – that is, no new non-white immigration except for spouses and children joining those already in the country. The immigration controls introduced from 1962 to

1971 also had the effect of recasting the terms of British nationality. No longer did it stretch to the corners of a multiracial empire or Commonwealth; now, it was only fit for whites.[27] Rather than the end of empire in the 1960s bringing with it the end of racism, a new racism was introduced into the structures of the state, through immigration laws that implicitly defined Britain as white.

In this way, the first half of Powell's programme was successful even as Powell was condemned by his party leader Edward Heath for extremism. While repatriation was rejected as impractical, the thinking behind it was accepted: the period of non-white immigration was now construed as a one-off, a momentary error not to be repeated. On the streets, there were many who had already taken this logic as a green light to launch campaigns of harassment against 'coloured immigrants'; racist attacks and abuse threatened to carry out by other means the repatriation programme that the 'liberals' in Westminster had rejected. By now, Britain preferred to forget that its own empire had made peoples of Asia, Africa and the Caribbean into British subjects and, in doing so, had given them the right to settle in the UK. Instead, their settlement in Britain was construed as an external intrusion into the British body politic. Refusing this convenient erasure of colonial history and its separation of imperialism from the black presence in the UK, the anti-racist writer A. Sivanandan coined the maxim, 'we are here because you were there'.

Officially, those who came while the door was 'absent-mindedly' left open would be given their due – efforts would be made at their integration – but further immigration was to be halted. It was the Labour home secretary Roy Jenkins who, in 1966, had sought to clarify what kind of integration was to follow, by defining it as 'equal opportunity accompanied by cultural diversity, in an atmosphere of mutual tolerance'.[28] There was, in other words, to be no active policy of cultural assimilation to British norms. Along with this policy of cultural *laissez-faire*, there was also the introduction of race relations legislation to outlaw discrimination, first, in an extremely meagre fashion, in 1965, then in 1968 and, more fully, in 1976. This notion of 'integration' thus formed the other half of a two-part consensus – zero primary immigration coupled with Jenkins-inspired integration policies – that would form the basis of British race relations for the remaining years of the twentieth century.

Yet, at the heart of this official consensus was a paradox. Controls against 'coloured immigration' were justified as a necessary part of a programme to reduce racism, which included the promotion of a mood of tolerance and equality. The laudable aims of equal opportunity, tolerance and diversity were undermined by the fact that their achievement was seen as dependent on strong immigration controls, which were, in turn, premised on racism. Roy Jenkins had said, 'There is a clear limit to the amount of immigration this country can absorb and it is in the interests of minorities themselves to maintain a strict control.'[29] But this remark could only refer to the non-white immigrants who formed the racial 'minorities' in Britain: white immigrants were not really thought of as immigrants at all. While immigration control was talked about exclusively in terms of stopping non-whites getting in, it was outright hypocrisy to speak at the same time of promoting racial harmony. The result was that the new consensus on immigration had racism encapsulated within it, a racism that was now 'respectable and clinical' because it had been institutionalised with 'the sanction of the state'.[30] The legal powers introduced by the 1971 Act remain the basis on which migrants are today arrested, detained and deported. But, equally importantly, the political balancing act of 'strong controls coupled with integration', which the Act confirmed, defined the way in which immigration and race were officially linked for the next thirty years, even while the issues were less loudly debated in British politics.

Every time politicians, from Roy Jenkins to Douglas Hurd[31] to Jack Straw, repeated the argument that immigration controls were necessary to prevent racism, there was, just below the surface, a series of unspoken implications: immigration controls are about stopping non-white people getting into Britain; racism is caused by too many non-whites getting in; the way to stop racism is to stop non-whites getting into Britain; a little bit of racism in immigration controls helps avoid much worse racism in wider society. The double standards of late-twentieth-century British racism were thus set in place: occasional fine-sounding words in public, combined with innuendo, whispering and silent rejection. It was on these terms that the politics of race and immigration were 'settled' in Britain in the early 1970s, leaving in place a kind of official 'polite racism'. At the heart of this fragile political consensus there was always the risk that the balancing act would falter and the double standard prove untenable – and thirty years later it did just that.

REFUGEE PROTECTION

While the question of empire complicated the post-war framework of national sovereignty, it was the new framework for the protection of refugees that constituted an even clearer exception to the principle that a nation had no responsibility to foreign nationals outside its borders. There were millions of people in Europe at the end of the Second World War who did not fit into the compartmentalised national borders imagined by the United Nations. Many of the 30 million or more people in Europe who had been displaced were unable to return home.[32] It was more than just a practical problem. The displaced Europeans were thought of not just as refugees but as 'stateless' persons, deprived of national belonging itself, not just the material loss of home and possessions. In losing their nationality, they had lost the protection of any state. They were therefore a challenge to the framework of national sovereignty that the United Nations had set out to embody.

The Second World War had shown the need for states to have responsibilities to refugees. It was known that the Allied powers could have saved many more people from the Holocaust were it not for their own anti-Semitic attempts to limit the entry of Jewish refugees. The British government, for example, could have rescued tens, even hundreds, of thousands of Jews if it had not pandered to anti-Semitism on Britain's streets and in the press, by making it harder for refugees to enter the UK in the late 1930s. Both the *Mail* and the *Express* called for Jews to be denied entry, using the same language that they use today against asylum seekers.[33] For every Jew the British let in during the 1930s, Jewish associations had case files of seven others who were refused. When Austria was annexed by Nazi Germany in 1938, for example, putting thousands of Austrian Jews at risk, the British government introduced strict visa controls to make it harder for them to escape, a tactic that would be repeated by British governments right through to the present day. More than 65,000 Austrian Jews were murdered in the Holocaust.[34]

It was to the question of 'stateless' persons that the newly formed UN turned in 1950, calling for a convention to be held in Geneva the following year.[35] Hanging heavily over the proceedings was the deadly failure of earlier refugee policies to respond to the challenge of Nazism. The convention that was eventually drafted in Geneva was intended as an international safety-net for those who fell through the cracks in the system of nation-states. Its aim was to readmit these people back into the fold of national belonging. The mechanism that the convention chose was to place an obligation on nation-states to cede their own sovereignty over immigration decisions, to allow for the 'resettlement' of refugees, in certain limited circumstances. In putting this obligation on nation-states, it created an exception to the general principle that states should have sovereign control over their own borders. But it was an exception that was justified by the need to deal with an exceptional problem – the persecution of people by their own nation. The failure to give refuge to Jews in the 1930s had shown that it was necessary to set down clear, international principles for decision-making on refugees' claims, so that decisions could be removed, as far as possible, from the purview of short-term political calculations by individual governments. Refugee protection was therefore internationalised and made the responsibility of the entire 'community of nations' – hence, the 'spirit of international co-operation' spoken of by the convention's drafters.

Whereas the United Nations was primarily concerned with relations among states, the Geneva Convention was unusual in being concerned with the relations between states and individuals. It was a product of the nation-state system but also, potentially, in contradiction with it, as it created a domain within which the nation-state alienated a degree of authority to a higher, international body. It thus anticipated the later development of human rights conventions that sought to place general obligations on states in regard to the treatment of individuals.[36] In granting to any refugee clear rights to protection, the Geneva Convention also served to blur the line dividing the rights of citizens and non-citizens. Although the principle of national sovereignty held that no state had any particular responsibility to foreigners outside their own borders, under the Geneva Convention a refugee was entitled to claim the same protections and benefits as national citizens. In effect, refugees became subjects of a nascent international realm, where rights were defined universally, even as this international realm sought immediately to resettle refugees back into the embrace of national belonging. In this way, the convention shared in the general tension of the nation-state system between an implicit universalism and the need to contain that universalism within the framework of nations.

2
From Dependency to Displacement

When a criminal kills someone for an unpaid debt, the execution is called a 'settling of accounts'. When the international technocracy settles accounts with an indebted country, the execution is called an 'adjustment plan'. – Eduardo Galeano, 1998[1]

The principles of refugee protection and national sovereignty were pretences. In the case of both, the formal equality of all peoples, proclaimed by the post-Second World War settlement, did not extend outside the West. Refugee protection was initially limited to European refugees, particularly those fleeing from Communist totalitarianism, who proved useful icons of Cold War propaganda and, in the 1950s, could help meet the demand for white labour in Western Europe. By 1967, the overt racism of a whites-only Geneva Convention was untenable and its provisions were extended to refugees from anywhere in the world. But, as soon as refugees from Africa and Asia took up this right, mainly from the 1980s, European governments began to find oblique ways of restricting their access to asylum. History was destined to repeat the Jewish refugee experience time and time again for victims of persecution in Africa and Asia.

The undermining of the protections nominally afforded to non-Western refugees was mirrored in the subversion of the national sovereignty that had been fought for by anti-colonial movements, although at first this was not apparent. India and Pakistan gained political independence from British rule in 1947; colonialism in Sri Lanka ended the following year. In 1957, Ghana, led by Kwame Nkrumah, became the first British colony in Africa to free itself from colonialism. Ho Chi Minh's defeat of the French Expeditionary Corps at Dien Bien Phu in 1954 indicated the beginning of the end for the French empire. It would take two more decades before Portugal's colonies too would be liberated. But political independence did not bring with it economic independence and, in the end, this proved its undoing.

Imperial rule had fostered a disorganic capitalism in the colonies, in which the potential for development had been distorted to meet the needs of Europe.[2] It produced a capitalism that was uneven and unbalanced, with its centre of gravity lying in London, Paris or Brussels rather than with the needs of colonised peoples. The extraction of raw materials to supply Europe's industries was encouraged while indigenous growth was quashed. Contrary to the myth of colonialism bringing the railways to a pre-industrial society, existing industries, such as textiles and metal-working in India, were destroyed to make way for European imports while the railways themselves were built to reorient the economy around the extraction of cheap raw materials.[3] As food production was conscripted to European interests, the advance of famines was accelerated. Tens of millions may have died in India in the last quarter of the nineteenth century as a result of famines induced by colonial 'free trade'.[4] Following political independence, the challenge for the new post-colonial elites was how to reduce dependence on foreign capital. In some cases, the economic underdevelopment imposed by Europe was left intact by the new leaders, who just placed their own personnel in the ministries recently vacated by the colonisers, so as to enjoy the same unfair advantages. The national consciousness with which political independence had been won was then reduced, in Frantz Fanon's phrase, to 'an empty shell' unable to crystallise 'the innermost hopes of the whole people'.[5]

In other countries, the nationalist leaders of newly liberated states attempted to pursue economic independence, through various forms of import-substitution policy, designed to relieve their dependence on foreign imports and, therefore, on loans of foreign currency to pay for them. This economic independence, it was thought, could then be the basis for planned development that responded to the needs of the masses rather than to the logic of colonialism. It could also provide the economic foundation for a programme of 'Third World' solidarity and non-alignment in the Cold War. At the 'Asia-Africa Conference' in Bandung in 1955, nationalist leaders had come together to proclaim such a programme, among them Nehru of India, Nasser of Egypt and Sukarno of Indonesia, the host nation. The prospect alarmed the elites of Washington and Westminster and, in the midst of the Cold War, Third World nationalism was mistakenly denounced as Communism by another name. At stake were the resources that the West depended on economically, particularly oil in the Middle East, but also the raw materials that had fuelled colonialism in Asia and Africa. The need to secure control of these resources made nationalism a threat. For their part, the Soviet leaders also had strategic ambitions to secure the resources of Third World nations, such as Afghanistan, that were regarded as within their 'sphere of influence'.

Thus, the neat national boundaries of sovereignty imagined by the United Nations and on which the Bandung ambitions had been based did not pertain. Instead Third World nations found themselves trapped in the teeth of two giant gears of late twentieth-century history. The first of these gears was the gradual attaching of the lives of people in Africa, Asia and the Middle East to a world market system anchored in the growing power of multinational corporations and international financial institutions. This led, through a series of intermediary causes, to the collapse of the ability of most nations in these regions to plot their own political or economic course and tied poorer nations into relations of abject dependency on the new international financial architecture that had been agreed at Bretton Woods, New Hampshire, USA, in 1944 – the International Monetary Fund and the World Bank – which were able to impose their own narrow economic formulae on debtor nations. The second gear that undermined national sovereignty was the orchestration of state terrorism, regime change and proxy warfare in the name of, first, the Cold War and, later, the 'war against terror'. This was done through the sponsorship of authoritarian and brutal 'favoured' regimes and the covert use of assassination, terrorism and warfare to destabilise 'uncooperative' states, no matter what the human rights costs and long-term effects on those societies. In the meshing of these two gears, the formal principles of national sovereignty were shredded while the long-term structures of Third World underdevelopment, instability and violence were given their familiar shape. In each specific case, local factors gave a different form to the general pattern. In some places the turns of the gears would be felt abruptly while, elsewhere, they would be prolonged but, across different times and places, it was still possible to trace the same basic processes. Chief among these was a change in the nature of the state's relationship to its citizens. As the role of the state in leading a joint national project of social and economic development gave way to the supremacy of the market and of the individual, so too was there a decline in the sense of a shared citizenship that underlay national belonging. In its place came either the politics of ethnicism, as the state attempted to bond itself to (some of) the people through ethnic identity politics, or the use of terror and repression, as elites tried to hold on to power in the face of the escalating social tensions that accompanied the state's subsumption to global vested interests. Both courses ultimately risked the collapse of the state itself and the descent into wars for the control of diminishing national resources, in which mass civilian killing, intimidation and forced displacement became military objectives, not just side-effects of war.[6]

DEBT AND DEPENDENCY

Ostensibly, the International Monetary Fund (IMF) and the World Bank existed to help the governments of economically weak countries by making available loans for development. But the embedding of these institutions in the elites of Washington and the creation of a decision-making process of one dollar-one vote ensured that they remained entirely unaccountable to the people on whom they had the greatest effect.[7] IMF and World Bank loans created a vicious cycle. In order to industrialise and escape from the colonial legacy of uneven development, it was necessary to buy foreign machinery, which meant buying foreign currency, which meant foreign loans. These were to be paid back through exports. But if the value of exports fell, as was likely if the only export was a single raw material whose price was set in foreign markets, then the debt would build up. To service the debt, the government would have to cut off investment, leading to still lower revenue from exports and ending in a 'debt trap' that would grip African, Asian, Caribbean and Latin American nations, one by one, from the 1950s onwards. By the late 1970s, the IMF and World Bank had a cookbook of economic policies that would come to be known as 'structural adjustment programmes' (SAPs). SAPs initially meant privatisation of state assets and the abolition of state subsidies on, for example, food products. But by the 1980s, they represented a complete economic package of deregulation, privatisation, free trade, unfettered capital movement, low taxation, fiscal austerity, cutbacks on social provision and the creation of so-called Free Trade Zones – enclaves where labour could be cheaply exploited by multinational corporations without fear of trade unions. SAPs were presented as the necessary 'shock treatment' that an economy needed to get it back on its feet after a debt crisis. But they produced permanent immiseration in the public and private sectors alike, while clearing the ground for multinational corporations to plunder whatever assets remained. Austerity measures threw state employees out of work and destroyed health and educational provision. At the same time, the removal of capital controls, tariffs and subsidies unleashed foreign competition on to domestic industry and agriculture. Furthermore, this competition from Europe or the US was itself often boosted by the very state subsidies that SAPs had abolished in the rest of the world. But because indebted nations were dependent on the IMF and World Bank for foreign currency credit, they had no choice but to accept structural adjustment. The loans had become, in effect, political levers that were used by the international financial elite to accelerate the 'integration' of the Third World into global free markets and promulgate the 'neoliberal' economic policies of privatisation, removal of subsidies and tariffs, withdrawal of trade union rights and retrenchment of the welfare state.

Ghana, for example, won independence from Britain in 1957 but its underdeveloped economy remained entirely dependent on the export of cocoa. It used revenues from these exports to fund attempts at industrialisation and diversification. The price of cocoa, though, was to fall, leaving Nkrumah's nationalist government with a balance of payments crisis that only foreign loans could resolve. It was the opportunity that his opponents, backed by Western governments, were looking for, and a regime more favourable to foreign capital was installed in 1966. Nkrumah's policies of economic independence were reversed and national assets were offered up to privatisation and foreign ownership. In the ensuing decades, Ghana would plunge ever deeper into debt-dependency. The need to meet IMF and World Bank dictates would haunt all future governments and keep them in hock to the needs of Western capitalism, whatever the colour of their own political rhetoric.[8] By 1990, having completed sixteen structural adjustment programmes with the World Bank and IMF, Ghana had an external debt of $3.5 billion and was still, as it had been at independence, entirely reliant on cocoa exports. As demand was finite, the more cocoa that was exported, the more its price fell, leaving little opportunity for growth. Then, Ghana's other raw materials were opened up for extraction – specifically, timber. Ghana's tropical forest was reduced to just a quarter of its original size, in the process killing both the wild game that provided food for the majority of the population and the supply of fuel and medicines that was previously harvested from the trees.[9] Meanwhile the privatisation of education, as dictated by SAPs, forced two-thirds of children in rural areas to stop attending school.[10] Absolute poverty, inequality and dependence on foreign imports of food had all risen, in what was nevertheless described by the IMF as one of its few success stories in Africa.[11] And still the plunder in Ghana continues: recently, at the behest of British companies, backed with funds from the UK government, plans to privatise Ghana's water supply have been set in train, which will lead inevitably to prices that are beyond the reach of those most in need.[12]

Across Africa and Asia, the abolition of state subsidies and protection for agriculture – which SAPs described as the 'integration' of farmers into the world economy – resulted in the ripping apart of the social fabric of rural economies and uprooted great swathes of the world's population from the traditional subsistence farming that had been the lifeblood of their societies. The famines that devastated parts of Africa in the 1980s had their roots in this process, as much as in 'natural causes'.[13] Unable any longer to reap a living from the land, these rural evictees put their hopes for survival in the cities. But the cities could not provide jobs even for their existing workforces, as cutbacks in the public sector took hold. There was, then, only the makeshift economy of street vendors and day labourers and a life of surviving hand-to-mouth in slums, which had become a permanent feature of Third World cities. As more and more resources went on servicing foreign debts, Third World states were less and less able to deal with these, the social consequences of 'integration' into a global capitalist economy.[14] By the mid-1980s, there was already more money leaving African and Asian countries in debt repayments than was flowing in as further loans, investment or aid.[15] By 1992, Africa, Asia, Latin America and the Caribbean were together paying Britain £2,493m more annually than they got in official grants, voluntary aid, export credits, bank loans and direct investments from the UK.[16] By the new millennium, Oxfam estimated that the West's unfair trade policies and subsidies were costing developing countries $100 billion a year.[17] The result was a world of vast inequalities, underemployment and human devastation, with a billion people living on less than one dollar a day and ten million children dying each year as a result of preventable diseases.[18]

Across the world, people took to the streets to protest against the poverty imposed by IMF and World Bank structural adjustment policies. By the 1990s, these protests coalesced into a global movement for social justice, a movement that began to register in the mainstream Western media after the disruption of the World Trade Organisation (WTO) meeting at Seattle in November 1999. Whereas the anti-WTO protests were portrayed as a new kind of Western, middle-class, student politics, in fact, it was a movement of a thousand strands, the strongest of which reached out from those countries most impoverished by global capitalism – for it was there that its fiercest critics were to be found.[19] As opposition mounted, the structural adjustment policies of the 1980s and 1990s were rebranded as 'poverty reduction' strategies. The emphasis now was on achieving 'good governance' but in practice these strategies merely repeated the same mistakes as before. New leaders might replace old but they had no more economic leeway than those who had come before. For the poorest countries, the scale of the debt was such that there was never any hope of paying it all back – the debt would remain as a permanent sword of Damocles hanging over them. Even when campaigning by the global justice movement led to the discussion of debt-cancellation plans, 'conditionalities' were attached, which ensured that, in return for cancellation, further structural adjustment would be embarked upon. In any case, by this time, a new set of global trade structures, such as the World Trade Organisation, had been constituted, which locked countries into adopting the neoliberal policies of structural adjustment programmes, irrespective of their dependency on IMF and World Bank credit. Focusing on the select number of exchanges that have been beneficial for poor countries, neoliberal globalisation was celebrated as a win-win situation for rich and poor alike. But the bigger picture was a structure of exploitation and unequal exchange. In most parts of the world, it was only tiny elites who benefited from globalisation as currently construed. The two countries that were presented as successfully emerging out of poverty – India and China – were in fact the two that had, in the past, been the most resistant to neoliberal policies.

STATE TERROR

The post-colonial leaderships that emerged after political independence had been formed by the anti-colonial struggles for national sovereignty. But debt and dependency had cut many of them free from the aspirations of their people. The new elites began to breathe in the air of the multinational corporations on which they depended and bask in the ideology of the international financial class. An ideology of development, endorsed by the World Bank and IMF, implied that the only way forward was to catch up with the West by importing its experts, its corporations and its economic models. Post-colonial elites found a new role for themselves as local satraps for a global empire of commerce and they delivered back, to their new governors, nations that they had recomposed to the needs of foreign capital. Those leaders, on the other hand, who refused this role and cast around for alternative ways of developing their countries, were seen as obstacles to the strategic interests of Western governments, were labelled Communists and were destabilised, in the name of the Cold War. They faced subversion, not only by the economics of dependency but also by the politics of covert action: coups, assassinations and terrorism, sponsored by one wing or another of the US or European intelligence agencies.

In Iran, the government of Muhammad Musaddaq was overthrown in a coup sponsored by the British and US governments, which had intervened after his nationalisation of the Anglo-Iranian Oil Company in 1951. In his place, the Shah was installed. The death of five thousand, mostly members of the Iranian Communist Party who had supported Musaddaq, followed immediately and the brutal suppression of dissent, which would characterise Iranian politics to the present day, was set in train. Savak, the Shah's notorious secret police force, was established with the help of the US and Israel at this time. The regime change in which Musaddaq was overthrown 'destroyed any chance that Iran had of evolving as a Western-style democracy'.[20] In Congo, the democratically elected left-wing leader, Patrice Lumumba, was killed in 1961 in a Belgian-sponsored assassination at the very outset of independence, poisoning the political life of that country for decades to come.[21] In Indonesia, the nationalist Sukarno, who had led the country since independence from the Dutch in 1949, became a target for British and American ire. His government opposed British colonialism in Malaysia, refused the involvement of the IMF/World Bank and was partly supported by the Indonesian Communist Party (PKI), then the largest communist party outside China and the Soviet Union. In 1965, General Suharto launched his seizure of power over the country, in a coup that received logistical support from the US and backing from Britain. Between 500,000 and one million members of the PKI were killed by Suharto's forces, which, it later emerged, had been supplied by US officials with the names of those they wanted dead.[22] With Suharto in control, Indonesia's wealth was handed over to the giants of Western capitalism, its workforce became fodder for the Free Trade Zones where unions were banned and health risks ignored, while the general and his placemen amassed their own private fortunes. He was supplied with arms from Britain right up to his removal from power in 1998, despite the Indonesian army's slaughter of thousands in East Timor. In New Labour's first year of office, eleven arms deals were approved.[23] Underwriting the whole Suharto racket was the IMF and the World Bank.

Those leaders who, like Suharto, became local conduits for global capitalism faced the risk of rebellion by their own people. For it was the masses who would take to the streets to demand that their leaders deliver on the promise of freedom from colonialism. These demands became more desperate as structural adjustment programmes were imposed, leading to the removal of state subsidies and the consequent spiralling of food prices. The Suharto regime had demonstrated that the economics of neoliberalism – privatisation, ending of subsidies and tariffs, withdrawal of trade union rights, retrenchment of the welfare state – predicated the politics of repression. The Free Trade Zone needed a police state to guarantee the 'freedom' of trade and to contain the social fall-out from the inevitable economic turmoil that free trade induced. As the divide between the elites in power and the masses grew ever greater and the optimism of the post-independence period gave way to disappointment, state authoritarianism set in. The apparatus of repression had, anyway, been inherited from the colonial system and post-colonial governments found numerous corporations and agencies that were happy to 'modernise' their police forces with new weapons and training. In the post-colonial arms trade, Britain found a way of recycling its imperial legacy, becoming second only to the US in the size of its arms industry. Thus, the Suharto regime provided the blueprint for a combination of neoliberalism and authoritarianism that took hold across the world from the 1970s onwards. In each country, the consequences varied according to local circumstances. In some, the neoliberal/authoritarian formula was consolidated into a military/police state that could survive in the long term only through repression, as it had in Indonesia. This was Chile under Pinochet (where Thatcher's economic policies had a 'dry run') and Kenya under Moi (where Britain had billions of pounds invested). In both countries, state violence and human rights abuses went hand in hand with backing from Western states and corporations.

It was in Nigeria, though, under General Sani Abacha that the connection of corporate interests with state authoritarianism was most glaring. Shell and BP had jointly held a virtual oil monopoly in Nigeria under the guard of British colonialism from 1938 and, after independence in 1960, Shell had maintained its dominance, as Nigeria became one of the world's biggest oil exporters.[24] But the wealth from the oil failed to 'trickle down' to the mass of the population and this, along with the effects of a structural adjustment plan in 1986, led to mounting opposition to the post-colonial state. In 1993, the military responded to growing unrest by annulling the presidential elections and General Sani Abacha took command of government. A ban on all opposition parties was brought in, trade unions were dissolved and martial law imposed. In the first two years of this military dictatorship, around nine thousand Nigerians claimed asylum in the UK. Yet Britain placed Nigeria on a list of 'safe countries' and refused to acknowledge that there were any human rights problems. The Home Office's internal briefing paper on Nigeria described it as a country where 'rights are generally respected', 'unfair trials' of opponents are unknown and minorities face no special persecution.[25] Out of a total of two thousand decisions made on their asylum applications, only four were granted refugee status, with a further fifteen afforded 'exceptional leave to remain' – temporary permission to stay in Britain.[26] To accept the claims of these asylum seekers would have meant publicly declaring that the Nigerian government was oppressive, something that would have soured relations with Abacha, and Westminster needed to remain on good terms with him in order to facilitate the profitable trade in arms and oil. To protect Shell's oil production, the Nigerian police and military had clamped down on protesters in the Ogoniland region, where hundreds of thousands of supporters of the Movement for the Survival of the Ogoni People had taken to the streets to demand a share of the oil wealth. British trade with Nigeria at this time was worth £400m a year, with companies such as Unilever, ICL and Lonhro investing there. There were also British arms dealers supplying the military regime with weapons including CS gas and rubber bullets, under licence from the government.[27]

Nigeria was only taken off the British government's list of safe countries when the high-profile writer and dissident Ken Saro-Wiwa was executed by Abacha's government. Nevertheless, deportations of those who had sought asylum in Britain continued, even of Nigerians who had been resident in Britain for sixteen years.[28] Nor did this complicity end with the much-heralded transfer to civilian rule in 1999. Foreign secretary Robin Cook visited Nigeria in that year and proclaimed that the country would be rewarded for its return to democracy. Yet human rights abuses and authoritarianism continued. The 'transition' government was friendly to the transnational corporations and provided enough of the trappings of democracy to offset criticism in the West; but not enough for the Nigerian people themselves to actually challenge the plunder of their country's resources. Democracy was thus confined to a leadership choice in elections that were carefully managed by the corporate-friendly ruling elites. It was no surprise that a virtual civil war continued in the oil-rich regions where local communities continued to fight for a share of the wealth.[29] The presence of oil in Nigeria, as in Algeria and Angola, meant that it was convenient to ignore these problems and pronounce these countries as safe for business.[30]

The contradictions of neoliberal economics and structural adjustment were not always to be resolved by police and military repression alone. Often, the state turned, also, to the politics of sectarianism to provide a fragile cohesion. Here, too, the colonial legacy provided an opportunity for post-colonial autocrats. Colonialism had 'divided in order to rule what it integrated in order to exploit'.[31] It brought together peoples with distinct ethnic or clan identities into a single polity and then kept those peoples apart in order to rule over them more effectively. Therefore, the populace had, often, already been coalesced into distinct camps at the moment of independence. There was always the possibility that post-colonial nationalism could degrade itself into a struggle over sectarian privileges, particularly over the allocation of government jobs and contracts, which was, at this time, the major passport to advancement. As structural adjustment programmes meant that state resources were progressively squeezed, patronage and ethnic or clan loyalty increasingly determined their distribution. Governments that were vulnerable to rebellion or electoral defeat found that they could muster an easy following through sectarian politics. Ultimately, groups that were excluded launched secessionist movements, which challenged, often violently, the borders of the state that had been inherited from colonialism.

Such was the fate that befell Somalia under the combination of IMF/World Bank 'reforms' and clan-based authoritarianism. General Mohamed Siad Barre had taken power in 1969, nine years after independence from Britain and Italy. Initially he had been backed by the Soviets before becoming a US ally and instigating an invasion of Ethiopia in 1977.[32] Till the 1980s, Somalia had been self-sufficient in food production and the livelihood of most people had rested on nomadic herding and small farming, the main economic threads holding the country together. But a structural adjustment programme, brought in from the early 1980s, tore the economy to shreds. Subsidies on grain were removed, water was commercialised and the emergency animal feed provided by the Ministry of Livestock was phased out. These measures effectively destroyed the pastoralist economy and reinforced Somalia's dependence on imported food. At the same time, the urban population was thrown into unemployment as schools, hospitals and the civil service were shut down at the behest of the IMF. The groundwork was thus laid for the famine and civil war that would later envelop the country.[33] By the mid-1980s, facing growing opposition, Barre's regime was no more than a clan-based autocracy, detaining and executing prominent leaders of other groups. The US government supplied Barre with millions of dollars of arms throughout the decade in spite of the regime's well-known record of abuses, and trained the military officers who would become torturers and mass killers.[34] It was a level of outside military assistance unmatched in Africa's history. But in 1988, the economy collapsed as Somalia's failure to repay loans led to the withdrawal of IMF credit. The vast military arsenal Barre had amassed under US patronage was now deployed against the secessionist movement in the former British 'protectorate' of the north. A bombing campaign – using British-made fighter planes – was launched against civilians, leaving tens of thousands dead.[35] Half a million refugees left Somalia in 1988 and 1989, mostly to neighbouring countries. A small number came to Britain, adding to existing Somali communities in port-towns and in Sheffield.[36] In 1991, the north of Somalia (Somaliland) succeeded in breaking away and Barre was expelled from power, leaving behind a bankrupt, starving, war-torn country. The politics of clan identity had hollowed out the state itself, fragmenting the nation into various armed clan factions, which now fought for control of Mogadishu. The ensuing devastation left 30,000 dead and ten times as many lost to famine.[37] An attempt by the US, at the end of 1992, to invade Somalia, in what was the first of that decade's 'humanitarian interventions', resulted in the killing of up to 10,000 Somalis.[38] Since then, the country has had no functioning central state. The militarised clan structures are the only institutions able to offer protection from violence but many people are caught between the various warring factions.[39]

Though the specifics of Somalia's collapse were tied to its particular history of clan identity and rivalry with Ethiopia, an underlying pattern could be discerned that was repeated during the 1980s and 1990s across Africa, in particular, but also in parts of Asia. There was the disintegration of the social fabric as large numbers of people were forcibly 'integrated' into the economy of global capitalism. There was subsequent political repression, violence and abuse of human rights to maintain control of the state in the face of dissent, often fuelled by strategic interventions and supplies of arms from the West.

And there were the chains of migration, from the collapsing rural economies to the restless cities and from the terror of warfare directed at civilians to hastily erected refugee camps in neighbouring areas. For a few, there was the attempt to reach Europe or North America. Around 36,000 Somalis applied for asylum in Britain from 1992 to 2001 but these asylum seekers were seen in the West as, at best, charity cases, fleeing from a mess that had been created entirely by Somalis themselves.[40] It was more convenient to present the Somalis as uncivilised 'barbarians', who had a natural propensity to tribal warfare, rather than to acknowledge the West's own hand in Somalia's collapse in the 1980s. As A. Sivanandan put it, in a sentence directed at the West's leaders: 'It is your economics that creates our politics that makes us refugees in your countries.'[41]

Sri Lanka followed another variation on this pattern. Following independence in 1948, Ceylon, as it was then named, had a free health service, free education, rice subsidies and strong trade union rights. The country, though, was split into two different communities as a result of the 'divide and rule' politics of British colonialism. On the one hand was the dominant Sinhala majority, on the other, the Tamils of the underdeveloped north and east. Gradually, the electorate was 'communalised' into separate camps, as the main political parties used Sinhala chauvinism as a short cut to electoral power. By the early 1970s, the revenue from tea, rubber and coconut exports was not bringing in enough foreign currency. Loans from the IMF were sought and the welfare state system increasingly gave way to a 'free market' economy; by 1978, Sri Lanka had its first Free Trade Zone on the Indonesian model. Violent protest had taken hold among young Sinhalese who felt deprived of the jobs and contracts in the state sector on which they had, till then, depended. The state responded with terror and repression. But to reassure the restless Sinhala youths, the government introduced a programme of 'standardisation' in education, which meant that those sitting exams in the Sinhala language needed fewer marks to get into university than those sitting in Tamil. Discrimination against Tamil speakers was thus institutionalised in schools, excluding them further from the diminishing resources of the country. Education had always been seen as the primary opportunity that Tamils had for escaping the dead economy of the north and east. 'Language and learning – these were their land, their livelihood, their legacy, their sense of civilisation.'[42] As Tamil insurgency spread, responding to the climate of hostility against them, the state once again escalated its repression. The entire

Tamil population was considered by the state a threat to the nation. By 1983, anti-Tamil pogroms were raging, forcing refugees to flee to India and further afield. 'A culture of violence had now settled on the land' and the country descended into civil war.[43] In an echo of the visa controls imposed on Jews fleeing to Britain from Nazism a half century earlier, visa controls were imposed on Sri Lankans in 1985 when Tamils began arriving in Britain to claim asylum.[44] This made it impossible for them to seek refuge in Britain unless they were able to enter Britain illegally or travel through a virtual war-zone to the capital Colombo to obtain a visa; even then, it would almost certainly be denied them. It was the first time that visitors to Britain from any Commonwealth country had been required to obtain a visa.

3
Seeds of Segregation

Before a group can enter the open society, it must first close ranks. By this we mean that group solidarity is necessary before a group can operate effectively from a bargaining position of strength in a pluralistic society. – Stokely Carmichael and Charles V. Hamilton, 1967[1]

The racism against Asian, African and African-Caribbean 'New Commonwealth immigrants' to Britain had been tied to a contraction of British sovereignty: after the defeat of the empire, those who had settled in Britain as its colonial or ex-colonial subjects were to bear the brunt of a post-imperial rebirth of racism. Doing the jobs at the bottom of the economy that whites did not want, they were the cheap factory workers needed for post-war reconstruction, the nurses and doctors without whom the NHS would collapse. Racism determined these workers' economic status as much as it shaped the other aspects of their lives – in particular, where they lived. In law, they were British subjects but in practice they were 'coloured immigrants'. Soon the law 'caught up' with practice and, through the Immigration Acts passed from 1962 to 1971, British citizenship was implicitly aligned with being white. But the settlers who had already arrived had formal rights, even if they did not yet see them realised. They had the right to vote and stand in elections, access the welfare state and join a union. And because they arrived at a time of growing equality across society and expanding public services, they were able to use this foothold of rights – proclaimed but not practised – to mount the beginnings of a struggle against the injustices they faced. It was in Britain's response to this struggle that the seeds of segregation were planted.

At first, the basis on which this struggle would be waged was not apparent. African-Caribbean and Asian settlers tended to be recruited into separate spheres of work, according to the precepts of an ethnic division of labour. What united them was a common experience of anti-colonial politics in their home countries and the fact that the term 'coloured' was foisted on them all, irrespective of their different origins. But, by the end of the 1960s, a political movement had been built in these communities, influenced by the Black Power politics of the US and the liberation movements of Africa and Asia. It was a movement that had been forged out of a decade of resisting racism in the workplace, in immigration laws and on the streets and, in doing so, it had created a unified black political identity that incorporated the Asian, African and Caribbean experiences.[2] This was a politics that was as unique to the British context as the racism it sought to eradicate and, in its influence over the coming decades, would force on Britain a complexion of race relations that was entirely different from that which obtained in the rest of Europe.

For this movement, calling oneself 'black' was as much a statement of belief as it was of belonging. It did not primarily indicate an affiliation to a particular ancestry or ethnicity but to a politics of collective struggle against racism and colonialism, premised on the possibility of solidarities across ethnic or cultural differences. But it also placed an emphasis on cultural liberation as an integral part of its anti-racism. Anti-colonial movements had drawn attention to the ways in which colonialism internalised a sense of inferiority in the minds of the colonised. The colonial mindset held that only European culture had value: other cultures were, at best, frozen at earlier stages of civilisation; at worst, they had never produced anything of merit. Even with the defeat of direct colonialism, this kind of racial superiority went largely unchallenged as the common sense of the day. The upshot for non-white peoples was what the poet Langston Hughes had earlier called 'that old whispering "I want to be white"' – the belief that progress consisted in wearing the 'white masks' that had been denounced by Frantz Fanon, the radical anti-colonial psychologist.[3] 'The colonized is elevated above his jungle status,' he wrote, 'in proportion to his adoption of the mother country's cultural standards.'[4] Both the Black Power movement and anti-colonialists emphasised that the fight against racism and colonialism demanded a decolonising of one's mind from the 'alien gods' of white culture,[5] helping 'the black man to free himself of the arsenal of complexes that has been developed by the colonial environment'.[6] Black Power had started from the premise that, before one's community could be integrated into a plural society, such as the USA, it had to strengthen its own group identity and pride. Otherwise, integration would amount to a process of simply abandoning one's identity and, in defining individual and collective success in terms of mainstream acceptance, the idea of white society as automatically superior would be reinforced.[7] In the British context, this meant that

Asians, Africans and African-Caribbeans could not simply subsume themselves into the existing institutions and struggles of the working class. Rather there was a need for an independent struggle against racism – not as an alternative to class politics but on the principle that 'the unity and autonomy of black struggle could only enrich and politicise the struggles of the class as a whole'.[8] Therefore, what would today be taken as separate 'cultural' campaigns, such as for the right to take a prayer break or to wear a turban at work, were then seen as an integral part both of anti-racism and the fight for workplace rights. On a philosophical level, it prompted a search for alternative value systems in African and Asian traditions, which could be counterposed to a Western culture that was perceived through the lens of colonial experience as hierarchical, materialist and dehumanising. While this prompted a rediscovery of cultural heritage, the focus remained on culture as a vehicle of collective political change rather than as a political end in itself. As far as the political value of culture was concerned, it was measured by its ability to support radical change and revamp society. In this way, a black political identity was able to combine cultural diversity with political solidarities of race and class.

THE NEW RIGHT AND MULTICULTURALISM

As the politics of African-Caribbean and Asian communities became radicalised, mere survival in Britain was not enough. Those who were born or grew up in the UK wanted to remake society, not just be tolerated within it. The uprisings of the early 1980s were the most obvious expressions of this shift as, from 1981 to 1985, youths in a number of urban areas in the UK exploded into conflict with the police. As demands for change became louder and stronger, especially among the young, the *laissez-faire* approach to 'cultural diversity', which had been a part of Roy Jenkins's 1966 definition of integration,[9] was subjected to an ideological attack by the so-called 'New Right', a grouping of conservative writers and commentators who supplied an intellectual gloss to Thatcherism in the 1980s, and the state engaged in increasingly active attempts to manage 'minority culture' and suppress its radical political elements.[10] Echoing Enoch Powell's shift from a belief in an imperial racial hierarchy to focusing defensively on white national identity, the New Right placed a strong emphasis on Englishness as both a racial and a cultural identity. It was in this blurring of race and culture that ethnic identity became a major theme of Thatcher's neoliberal transformation of Britain. By basing nationality on a racial idea of culture, centuries-old ideas of 'Anglo-Saxon decency' were revived and given new life as the unchanging qualities of an essentially English pre-political shared culture that held the nation together in the imagination, even as, in reality, it was breaking apart. The failure to see the United Kingdom as a multinational state, of which England was one nation, was a recurring feature of this discourse. Filling the vacuum left by the Thatcherite dismantling of public services, this conservative English identity, an ethnicity of Englishness in all but name, replaced the sense of citizenship that the downsizing welfare state could no longer embody. State and citizen were not to be bound together by the pursuit of collective well-being but by their sharing a common culture of unchanging Englishness. African-Caribbean and Asian communities were cast as an 'alien wedge' threatening to disrupt the homogeneity that was supposedly essential to the national order. Margaret Thatcher had already expressed this idea a year before she took office, when she stated in 1978 that the British people were worried that 'this country might be rather swamped by people with a different culture'.[11] If repatriation was impractical, the argument ran, certainly any acceptance of ethnic pluralism within a single state, as Roy Jenkins had proposed, amounted to national suicide. Social cohesion required cultural uniformity, and the state had a duty to defend the majority cultural identity from internal and external threats. For those 'ethnic minorities' already in Britain, the state ought to insist on allegiance and acceptance of what were imagined as uniquely English traits of civility. In Norman Tebbit's 'cricket test', a popular way of expressing this idea of assimilation was found.[12]

The underlying assumptions of this 'new racism' seeped into public life with limited opposition in the 1980s.[13] In place of overt statements of racial superiority came the idea of innate cultural differences between ethnic groups; immigration by people of a different ethnicity threatened the cultural identity of the nation and had to be halted in the name of national cohesion rather than a biological notion of 'racial health'.[14] In the influential *Salisbury Review*, academics such as John Casey of Cambridge University wrote of how race should be thought of in terms of a cultural, rather than purely biological, identity. This idea of race involved shared language and customs as well as physical appearances; it was feelings of loyalty to race understood in this sense that could provide the only true basis for political order. Casey concluded that the African-Caribbean youths exploding into rebellion in Bristol, Brixton and Toxteth had an innate cultural propensity to disorder, even a primitive fascination with fire. Repatriation, he argued, was necessary to restore to England the cultural purity of its own traditions of respect for authority and social decency.[15]

It was in schools that the New Right waged its battle for cultural homogeneity most fiercely. Ray Honeyford, an affiliate of the *Salisbury Review* set and head of a Bradford school with a majority-Asian intake, became a *cause célèbre* for the New Right after writing articles arguing that, through a process of minority intimidation, the decent and tolerant majority culture was being eroded in schools. African-Caribbeans suffered from a flawed 'family structure and values' and came from homes that lacked 'educational ambition'; Asians displayed a 'hysterical political temperament' and were 'obstinately backward'. The 'fundamentally decent' whites had been abandoned by the authorities to the disorder and confusion that immigration had introduced.[16] The solution was a reassertion of a homogeneous 'English' culture. The government heeded this call with the 1988 Education Reform Act, which brought in a nationalist national curriculum and made 'a daily act of collective worship' of a 'predominantly Christian' nature compulsory in schools.

While one half of the official response to the riots was a misguided New Right attempt to impose cultural homogeneity, the other half was an attempt to soften the sharp edges of black politics through official multiculturalist policies that focused on managing the 'ethnic identity' of different communities. In the context of the New Right's attacks on ethnic pluralism, a concept of multiculturalism was essential as a demand for the survival of non-white communities in Britain and as an effective bulwark against an illusory English purity. Yet, the policies that were implemented in the 1980s in the name of multiculturalism were a mode of control rather than a line of defence. Multiculturalism in this sense referred to a set of policies directed towards taking African-Caribbean and Asian cultures off the streets – where they had been politicised and turned into rebellions against the state – and putting them in the council chamber, in the classroom and on television, where they could be institutionalised, managed and commodified. Black culture was turned from a living movement into an object of passive contemplation, something to be 'celebrated' rather than acted on. The method for achieving this was the separation of different ethnic groups into distinct cultural blocs, to be managed by a new cadre of ethnically defined 'community leaders', and the rethinking of race relations in terms of a view of cultural identity that was rigid, closed and almost biological; all of which aimed at adapting what were now called 'ethnic minorities' to the British body politic in an unthreatening way and preventing any one group's militancy from infecting the others. Thus, it was thought that multicultural policies would absorb protest and avoid more radical change. William Whitelaw, the home secretary at the time of the Brixton rebellion, hinted at this in his observations on the benefits of introducing 'multicultural' television programmes on the new Channel 4:

If you are Home Secretary in any government, you are going to take the view that there are a lot of minority interests in this country, [for example] different races. If they don't get some outlet for their activities you are going to run yourself into much more trouble.[17]

It was in keeping with this approach that the 'liberal' Scarman report into the Brixton riots of 1981 had discounted the existence of institutional racism in the police and highlighted the instability of the 'West Indian family' as the underlying 'ethnic disadvantage' facing African-Caribbean communities.[18] The problems of British race relations were to be officially located in the different 'ethnic' characteristics of each minority, rather than in the racist institutions that British society had produced. Similarly, the Swann report of 1985, a major official investigation into the future of education in a multicultural society, recommended that schools intervene to correct the 'rootlessness' that a weak family structure had passed on to African-Caribbean children.[19] By the end of the decade, the idea had been entrenched in the public mind that African-Caribbean families had a cultural propensity to failure, with disproportionate numbers of single, unemployed mothers bringing up children likely to end up in crime.[20] If it was their 'alien' culture that was the primary cause of African-Caribbean poverty, then British society could absolve itself of responsibility. Moreover, the state was justified, according to this argument, in mounting ever greater intrusions into the everyday lives of African-Caribbean youths, to enforce a civility that their families had supposedly failed to provide – so continuing the criminalisation of young African-Caribbeans that had begun in the 1970s. That African-Caribbean culture contained its own strength that could be mobilised for the good of young people was entirely left out of this picture. By the mid-1990s, young African-Caribbean men in England and Wales were five times more likely than whites to be stopped and searched by the police and nine times more likely to be in prison.[21] Those in custody were also more likely than other groups to end up being killed in excessive use of force by police or prison officers. The extent to which officials were willing to go to excuse the institutional racism they presided over was revealed when the head of the Prison Service blamed the disproportionate death rate of African-Caribbean men in prison custody on their being genetically more likely to die than whites when restrained.[22]

Whereas the African-Caribbean family was construed as having too little culture, the Asian family had too much. For Asian children, the problem was that they were caught in an apparent identity crisis, falling between the cultures of their parents and British society, such that neither commanded authority and rebelliousness resulted; such was their 'ethnic disadvantage'. Here too, teaching Asian culture in schools was seen as a way of overcoming this problem, by giving the parents' culture the respectability of a place in the school curriculum. For Asians and African-Caribbeans, it was thought that schools had good reason to assist 'the ethnic minority communities in maintaining their distinct ethnic identities'.[23] Unfortunately, the 'culture' taught in schools was based on hackneyed formulae of steel bands, samosas and saris and a particularly desiccated view of ethnic identity, in which different cultures were static and closed. And because white working-class children were usually perceived by teachers as having no culture of their own, it seemed as if they were losing out in multicultural schools. In these ways, genuine education about other people, their histories and their struggles, was replaced with the grim essentialism of identity politics, as each group competed for 'ethnic recognition' in the classroom. While the error of the New Right was to confuse national cohesion with cultural uniformity, the error of multiculturalist policies was to confuse anti-racism with a superficial sort of cultural recognition.

Alongside multiculturalist policies in education was the local authority practice of 'ethnicised' funding, which had the effect of segmenting and dividing communities from each other.[24] The state's strategy, it seemed, was to re-form non-white communities to align them with the British class system, as a parallel society with their own internal class leadership, which could be relied on to maintain order. A new class of 'ethnic representatives' entered the town halls from the mid-1980s onwards, who would be the surrogate voice for their own ethnically defined fiefdoms. They entered into a pact with the authorities; they were to cover up and gloss over community resistance in return for free rein in preserving their own patriarchy.[25] It was a colonial arrangement, which prevented community leaders from making radical criticisms for fear that funding for their pet projects would be jeopardised. Different ethnic groups were pressed into competing against each other for grants for their areas. The poor and the still poorer fought over the scraps of the paltry regeneration monies that the government made available to keep them quiet. Money that did come in was spent, after empty 'community consultation exercises', on projects that brought little benefit, particularly to the increasingly restive youths. As A. Sivanandan put it, 'equal opportunities became equal opportunism'.[26] The result was that community representation became fragmented by ethnicity. Worst of all, the fight against racism came to be redefined as a fight for ethnic recognition, as if funding an ethnic project, any ethnic project no matter how dubious, was to tackle racism. The cost to Asian communities of such set-ups was huge, measured not only in political subjugation, but also in cultural stagnation. The version of culture promoted by multiculturalist policies was largely defined in terms of a fixed identity, unchanged in its transmission from 1960s India or Pakistan to 1980s Britain. The often conservative community leaderships tried to insulate their clans from the wider world, not, as the Black Power movement had intended, in order to strengthen group identity prior to entering a pluralist society, but rather to protect the structures on which their power depended. Ethnic identity became an escape from a racist society rather than the basis for a challenge to it. The defensiveness that racism induced tended to discourage internal critics of the community; those that did voice concerns were considered disloyal. The dirty linen of Asian communities – the deep-seated gender inequality, the family authoritarianism, the forced marriages – was washed neither in public nor in private. Whereas earlier political movements in Asian communities had begun to talk about tackling these issues, such initiatives were squeezed in the 1980s between conservative state-sponsored community leaderships, on the one hand, and an increasingly racist society, on the other – a loss to Asian communities that is rarely acknowledged.

While local authority 'multiculturalist' policies of the 1980s fragmented the politics of non-white communities into distinct ethnic blocs, a growing geographical segregation of communities resulted, in certain areas, from the interaction between industrial decline and institutional racism. It was in their workplaces that Asian and white working-class men had occasionally been bound into a single social fabric, albeit unequally. In the Lancashire and Yorkshire mill towns, for example, from the 1960s onwards, Pakistanis had been recruited to work night shifts, which were unpopular with the existing white workforce. But as the machinery developed, the need for labour diminished, and such labour as was needed could be got for less elsewhere. The work once done cheaply by Asian workers in the north of England could now be done even more cheaply by Asian workers in Asia. As the mills declined, entire towns were left on the scrapheap. White and Asian workers were united in their unemployment. The only future now for the Asian communities lay in the local service economy. A few brothers would pool their savings and set up a shop, a restaurant or a take-away. Otherwise there was minicabbing, with long hours and the risk of violence and racist abuse.[27] With the end of the textile industry, the largest employers were now the public services but discrimination kept most of these jobs for whites. Industrial collapse led each community to turn inwards on itself. The depressed inner-city areas, lined with the old 'two-up-two-down' terraced houses that had been built for mill-worker families, were abandoned by those whites that could afford to move out to the suburbs. Others took advantage of discrimina-tory council housing policies that allocated whites to new housing estates cut off from Asian areas. At the end of the 1990s, just two per cent of Bradford's large stock of council housing had been allocated to Asians.[28] In Oldham, the local authority operated a housing policy in which Asians were systematically steered into separate and inferior accommodation.[29] Those Asians who did get council accommodation on predominantly white estates soon found their homes targeted, bricks thrown through windows, sometimes petrol and a lighted match through the door. The fear of racial harassment and violence meant that most Asians sought the safety of their own areas, in spite of the overcrowding, the damp and dingy houses, the claustrophobia of a community penned in. With whites in a rush to flee the ghettoes, property prices were kept low, giving further encouragement to Asians to seek to buy their own cheap homes in these areas. It was 'white flight' backed by the local state. The geography of the balkanised northern towns became a chessboard of mutually exclusive areas.[30]

In schools, segregation was encouraged through the mechanism of 'parental choice' that had been enshrined in the 1988 Education Reform Act and which enabled parents to choose other schools for their children if they decided that the nearest school had an excessive number of children of a different ethnic background from their own. The year before the Act was passed, a group of white parents in Dewsbury, with the support of the right-wing Parental Alliance for Choice in Education, had withdrawn their children from a school on the grounds that the majority of other pupils were Asian.[31] After the 1988 Act, it became more common for white parents to send their children to majority-white schools a little further away, rather than a nearer school with a mixed intake. What resulted were Asian 'ghetto' schools in which expectations of failure were common and poor results could be explained away by invoking 'cultural problems'. The minority of teachers willing to tackle these issues found themselves struggling against a mass of institutionalised preconceptions.

THE POLITICS OF ETHNIC DIFFERENCE

The New Right's emphasis on an ethnically defined national identity was matched on the left by a new emphasis on ethnic difference, which dovetailed neatly with contemporary intellectual trends. The defeats suffered by working-class politics in the West left a vacuum into which identity politics flowed during the 1980s and 1990s. The apparent collapse of class politics was attributed to its failure to accommodate a more diverse range of identities: 'ethnic minorities', women, gays and so on. All these groups had been forced to fit themselves into a class-based mould, in the name of solidarity, rather than express themselves according to their own cultural imperatives. At its core, the new embrace of cultural pluralism expressed an important truth: that people should not be expected to assimilate into a 'universal' public sphere that was imagined as neutral when its norms were, in fact, parochially male and white. The danger, though, was that in throwing out false universalisms, an inward-looking, reductive and conservative notion of identity would take hold. The important idea that our culture or ethnicity was a central aspect of who we were did not imply the mistaken idea that our ability to transcend that culture in identifying with others was fatally limited – but it was sometimes assumed to. This was especially the case when culture came to have an anthropological meaning: a distinctive way of life in which a people was rooted, organically, holistically and traditionally.[32] On this view, interaction between cultures could easily be seen as a contamination of each culture's uniqueness. Such an argument could be pitched as a radical defence of the right of 'minorities' to preserve their own identity. But it could equally be used to argue that white cultural identity needed to be defended against the contamination of 'immigrants', which led to policies of assimilation and repatriation.

If genuine interaction between cultures was not possible then solidarity could only exist between those of the same ethnicity, and this would imply that, in place of anti-racist unity, there would be a new politics of ethnic difference. By the 1990s, such arguments represented a new intellectual orthodoxy. The leading sociologist Tariq Modood argued that Asians could not identify with a black political identity:

because ... 'blackness' has so much of the history, sorrow, hopes and energy of descendants of African enslavement in the Atlantic world ... it cannot have the same meaning or equally give strength to those who can identify with that history and those who cannot.[33]

On one level, this was an obvious truth. Asian identity, defined by Modood as 'some share in the heritage of the civilisations of old Hindustan prior to the British conquest', had its own distinct symbols of identification, even if these were hard to spell out. (Modood thought that Asians were 'those people who believe that the Taj Mahal is an object of their history'.[34]) On another level, the argument was mistaken in its assumption that identities were primarily about cultural symbols shared by a single ethnic group. The black political identity that had been forged in the late 1960s was based on a shared political stance rather than on the specific history of a particular ethnic group. The way in which it was misinterpreted by Modood and others was itself a reflection of the extent to which identity politics in the 1990s had jettisoned any notion of social or political solidarity. It was true that, by the 1990s, the social context that had made a political black identity possible was ebbing away with a growing fragmentation in and between Asian, African and African-Caribbean communities. But the end point of this line of thinking was the implication that one could only unite with someone whose ethnic identity was exactly the same as one's own, which of course would rule out any kind of genuine political solidarity at all.

Under the influence of the post-structuralist philosophy that was in vogue among left-wing academics in the 1990s, many took this to its logical limit. The problem, argued post-structuralists, was with any social category at all, such as 'the working class', 'black' or 'Asian'. The model of the working class as a 'universal subject' was doomed to fail all along because such an approach ignored the fact that identification itself was a highly unstable practice. Any collective social identity ought to be treated as a suspiciously dangerous 'universal'. Allied to this line of argument was the idea that social realities such as racism were actually discursive in nature, that is to say that they were best understood and challenged as forms of discourse or as 'texts'. Behind this was a genuine insight: there was a growing realisation that the lines dividing East and West or black and white were, to some degree, imaginative, not in the sense that they did not exist, but in that they were not fixed by nature but produced by human discourse. But post-structuralism tended to argue that there was nothing beyond the discourse that produced these terms; they thus floated freely in the air, adrift of any possible social referent. This implied that identities could only ever be ambivalent, shifting and contingent: these were the 'new ethnicities' that were championed by Stuart Hall.[35] All this had huge consequences. Methodologically, it meant 'bracketing' the question of what the black experience, however multi-faceted, actually was and instead focusing on how the meaning of 'blackness' had itself been textually constructed. Politically, it meant that expressing one's ethnic identity was inherently an act of defiance and an end in itself, simply because to do so was to destabilise the 'mainstream discourse'. Finally, it meant that left-wing academics were, rather conveniently, placed at the forefront of anti-racism, uniquely equipped as they were with the ability to 'deconstruct' racist texts. A whole host of concepts – struggle, solidarity, social structure – that had previously been thought essential to political liberation were now seen as a hindrance.

This argument reached its apotheosis in the work of the post-structuralist critic Homi Bhabha, for whom political or social action was understood as a form of 'writing', the meaning of which was always incomplete.[36] In place of political struggle, there was the constantly shifting 'indeterminacy' of signifying processes. There was no opposition to racism as such; even oppositional discourses operated from within the same terms of reference. Instead, there was the transgression that resulted from an inherent indeterminacy in racial discourse. But this destabilisation of racial discourse did not need political struggle to activate it; it was simply an automatic feature of signifying practices themselves. Thus racism generated its own anti-racism in the process of its 'texts' being read. For a Left academia experiencing political defeat, this was no doubt an appealing idea. But for 'ethnic minority' communities it was disastrous. They had become officially defined not by colour or nationality or immigration status but by culture – which was proving to be the most ambiguous of concepts. And there was little in the Left's interpretation of culture that could be used to further their struggles for racial justice.

COMMUNITIES OF FEAR

The result of the New Right's politics of national identity and the state's attempts to manage 'ethnic' identity through 'multicultural' policies had, by the 1990s, produced two entirely different experiences of multicultural Britain. In popular culture, black culture had stepped into the mainstream of British life, albeit in a form that blunted its most radical edges. A glitzy image of 'Asian cool' was promoted in music, fashion, films and comedy, and Asian millionaires were fêted by leading politicians and glamourised in the media – the closest thing that Britain had to the American 'rags-to-riches' immigrant dream. It was all this that was summed up when non-white communities were described as 'vibrant' and when 'diversity' was described as something new and exciting for Britain. Yet the majority of young Asians and African-Caribbeans were excluded from this trendy coterie. For them, the public acceptability of a small number of high-profile faces only compounded their own sense of alienation. For them, multicultural Britain continued to be marred by a deep-seated racism, which not only excluded at every turn but also threatened them with violence on the streets.[37]

From Oldham, Burnley, Accrington, Blackburn and Preston to Bradford and Leeds, a generation of whites and Asians was now growing up whose only contact with each other was through uncertain glances on the street or through the pages of local newspapers. The schools they passed through had failed to give them an understanding of each other's history. Among Britain's most impoverished one per cent, these were communities that had sunk well below the radars of both the Blair administration and the wider Left. The politics of ethnic difference ensured that there was little sense that deprivation was an issue shared by different communities. Whereas Indians and Asian refugees from East Africa were both more likely to have had experiences of urban living and higher education before they settled in the UK, those who came into the working-class Asian communities of the northern towns brought with them much less in the way of cultural and financial capital. With roots in rural areas of Pakistan and Bangladesh (Mirpur and Sylhet), it was easy to interpret the poverty experienced in these communities simplistically as a direct function of their ethnicity or their Muslim faith. In Britain as a whole, 54 per cent of Pakistani and Bangladeshi homes survived on income support and a third of young Muslims were living in a household where no adults worked.[38] Many of these young people had been failed by an education system that expected them to fail, leaving them without any of the skills they would need to get the kinds of jobs that were now being created. And racism prevented many of those who did have qualifications from accessing the job opportunities they deserved.

These communities also continued to be the most likely to suffer racist harassment. The failure of the police to tackle racist gangs meant that violent confrontations between groups of whites and Asians were common in Lancashire and Yorkshire towns. Inevitably when the police did arrive to break up a mêlée, it was the young Asians who would bear the brunt of police heavy-handedness.[39] As such, Asian areas became increasingly targeted by the police as they decided that gangs of Asian youths were getting out of hand. The real crime problems faced by Asian communities – not only racist incursions but the growing epidemic of heroin abuse – were ignored. Among young Asians, there grew a hatred of police forces that left them vulnerable to racism, on the one hand, and, on the other, criminalised them for defending themselves. Taking their cue from the police, local newspapers marginalised the regular racist violence against Asians, while Asian crime on whites was sensationalised and interpreted as racially motivated.[40] The segregation of communities came to be perceived as 'self-segregation' – the attempt by Asians to create their own exclusive areas or 'no-go areas' because they did not want to mix with whites. It was a self-fulfilling prophecy.

When the police responded to white racists going on a rampage through the Asian area of Glodwick in Oldham in May 2001 by donning riot gear, arresting Asians and attempting to disperse the increasingly angered crowds of local residents, Asian youths responded using stones, burning cars and petrol bombs to drive the police, dogs and vans and all, off their streets. It took the police six hours to regain control of the area. Then, the following weekend, in the week that Tony Blair became the first ever Labour Party prime minister to win a second term of office, rioting erupted in Leeds. After police used pepper spray on a local Asian man, whom they accused of not paying his car tax, hundreds of youths surrounded the local police station and fought with officers for six hours. Two weeks later, a racist gang of football hooligans and members of the National Front attempted to march through an Asian area of Burnley, Lancashire. Around two hundred Asians assembled to prevent the gang from entering their streets but, instead, riot police advanced against them and another night of rioting between police and young Asians ensued. Then at the beginning of July, Bradford re-enacted the now familiar script. This time the riot resulted in injuries to hundreds of police officers and many buildings firebombed. It took one thousand police officers eight hours to regain control of the narrow streets. If the streets had been wider, the police said later, they would have used water cannon tanks to disperse the crowds.

In the scale of the damage caused and the shock they delivered to the nation, the fires that burned across the north of England in the summer of 2001 were the worst riots in Britain since the early 1980s, when African-Caribbean youths rebelled against racist policing in Britain's inner cities. Whereas earlier generations had risen up against the police as a community united in their anger at the 'heavy manners' of the police, the fires this time were lit by the youths of communities falling apart from within, as well as from without; youths whose violence was, therefore, all the more desperate. It was the violence of communities fragmented by colour lines, class lines and police lines; it was the violence of hopelessness. Hundreds of voices rushed to condemn the rioters in Oldham, Burnley and Bradford, while little was heard from young mill-town Asians themselves. The community leaders blamed a lack of discipline, a decline in Muslim values and the undue influence of Western culture. The popular press blamed the community leaders who had failed in their allotted role: to control 'their people'. Then it was the inherent separatism of Islamic culture that was to blame – these people did not want to integrate; they were 'self-segregating'. A people that had been discarded for their class, excluded for their race, stigmatised for their religion, ghettoised and forgotten, was now blamed for refusing to mix.

4

We Are Here Because You Are There

[T]he refugees, migrants and asylum-seekers, the flotsam and jetsam of latter-day imperialism ... are the new underclass of silicon-age capitalism. It is they who perform the arduous, unskilled, dirty jobs in the ever-expanding service sector ... They are, in a word, the cheap and captive labour force – rightless, rootless, peripatetic and temporary, illegal even – without which post-industrial society cannot run. – A. Sivanandan, 1989[1]

By the 1980s, countries in Africa, Asia and the Middle East were increasingly enmeshed in the emerging neoliberal economic order that had come to fruition with the election of Thatcher and Reagan in the UK and the US respectively, both of whom promoted neoliberalism around the world. Existing social bonds declined or broke asunder and the lives of billions of people were gradually conscripted into a new version of capitalism geared to the power of global markets. The new global capitalism was built on the legacy of structural adjustment programmes and Cold War interventions to subvert 'nationalist' states. In this new capitalism, global financial elites held sway over poorer nations. Unless prepared to break the rhythm of these new forces, governments in these countries had to dance to the tune of foreign investors, whatever the needs of their own people. The contemporary revolution in information technology offered the chance for capitalism to recompose itself around new imperatives. The defeat of organised labour in the West and the removal of post-war 'Keynesian' ideas of state investment allowed for production to shift to a new paradigm based on global chains of production, in which investment flowed freely across borders. Remaining restrictions on the free movement of money were removed by the pressure of international financial institutions that held the purse strings of debt-ridden regimes across the world. Capital was enabled to roam freely across borders, finding new workforces, new markets, new resources to exploit. The 'self-regulating market' that Karl Polanyi had written of spread to every corner of the world and into every sphere of life.[2] With the end of the Soviet system in 1991, the last great obstacle to this new global capitalism was removed. A series of new transnational structures, such as the World Trade Organisation, sought to give free market principles a quasi-constitutional status over the long term, thus locking poorer nations into unfairly weighted trade rules, not just on commodities but also on public services, such as health and education, and cultural wealth which, till then, had generally been exempted from international market forces. The role of the nation-state changed from that of a mediator between a national capitalist class and its labour force to a transmission line between global capital and a local population. In all countries subject to the rise of a neoliberal version of globalisation, the gulf between the people and their politicians spread wide open and earlier notions of a national community were shattered. In most nations, the ruling class became, more often than not, part of a globalised ruling elite to which ideas of sovereign national development were foreign. Whereas before, national sovereignty could be seen as a prerequisite to popular sovereignty, the neoliberal state no longer belonged to the nation but to global capitalism. What had been a world of sovereign nations made up of citizens became, increasingly, a world split between those with the power to consume and those without. The borders that had once denoted the boundaries between sovereign states now traced the lines between separate but integrated markets. The whole balance of rights, obligations, citizenship and sovereignty that had defined the nation-state system was thrown up in the air.

As Philip Bobbitt has argued, the ascendancy of a globalised version of capitalism diminished the credibility of nation-states as vehicles for the incremental improvement of people's welfare. This, in turn, led, in the US and the UK, to the emergence of a new principle of state legitimacy, replacing the welfare model of nation-states that was defined in the heat of industrial capitalism's class struggle. Bobbitt calls states that operate according to this new principle 'market-states': 'Whereas the nation-state justified itself as an instrument to serve the welfare of the people (the nation), the market-state exists to maximize the opportunities enjoyed by all members of society.'[3] The market-state does not intervene in the labour market to generate demand for jobs with the Keynesian aim of creating full employment; instead it seeks to enhance the potential of individuals to participate in the labour market, through training schemes and education. The well-being of social groups is no longer the responsibility of the state; its responsibility is to maximise the choices available to individuals. Market-states engage in a Dutch auction for foreign investment, offering ever-worsening protections for their populations in the name of 'competitiveness'. Public services shift from welfare provision to a focus on 'enabling' individuals to re-enter the labour market, through 'welfare to work' programmes, such as those pioneered by Bill Clinton and imported to Britain in the mid-1990s. Welfare rights are diminished while the responsibility of welfare recipients to adapt themselves to market demands is increased (see Chapter 5). And if markets cannot find a use for an individual, then neither can society. Insecurity and vulnerability are the hallmarks of this new order, in which entire communities can be socially abandoned by the state to poverty, low-level violence and disorder. In Britain, these abandoned communities – whether marked out by race or class – are entirely disenfranchised by the market-state and can no longer be held together by traditional working-class or immigrant culture. It is the children of this underclass, disdained as 'chavs' and 'hoodies', who are being imprisoned in their thousands under powers designed to tackle 'anti-social behaviour'.

THE NEW MIGRANT UNDERCLASS

The new version of globalised capitalism that had produced the market-state and an abandoned underclass in Britain's cities had also planted the seeds of a revolution in patterns of migration, altering the parameters of a long-standing association between migration and the rise of capitalism. On the one hand, migrants have in the past made up pools of 'reserve' workers on the margins of the labour market, who could be absorbed into production during economic upturns and ejected from work in subsequent downturns.[4] These reserve workers were the shock absorbers of industrial capitalism, a 'surplus population' whose lives were defined by an economic insecurity that was the product of inevitable fluctuations in the economic cycle. Their defining characteristic was their subjugation to the dictates of an expanding and contracting labour market. On the other hand, the growth of capitalism itself often produced migration. During periods of intense transformation, as pre-existing social relations were swept aside, people were forced to migrate in order to survive. In nineteenth-century Britain, as growing international competition in agriculture meant that work was harder to find on the land, people migrated to towns and cities. When even towns and cities proved unable to accommodate this 'surplus' labour, migration went further afield. In the eight decades from the middle of the nineteenth century through to the first quarter of the twentieth, just under 17 million emigrated from the British Isles, about 41 per cent of the 1900 population. Many took up positions in the expanding outposts of the British Empire but the majority of these economic migrants went to North America or Australia.[5] This mass emigration to the Americas and Australasia provided a 'dynamic safety-valve' to the uprooting of Britain's rural and urban unemployed.[6]

At the same time as British capitalism was generating a 'surplus population' that was available to migrate to the New World, it was also finding new workers to enter Britain from Ireland to carry out the poorly paid, menial tasks for which there were too few willing English workers – but which the industrial revolution nevertheless depended on. In 1841, between one-fifth and one-third of the working populations of London and Manchester was Irish.[7] These reserve workers were always stigmatised, as if the dirty and dangerous work that they undertook was a sign of their own dirty and dangerous character. A hundred years later, after the Second World War, the 'New Commonwealth immigrants' from Asia and the Caribbean joined the Irish in this role. A fully fledged racial division of labour placed Asian and African-Caribbean workers in jobs at the bottom of the economy in mills, foundries and factories. It was a division that reflected a global racial hierarchy entrenched by colonialism.

By the 1980s, with industrial production freed to relocate to other parts of the world, the potential pool of reserve workers also became globalised. Transnational corporations could prowl for cheap labour around the world, rather than be confined to national boundaries. Underlying the power of this new global capitalism was the threat of 'capital flight' – closing down an investment in one place and relocating it elsewhere. It was this that forced workforces across the globe to compete with each other on wage levels, undermining their collective strength and minimising wage inflation. This transformation meant that capital could find pools of reserve workers anywhere in the world. It also meant the generalisation of the economic insecurity that had been experienced by reserve workers in the era of industrial capitalism. The use of short-term, non-binding workforces became a routine business strategy. Job creation at the bottom end of the labour market was henceforth strongest in those sectors that were necessarily rooted in a particular place and so less vulnerable to 'capital flight' – for example, catering, cleaning, nursing, personal services, food processing. The principle of this post-industrial labour market was 'flexibility': deregulation made it easier for workers to be hired and fired at will and created a boom in part-time jobs, temporary jobs, jobs that paid so little per hour that they were only feasible if long hours of overtime were added. Privatisation, subcontracting, the threat of dismissal or relocation were the means by which this new regime was established. The bottom layers of the economy became centred on what Larry Elliott and Dan Atkinson called the 'rotating worker, forever in danger of being revolved out into the market to be replaced by cheaper labour from outside'.[8]

But at the same time as demand for these new kinds of 'flexible' low-paid workers was increasing in the UK, there was a decline in the number of people in the existing population who were willing or able to take on this kind of work. Britain's post-industrial economy increasingly turned to migrant communities to meet its demand for a flexible, peripatetic workforce. Those from Asia and the Caribbean, who had earlier come to the UK to meet the post-war demand for cheap labour, were disproportionately concentrated in the manufacturing jobs that suffered most under Thatcher's programme of de-industrialisation in the 1980s. Many found themselves permanently on the dole or forced to eke out a living in what was called the 'service sector' – for example, working in taxis, restaurants or take-aways.[9] But there was also the growing recruitment of women from these communities into the networks of sweatshops and home-working that had been developed in the shadow of the textile industry. As suppliers in this industry found themselves increasingly under pressure to cut costs, they sought to reduce their overheads through subcontracting, not necessarily to cheaper workforces in the Third World but to Third World workforces in the First World – usually women workers from the poorest and most excluded of Britain's immigrant communities, with male entrepreneurs from these communities acting as agents. Victorian working conditions were revisited in post-industrial networks of subcontracting and outsourcing, while the women themselves were 'trapped between the racism of the host community and the sexism of their own'.[10] These practices became essential for the textile industry's ongoing existence in Britain.

By the 1990s, the supermarket–supplier relationship was undergoing a similar restructuring to that which had occurred in the textile industry in Britain. The food processing companies that supplied supermarkets turned increasingly to the exploitation of migrant labour, as supermarket chains sought, with ever greater vigour, to cut costs and order the food industry around their own needs. Behind the supermarket oligopoly lay an array of suppliers who were entirely dependent on the supermarkets for their own survival.[11]

Behind the suppliers lay a disposable labour force, picking vegetables, processing food and packaging it all up. As supermarkets demanded reduced prices from their suppliers, the suppliers in turn demanded cheaper workers. As supermarkets shifted to opening at evenings and weekends, so too did the suppliers; and so the pack-house workers had to be available at any time of the day or night, any day of the year. And as supermarkets embraced 'just-in-time' computerised ordering, based on hour-by-hour sales returns, so too did the workforce have to be arranged around 'just-in-time' principles. Orders changed at very short notice in response to every whim of consumer demand. If a bout of hot weather caused demand for lettuce to shoot up, the ordering system would quickly pass this information on to the supplier who would, equally rapidly, have to find thirty workers to pack lettuce. This demand for labour would pass through the chain of subcontractors down to a gang-master who had to be able to get these workers to the pack-house immediately.[12] For this to happen reliably and cheaply, a pool of disposable workers, rather than a permanently employed and properly protected labour force, was advantageous. It was natural, then, that this workforce would usually be made up of migrant workers, often indentured to a gang-master and dependent on him for work and residence. According to a study of the food processing sector in Sussex in the late 1990s, migrant workers from eastern Europe were paid £3 per hour before the gang-master's deductions for rent, transport costs and interest on the loans necessary to migrate to Britain. Work was not always available but, when it was, workers might be expected to do seventy hours a week. Threats, intimidation, fines and even physical violence were used to keep workers in order.[13] This intense exploitation and vulnerability effectively subsidised the shiny, supermarket culture of 'consumer choice' and the low inflation of food prices that the rest of Britain's population benefited from.

The supermarket-supplier industry is one example of a sector in which the post-industrial economy has become structurally dependent on regiments of migrant workers whose availability as a heavily exploited 'underclass' makes possible the way of life that Britain takes for granted. Another sector in which this dependence has emerged is in the creation of a new servant class of in-house 'domestics' to clean homes and care for children. The numbers of people in Britain able to afford domestic help shot up in the 1990s, with the amount spent on domestic workers quadrupling between 1987 and 1996, according to one report.[14] Increasingly, migrant women are recruited as live-in domestic workers.[15] A survey conducted in August 2002 by the campaign group Kalayaan illustrated the degree to which this work is often associated with humiliation and abuse. It found that two out of three domestic migrant workers suffered physical abuse from their employers, while nine per cent had been sexually abused. Although these women were working legally in Britain under the Home Office's domestic worker migration scheme, around half were estimated to have had their passport withheld by their employer, which meant that the ability to prove their immigration status rested on the goodwill of their employers. Employers often exploited this fact to enforce harsh working conditions, long hours and other forms of mistreatment.[16] In one case documented by Kalayaan, a Gambian woman who was invited to the UK by a British family found that she was expected to work from six-thirty in the morning till midnight or later, not just doing childcare as promised, but also cleaning, cooking and taking the children to school. For this work, she was initially paid £300 per month but, after a while, the family stopped paying her and threatened her with being sent home if she complained.[17]

In Britain, the architecture of immigration policy had, since the early 1970s, been built on the need to thwart the migration of workers from outside the EU. As such, the new migrant labour forces which, by the 1990s, were required to meet the demands of Britain's post-industrial economy, were to be found largely through clandestine immigration, the use of false papers and 'over-staying' on visas. There were those who entered Britain clandestinely without any legal documents and were unknown to the immigration authorities; those who entered legally as visitors but did not have permission to work; those who came to study but worked more than the allowed twenty hours per week; those who entered legally as workers or students but stayed longer than their visa allowed or switched from the job they were permitted to do; and those who entered to claim asylum but worked without permission.[18] Even those who were working legally in Britain under various work permit schemes experienced a measure of vulnerability as they were effectively tied to their employer and risked being rendered 'illegal' if their contract ended. It was through these categories of entry that the new underclass of migrant workers was established in the cleaning, nursing, construction, fast food and agriculture sectors, where trade unions had little presence and inspection systems were negligible.[19] The practice of subcontracting labour through gang-masters was found not only in the food processing sector but also across the hospitality and cleaning sectors and small-scale manufacturing.[20] This was an underclass that could be subjected to extremely long hours doing dangerous, dirty work; that could be made to bear excessive deductions supposedly to pay for accommodation, transport and administration; a workforce often without proper contracts, sick pay, holiday pay, maternity leave; and, a workforce that avoided complaining for fear of dismissal and, potentially, deportation.

These migrant workers are more likely to take on hard, dirty, irregular work; more likely to adapt to production peaks and troughs and seasonal variations. Usually here without family, they are more likely to work long shifts or nights or weekends. They are the idealised workers of pure capitalism, willing to offer up their labour wherever and whenever it is demanded, apparently unfettered by non-economic factors, their lives reduced to a never-ending cycle of chasing work and then recovering from it. The costs of creating and sustaining this unit of labour – the nurture, subsistence and education needed to provide Britain with a healthy, adult worker – are borne by another country, certainly a poorer country. As John Berger has put it:

They are not born: they are not brought up: they do not age: they do not get tired: they do not die. They have a single function – to work. All other functions of their lives are the responsibility of the country they come from.[21]

Hidden from view is a network of family ties and mutual dependencies. The man who seeks work abroad will often leave behind a wife struggling to keep the fabric of family life intact. The woman who emigrates often has to find a mother or sister to take on the unpaid domestic work she leaves behind. As a living, financial investment for an extended family, migrant workers are literally 'human capital'. Britain's hypocrisy is to want only the work and not the worker, creating an underclass that can service society without being a part of it. Effectively, this hidden underclass does not exist until some catastrophe, such as the death of twenty-three Chinese cockle-pickers at Morecambe Bay in February 2004, briefly exposes their plight – but, even then, it is portrayed only as a failure of Britain's border controls rather than as a consequence of Britain's deregulated labour market.

GLOBAL EXODUS

On 2 August 2004, thirty police officers, twenty Immigration Service officers and two officials from the Department for Work and Pensions raided a factory in Lancashire where frozen pizzas were made. They spent four hours checking the status of workers at the factory and arrested twenty-one people. Most of those arrested were 'failed asylum seekers', from Zimbabwe, Ethiopia and the Democratic Republic of Congo, all countries with well-known human rights problems. Seven of the twenty-one arrested were eventually jailed for using false documents. One of those arrested was Didier Motengo.[22] A graduate from the Democratic Republic of Congo, Didier had been arrested in Kinshasa two years earlier for his university political activities. He was taken to a detention centre, interrogated and beaten with rifle butts. Later, he managed to escape and, with the help of an agent, Didier fled to the UK to claim asylum. Although he was able to present evidence in support of his claim, Didier was refused asylum by the Home Office and was unsuccessful in further appeals. He was now a 'failed asylum seeker', forced to survive on the minimal level of support provided by the Home Office. Didier chose to work illegally, hoping that he could raise enough money to finance further legal action (the new rules on legal aid for asylum claims meant that he had no chance of access to public funds for legal representation). But the government was under pressure to clamp down on 'illegal working' among migrants and the numbers of raids on workplaces was increasing. Didier was unlucky enough to be caught in one of these raids. At his trial, the judge recognised that Didier and the other 'failed asylum seekers' were in a dire situation:

The desperate circumstances that you found yourself in led you into this dishonesty. I know and accept that each of you desperately wanted to stay in this country. I also accept that you resorted to dishonesty because of your desperate plight.

Nevertheless, the judge added that 'using a false document to gain employment strikes at the very fabric of our society'. Didier was sentenced to four months in prison.

Didier was one among the hundreds of thousands of migrants who have ended up in Britain's new underclass. Some, like Didier, have been asylum seekers, driven to migrate because of the warfare, ethnic conflict or political repression that have been symptoms of the fractured 'integration' of African and Asian nations into the global market, or the result of the Cold War's impact on the Third World (see Chapter 2). Others have aspired to escape, for a while, the underdevelopment of their own country, putting their skills at the disposal of richer countries' economic needs and matching supply with demand according to free market dictates. In an echo of the nineteenth-century emigration that accompanied the ascendancy of industrial capitalism in Europe, the globalisation of capitalism has resulted in epic social upheaval, this time on a worldwide scale. Again, millions have been driven to leave their homes as their existing livelihoods have collapsed around them, fleeing either to other parts of their own country or overseas, in the search for security. Governments caught in a debt trap have been unable to generate opportunities for their own young people, prompting a desire to seek work overseas. The remittances sent back by these migrants have then become essential to the government's finances and there has been no incentive to control emigration, either by policing or through the creation of indigenous opportunities. Contrary to the image of poor countries dependent on Western charity, the reality is increasingly one in which migrant workers generate the wealth needed for their countries to survive. According to the World Bank, migrant workers sent back over $200 billion to their home countries in the developing world in 2005, outstripping flows of development aid.[23] Thus, at the same time as a new version of capitalism has been pushing Britain to depend increasingly on migrant workers, so too has the globalisation of the new capitalism generated the conditions for large-scale emigration from many regions of the world, throwing up the migrant 'surplus population' that post-industrial economies like Britain need.

In the Philippines, for example, governments have cut down rain forests, destroyed coral reefs and squeezed the poor of primary healthcare, clean water and shelter – all in order to cope with debt repayments. Now, the Philippines is effectively kept out of bankruptcy by Filipinos working abroad sending back remittances. Filipinos in Britain sent back $260m in remittances in 2003.[24] But this injection of foreign currency needs to be balanced against the money exiting the country in debt repayments. The government spends eight times more on servicing its debt than the amount it spends on its own healthcare system. Nurses and doctors are underpaid and work excessive hours which, in turn, encourages further emigration and is causing a recruitment crisis in the Philippines' own hospitals. Even qualified doctors – some with sixteen years' specialist experience – are enrolling on nursing courses with a view to working abroad where demand for Filipino nurses is greater than for Filipino doctors. Two thousand doctors were said to have taken this route by 2004.[25] In private nursing homes in the UK, there are legions of qualified Filipino nurses who have come to Britain, after paying a 'finder's fee' to an employment agency, hoping to work in nursing. The job often turns out to be working in the kitchen or scrubbing the toilets rather than actual nursing. Often these workers, mostly women, hope to gain a British nursing qualification through working a six-month adaptation period. But the work permit system means that the threat of deportation hangs over them if they complain and nor is their pay protected. Although the work permit has a wage stated on it, agencies extract from nurses extra hours without pay or even force them to sign a new contract on a reduced wage. In two Glasgow hospitals, Filipino nurses have been found to be working for effective wages of just £8 per day.[26] While Britain's own health service is subsidised by this cheap migrant labour force, in the Philippines healthcare is starved by a combination of debt and emigration. And thousands of Filipino migrants suffer the human costs of degrading work and family separation to sustain this contorted economy.

Unlike the migrations of the nineteenth and early twentieth centuries, the large-scale migrations to the richer parts of the world in the current era of global capitalism have been met by a militarised system of worldwide immigration controls established to police this movement and regulate it on behalf of the wealthy nations. With a cruel irony, the very global forces that had thrown these migrants and asylum seekers into searching for security overseas also conditioned the hostile mood against them. The feeling that the state could no longer provide for the existing population made it all the harder for Britain to accept any provision for newcomers: 'we have to look after our own people first' was the headline in a thousand newspaper columns. It was not the numbers of asylum seekers and migrants coming to Britain that explained the adverse reaction to them. After all, the numbers were rising but they remained small compared to the overall population, and the places and times where the reaction was most virulent were usually where the numbers were smallest. It was rather that, thanks to the opportunism of media and politicians, asylum seekers and migrants had been made into potent symbols for the loss of a nation-state that once 'belonged' to its people and afforded them certain privileges as citizens. As power had shifted to the global level, citizenship had withered within national boundaries and it now expressed itself in a hollowed-out cry turned inwards towards new forms of racism rather than the outward-looking universalism of the post-war period. In this way, the icon of the 'asylum seeker' not only came to stand in for the new kinds of migrations that globalised capitalism had produced but also became a screen onto which wider anxieties associated with 'globalisation' could be projected. These anxieties coalesced around the diminishing credibility of the nation-state as a means by which the people's well-being could be increased. A diminished sense of national community was the psychic fall-out of the transition to the market-state.

Amid this upheaval, a popular myth grew up that asylum seekers were not coming to Britain to escape violence and persecution in countries such as Afghanistan, Iraq, Nigeria, Somalia, Sri Lanka and Turkey. Really they were all chasing economic betterment, by accessing the provisions of Britain's welfare state. Until 1985, nobody had taken much notice of immigration by asylum seekers who had, before then, usually been white and fleeing communism, both of which helped their acceptability. With the arrival of Tamil refugees from Sri Lanka in 1985, the issue suddenly flared up. When Home Office figures for that year showed that 5,444 people had applied for asylum, Douglas Hurd, the then Conservative home secretary, described the majority as 'disguised economic migrants', setting the template for a campaign against asylum seekers that would escalate relentlessly over the next two decades.[27] Not only was there a muddle between economic migration and asylum-seeking; there was also a refusal to examine 'push factors' in countries of origin (such as political persecution by UK-backed regimes) and the full range of 'pull factors' in countries of destination (such as Britain's need for migrant workers); all was reduced to the simple calculation that 'they' were coming to take 'our' riches. Of course, it was true of some asylum seekers that they were primarily coming to take up work in Britain that was better paid than in their own countries. But prevailing opinion tended to regard all migration, including asylum-seeking, in terms of a crude economic cost-benefit analysis; thus emerged the idea that across the poor countries of the world, there were vast hordes on the verge of migrating to rich countries, either to work or to obtain welfare benefits. As travel costs went down, these hordes would increasingly find migration economically viable. Yet the reality of migration has been far more complex. Of course, disparities in wealth have created incentives to migrate but, if human beings always made decisions about where to live on the basis of economic betterment alone, then everyone in Greece would have moved to Luxembourg where they could instantly double their wages, as they are legally entitled to do.[28] For most asylum seekers, it was not that poverty had led directly to their migration; it was rather that the embedding of poor nations in a world market system tended, in a variety of complex ways, to unleash political and ethnic conflicts which, in turn, forced people into fleeing violence. These asylum seekers were in genuine fear of persecution according to the Geneva Convention definition but were overwhelmingly rejected as 'economic migrants'.[29] As a route opened up of people seeking safety in Britain from these countries, there was then inevitably a minority who, though not in immediate danger of persecution themselves, trod the same asylum-seeking path to take up work in Britain, more often than not only for a short time before returning home.[30] But this economic migration was driven by demand in Britain for cheap workers rather than a supply in poor countries of acquisitive emigrants. And since UK immigration policy meant that there was no legal way for this demand to be met, clandestine migration – and possible abuse of other migration routes, such as the asylum system – was the inevitable consequence. In the end, then, the confusion between seeking asylum and economic migration became self-fulfilling. Those who were responding to Britain's demand for cheap migrant workers occasionally presented themselves as asylum seekers in order to remain in the country for a while, while those who were genuine asylum seekers were often, like Didier Motengo, forced to work illegally after their asylum claim had been rejected and they were left destitute.

BORDER CRIMES

In a speech on immigration given to the Confederation of British Industry in April 2004, Tony Blair referred in passing to his recommending Nicholas Winton for a knighthood, in recognition of his work saving nearly 700 Jewish children from Nazi-occupied Czechoslovakia.[31] Winton visited Prague in late 1938 and, alarmed by the danger facing Jews who were then filling refugee camps in a city set to be invaded by the Nazis, decided to make every effort to rescue the children. Back in Britain, the Home Office was persuaded to issue special visas allowing the children to travel to London, where they met foster parents. It is an episode hailed by Blair as an example of Britain's 'long heritage of welcoming those who are genuinely in need of our protection'.[32] What he neglected to mention was the fate of the parents of those children, who were refused entry to Britain and many of whom, one assumes, perished in the gas chambers. Whereas popular history recalls a proud history of Britain offering sanctuary, the reality was less salutary. The 'East African Asian' refugees – British subjects of Asian origin who fled from Uganda, Kenya and Tanzania in the 1960s and 1970s – were also cited by Tony Blair as beneficiaries of Britain's tradition of protecting refugees. Yet it was a Labour government that rushed through legislation in 1968 to block their entry.[33] In the case of Jews fleeing Nazism and East African Asians, Blair said, 'the evidence of persecution was all too clear, the case for asylum overwhelming'. Current asylum seekers were different though: 'since the early 1990s, the nature and volume of asylum claims to the UK has changed radically. It became increasingly apparent that our asylum system was being widely abused.'[34] Yesterday's refugees are always remembered more fondly than those seeking safety today.

Were he trying to save today's child victims of persecution, a present-day Nicholas Winton would have to become a people smuggler, risking prosecution and up to fourteen years in prison. There is only one way that today's Home Office admits refugees into Britain: through a 'resettlement' programme launched in April 2003. By October 2005, only 201 refugees had been brought to the UK on this scheme.[35] For the rest of the world's refugees – the millions in refugee camps in Iran, Pakistan, Jordan and Tanzania[36] – no matter how overwhelming the evidence of their persecution, nobody is going to examine their claims until they get themselves on to British soil. And the only way they can do that is by some form of clandestine entry into the country: either stowing away in a lorry or boat, clambering on the undercarriage of a moving Channel Tunnel train or using forged documents. 'Illegal immigration' is supposedly a serious crime. But it is a crime like no other. Although those suspected of it can be arrested, have their premises searched, be held in a detention centre for an indefinite period of time and have 'reasonable force' used against them, this 'crime' is recognised as a right by the Geneva Convention on Refugees. Article 31 of the convention allows that entering a country without documents is often necessary for refugees and stipulates that there should be no penalty for entering a country in this way. To seek asylum is therefore simultaneously a basic human right and an act that is virtually illegal. As Jack Straw put it, the Geneva 'Convention gives us the obligation to consider any claims made within our territory ... but no obligation to facilitate the arrival on our territory of those who wish to make a claim.'[37] This underlying paradox is rarely noted in the public debates about asylum and yet it provided the basis for a vicious circle of criminalisation that asylum seekers were caught in from the mid-1980s onwards, which pushed them into deception and, ultimately, the use of criminal networks in order to enter Britain to exercise their right to asylum.[38]

The vicious circle began with the selective visa restrictions imposed by Britain, first on Sri Lanka in 1985 and then consistently on every country from where refugees have fled;[39] the most recent country to face a visa regime has been Zimbabwe, after intensified repression by Robert Mugabe's government in November 2002. A visa is essential to entering Britain legally because airlines are careful to prevent passengers from flying without the proper documentation – they receive fines if they fail to do so. But to obtain a visa from a UK embassy is virtually impossible for would-be refugees. There has never been a special visa that those hoping to claim asylum can apply for, which means that, when applying for a visa, asylum seekers are immediately forced to conceal their real reason for wanting to enter the UK. In any case, visas are never granted where there is a suspicion that someone might claim asylum. An added problem is that those facing persecution in a country are unlikely to be able to obtain a passport from that country's government. In fact, those asylum seekers who do travel to the UK legally with a valid passport are told by the Home Office that they could not be a genuine refugee, on the assumption that the authorities in the home country would refuse to allow a genuine dissident to obtain one. Meanwhile, those who travel to the UK with invalid passports are told that the credibility of their asylum claim is undermined by the fact that they had a forged document. Either way, you are a 'bogus asylum seeker'. The effect of these kinds of measures was to drive more asylum seekers to use illegal means to enter Britain: either through clandestine entry to the country or through the use of forged documents. Just as migrant workers who were coming from outside the EU to meet Britain's labour demands were forced to use clandestine means, so too were those who wanted to assert their right to asylum in Britain under the Geneva Convention. Thus, the 'people trafficking' industry was created. Asylum seekers and migrant workers were driven into the hands of criminal networks. The system had turned them from migrants and asylum seekers into 'illegal immigrants'. In the process, the personal risks they themselves faced were drastically increased, having to cross not just deserts and mountains but minefields, electrified fences and straits patrolled by military craft. And everywhere the journey would bring them into contact with the local mafias and the associated risks of extortion, exploitation or violence.[40]

By the 1990s, the focus was on how these 'illegal immigrants' could be stopped from entering Britain. New criminal offences were introduced for those 'assisting illegal entry', criminalising those who arranged for asylum seekers to come to the UK, irrespective of whether their asylum claim turned out to be accepted. New arrest powers were given to immigration officers, justified by the need to intercept the 'trafficking gangs'. The 'traffickers' began to be considered serious criminal threats analogous to drug smuggling and other forms of transnational organised crime, ignoring the fact that illegal migration was the only way that the vast majority of those with valid asylum claims could reach Britain at all.[41] To criminalise people-smuggling out of existence without introducing significant other routes for would-be refugees to be admitted – as the government now sought to do – was, therefore, virtually to abolish the right to asylum. By 2004, legislation had been introduced that made it an offence not to be able to produce a valid passport when interviewed on or after arrival in Britain. Since those with genuine asylum claims generally were unlikely to obtain valid travel documents in their home countries, this effectively made a criminal offence of the only remaining practical method that genuine asylum seekers had of seeking sanctuary in Britain. In the first six months of this provision being in force, 134 asylum seekers were sent to prison in this way.[42] It was no surprise that those discovered trying to enter Britain were described by the media as 'suspected asylum seekers' or 'illegal asylum seekers', as if to seek asylum was itself a criminal offence.

This attempt to control flows of people across borders increasingly involved Britain's joining a common EU strategy of militarising border controls on Europe's periphery. Although the UK negotiated 'opt-outs' from many of the asylum and immigration policies being co-ordinated in Brussels and did not join the common border policy of the 'Schengen' agreement, Britain worked closely with other EU countries in co-ordinated border policing operations. In the Mediterranean, Royal Navy craft were deployed and supported by the RAF in intercepting migrants from Turkey and North Africa before their entry to EU territorial waters.[43] As desperate migrants tried to sneak their way through the gaps in Europe's borders, the seas that separated the continent from Africa and Asia became hidden war-zones, where the battle to enforce a global migration regime was being fought. The total death toll ran into the thousands, with an average in 2002 of 37 reported deaths per month of people trying to cross into Europe by sea; many other deaths went unreported.[44]

The policing of immigration was driven by a military notion of 'invasion', at the expense of any attempt to protect the welfare of people in desperate situations. In turn, the criminal market for people-smuggling burgeoned. The ninety lives that are known to have been lost between 1989 and 2004 as a result of people using dangerous and highly risky methods to enter Britain is testimony to this spiral of increasingly dangerous border crossings.[45]

As would-be asylum seekers perished on Britain's borders, the old canard of a proud British tradition of giving sanctuary to refugees sounded distinctly hollow. Yet asylum seekers do not ask for British charity; they claim rights as global citizens in an age when the national sovereignty of poorer nations has been eroded. Through its part in the empire of global capitalism, Britain carries with it a profound obligation to today's migrants, just as it had obligations to the 'New Commonwealth immigrants' of thirty years ago. It is an obligation that runs through the dirty politics of sponsoring foreign regimes that oppress their own people, in Turkey, Saudi Arabia, Nigeria and elsewhere. It runs through the wealth Britain continues to extract from Africa and Asia in debt-servicing, arms trading and the exploitation of natural resources. And it runs through the bloody catalogue of wars that Britain and, through the job-sharing of its 'special relationship', the United States, have fought to secure and protect those flows of wealth, both openly and by proxy, from Angola to Iraq. Ultimately, it is an obligation to treat today's migrants, not as scroungers or opportunists or victims of some self-created calamity of which little is known, but as global citizens. It is in the very processes of globalising capitalism, which Britain has led and profited from, that their global citizenship derives. We are here because you are there.

5
Asylum and the Welfare State

The British government does all it can to make asylum seekers feel at home – by treating them as badly as they were treated where they came from. – Jeremy Hardy, 1993[1]

By the mid-1990s, Britain had become a place in desperate need of change. Thatcher's energetic revolution-from-above, her attacks on the post-war Keynesian consensus, 'gentlemanly rule' and the old cultural elites, and their substitution with the values of middle-class entrepreneurialism and market forces, had waned. All that was left was John Major's reassurances to an ageing Home Counties audience that England would be forever village cricket, warm beer and old maids cycling to church through the morning mist. Many now looked to Tony Blair as harbinger of a much-needed 'modernisation'. Whereas previous Labour governments had based their right to rule on consensus and the better management of class conflict, Tony Blair's government claimed it was better placed to manage the needs of globalisation, because it was capable of *actively* 'modernising' society along neoliberal lines – something the Conservatives under John Major were unable to make progress on. At the heart of New Labour's modernising project was the concept of a 'knowledge economy'. Wealth was now to be created, not through mass production, with all its connotations of monotonous labour, alienation and exploitation, but with a workforce that was innovative, creative and flexible. Ideas, not machines, were the new forces of production; brains not hands the new wealth of nations. This presented a historic opportunity for the centre Left: capitalism, it was argued by New Labour, had discovered a vested interest in equal opportunity and education for all.[2] To actively intervene to bring the excluded into the labour market – through training programmes, for example – was to promote economic efficiency as well as social justice. For Third Way intellectuals, the knowledge economy seemed to promise the Holy Grail of social democracy, a reason for thinking that business and workers were no longer opposing forces. Both could be absorbed into a mutually beneficial contract of social inclusion.

Of course, such a project was only possible in the wake of two decades of neoliberal economics and the Thatcherite disaggregation of the working class. But whereas Thatcherism sought to minimise state intervention in the economy, Blairism envisaged a new basis for active, interventionist government, in the form of the market-state (see Chapter 4). The state's legitimacy was to be based on its role in maximising the potential of individuals to participate in the market economy. It would constantly intervene in the labour market to engineer a workforce that was fully adapted to the demands of a globalised, knowledge economy: a 'flexible' workforce with high job turnover and increasing precariousness. A cultural change in the workforce was required, embracing personal innovation, lifelong learning and adaptability. 'Welfare to work' policies, imported from Bill Clinton's America, would encourage these new attitudes among the unemployed.[3] Under previous Labour governments, there was taken to be a collective struggle against the poverty of unemployment; Keynesian fiscal policy was used to encourage demand in the economy and the creation of jobs, while the welfare state provided a universal safety-net when the economy failed. For the market-state, unemployment was not a failure of the market but of the individual – even a moral failure. The long-term unemployed, said Tony Blair, suffered from a 'culture of poverty, drug abuse, low aspirations and family instability'.[4] It was these that were holding them back from joining modern Britain, rather than institutional barriers or a disinclination to work long hours for a pittance. The idea of social security as a universal right no longer pertained; instead programmes of compulsory rehabilitation sought to inculcate 'responsibilities'. Refusal to accept a job or training programme would now be punished by the withholding of benefits. A personal advisor would talk through how best to return to work: the first step would be for the 'job seeker' to sign an agreement to undertake a series of steps to escape their plight; unemployment was to be tackled as if it were like alcoholism. In this way, the emphasis shifted from 'demand-side' management of the labour market to mandatory 'supply-side' measures; from directing the economy for the welfare of the people, to forcing individuals to adapt to the whims of the global economy. Whereas post-war Labour governments built the welfare state as the necessary bedrock of stability from which to go out into a risky world of social and economic change, in the age of globalisation and the market-state that bedrock was to be 'strong communities' and 'shared values'. The state had long since retreated from the ambition of protecting people from market forces *per se*. Nor was the state to leave individuals to survive alone in the market – that was, New Labour argued, the mistake of Thatcherism. Rather, the state's role was 'enabling' – to facilitate the strengthening of communities so that individuals had the confidence to endure market-driven social upheaval and embrace the opportunities that markets offered. It was shared values that allowed us to 'face the future without fear', Blair had said in 2000,[5] while David Blunkett had written that his politics was about the need to create a new sense of belonging that would serve as a 'counterweight' to the 'pace of technological change or globalisation'.[6] In this sense, New Labour's 'modernisation' was not just a political or economic project but also an attempt to produce new kinds of identity that were defined by the values of the market state.

The main hallmark of the post-war welfare state was the replacement of the coercive, discriminatory and stigmatising Poor Laws, and their associated machinery of surveillance into people's private lives, with a new ethic of social citizenship and universal inclusion. Access to the welfare state was not charity handed down from on high, to be carefully policed and allocated according to intrusive tests, but a right. But, gradually, the system of welfare provision had come to be associated with compulsion and restriction. The shift from welfare state to market-state, fully in train by the mid-1990s, meant that recipients of welfare were no longer bearers of rights but objects of surveillance and coercion, which aimed at inducing in them appropriate forms of behaviour. In this rebalancing of rights and responsibilities, recipients could no longer be allowed to passively consume services according to the principle of need. Instead, the state increasingly tried to use its powers to produce the kinds of active citizens it wanted, in line with the needs of the market, and sought to make the provision of welfare conditional on the adoption of a set of 'shared values'. And in order to enforce such an approach, the market-state accrued to itself a vast array of new powers to separate the legitimate receivers of state provision from 'abusers' and 'scroungers'. There was, of course, a decades-long history of media scapegoating, which played on fears that 'dole cheats' or 'single mothers' were running down the welfare state. And, since at least the 1970s, there had been newspaper campaigns against 'immigrant scroungers'. But, during the 1990s, the ebbing away of the remnants of the old welfare state meant that these fears reached a new intensity. It was asylum seekers that provided the obvious focus for such fears. The Geneva Convention had established a framework to provide refugees with sanctuary, irrespective of their ties to any particular nation. In doing so, it represented an exception to the post-war norms of national sovereignty and the welfare state that had symbolically tied entitlements to welfare with national citizenship. If the market-state was to move from welfare provision on the principles of rights and needs and instead focus on 'responsibility' and acceptance of 'shared values', then it was with asylum seekers that the gap between the old and new models seemed to be greatest. As 'aliens', they were perceived as having no notion of responsibility to British society and no understanding of the 'values' that defined it. They were abusing the system, breaking the rules, taking advantage of 'our' generosity.

Until the 1980s, the provision of benefits had not officially been subject to immigration status, although secret internal instructions to social security officers had been issued in the 1960s restricting benefits to 'any claimant who appears to come from abroad'.[7] The attempt to transform benefit office workers from providers of welfare into virtual immigration officers had only a limited success, as unions representing local authority workers challenged such practices, pointing out the dangers of turning the welfare state into an extension of the Home Office's immigration department. But from 1988, checking immigration status became institutionalised in social security offices with new income support regulations.[8] Non-whites, whether settled or born in Britain or newly arrived, carried 'their passports on their faces', in A. Sivanandan's telling phrase.[9] By virtue of their skin colour, they were forced to prove their immigration status before being granted housing or benefits – those who could not had their benefits cut. The Asylum and Immigration Appeals Act 1993 required local authorities to investigate the immigration status of benefit claimants if they were 'suspected' of being asylum seekers. Within two years, staff at social security offices were being trained in how to spot 'immigration offenders' so that they could pass this information on to Home Office officials.[10] The myth that large numbers of asylum seekers were exploiting loopholes in the system was increasingly circulated: the decent British principles of the welfare state were being mocked by conniving foreigners, exchanging tricks and scams in a hidden world of abusers. By now, it was widely believed that most asylum seekers were not genuine applicants under the Geneva Convention but 'benefit cheats', entering Britain illegally to access the welfare state; it was necessary, therefore, to make it harder for all asylum seekers to get housed. Neglect or even cruelty was permissible as a deterrent against those who were seeking to defraud. By making it harder to obtain benefits, housing, healthcare or other kinds of support, it was thought that 'bogus asylum seekers' – the phrase had been common in the press since 1991[11] – would be deterred from coming to Britain.

With New Labour in government from 1997 onwards, the focus on preventing foreign 'scroungers' from draining the nation's welfare state became a cornerstone of the politics of the market-state. The demand for new lines of demarcation between the legitimate British receivers of state support and 'foreign abusers' allowed for principles of need and rights to be discarded, in favour of a closer alignment between entitlement and national belonging and/or shared values. Ironically, in taking up the demand to protect the welfare state from overseas 'scroungers', the welfare state itself would have its principles eroded. The greatest threat to the welfare state was not from asylum seekers themselves but from the political response to their being scapegoated, which undermined the entire welfare state system far more effectively than they themselves had ever threatened to. New techniques of coercion and surveillance were applied to asylum seekers, and the acceptance of these measures for asylum seekers served only to set a precedent for the future possibilities that British benefit claimants might face. Compulsory ID cards were the most obvious example of a measure that could be tested in relation to foreign nationals and then expanded to the whole population in the name of defending public services from abuse. Misdirected fears of a diminishing welfare state effectively supplied the hook around which the state was able to legitimise its own agenda of neoliberal 'reform' of welfare provision.

The establishment of the National Asylum Support Service, a separate support system for asylum seekers introduced by New Labour's 1999 Immigration and Asylum Act, set a precedent for a second-class structure of housing and benefits provision. Support was given in the form of vouchers, rather than cash, and a policy of dispersing asylum seekers around the country was introduced. The 2002 Nationality, Immigration and Asylum Act unveiled the notorious Section 55 rule, which threw thousands of asylum seekers into homelessness on the grounds that they did not place their claims quickly enough after arriving in Britain. The policy was introduced as an even stronger deterrent against 'bogus' asylum seekers but, because there was no reason to suppose that late claimants were any more likely to be unfounded, it represented a collective punishment on all asylum seekers, whatever the merits of their claim. The result was that asylum seekers 'disappeared' into cardboard-box alleyways, surviving, where possible, on charity or the undocumented economy. With the Asylum and Immigration (Treatment of Claimants, etc.) Act 2004, the Home Office threatened to make asylum-seeking parents destitute and take their children into the care of social services if they refused to leave Britain 'voluntarily' after their asylum claims had been rejected. The same Act introduced the 'workhouse' requirement that claimants accept forced labour in exchange for benefits.

While some of these policies might have been about saving money in the short term, most could not be understood in terms of costs alone. Putting asylum seekers in detention centres, issuing them with vouchers rather than cash benefits or dispersing them around the country were all more expensive than allowing them access to the same benefits as everyone else.[12] And neither did these policies 'work' in terms of a deterrent to asylum seekers' coming to Britain. The Home Office's own research suggested that which country asylum seekers came to was determined by whether they had friends or relatives there; their belief that the country was safe, fair and democratic; previous links with the country, including through colonialism; and the language spoken. Asylum seekers had little knowledge of the benefits available.[13] And indeed, the number of asylum claims made in Britain rose steadily from the early 1990s to the end of the decade, in proportion to the progressive tightening of support entitlements. It would have been cheaper, fairer and simpler to enable asylum seekers to access the same benefits system as everyone else while increasing the availability of affordable temporary housing that asylum seekers, along with many others, needed. It was this shortage that was the real problem in the early 1990s, not large numbers of asylum seeker 'scroungers'.[14] And it was implausible that a few thousand asylum seekers were to blame for London's housing crisis. But, once the descent down the slope of deterrence had begun, it was harder and harder to remain stationary, let alone clamber back to saner ground. Each 'solution' only created more social problems, which needed more and more drastic 'solutions', which, in turn, fuelled the rise of destitution, racism and despair. It was a state of affairs that was destined to worsen for as long as the series of fantasies on which the policies were based went unchallenged. That the problems multiplied and the policies did not 'work' was not surprising, given their foundation on what were essentially myths of 'bogus asylum seekers' that had been circulated vigorously from the start of the 1990s by politicians and newspapers.

DOVER AND DISPERSAL

In the first half of the 1990s, around ninety per cent of asylum seekers were housed in London, usually in neighbourhoods where fellow nationals were concentrated. This at least had the advantage that asylum seekers were able to draw on local networks of community support. It also meant that asylum seekers were generally unnoticed among London's multiracial population. Their struggle was usually with the system rather than the people they lived side by side with. But there were exceptions. Panchadcharam Sahitharan was a young Tamil man, caught up in Sri Lanka's civil war. He arrived at Heathrow Airport in 1990, applied for asylum and was granted temporary permission to stay. The regulations prevented him from working or studying but his sister in east London put him up. On 29 December 1991, he was walking home when he was attacked by a gang of white youths and died four days later in hospital. The following year, Afghan refugee Ruhullah Aramesh was murdered in Thornton Heath, south London, by a gang of white youths armed with makeshift clubs and iron bars. In the same year, the Ahmed Dahirs, a Somali family, were attacked in their west London bed and breakfast accommodation by a racist gang. Eleven-year-old Abderahman was stabbed, requiring twenty-three stitches and his sister, Naseem, was also beaten. The reason that the family was particularly vulnerable was that the local authority had taken advantage of their status as asylum seekers and housed them in a racist area that other black families refused to accept.[15]

But for most, the greatest fears were arrest, imprisonment and deportation. Omasase Lumumba, the nephew of Patrice Lumumba, the first prime minister of Congo who was killed in a Belgium-sponsored assassination in the 1960s (see Chapter 2), had come to London to claim asylum, fleeing torture and detention in his homeland. He was arrested in Catford, south-east London, in 1991, on suspicion of stealing a bicycle, a charge that was never pursued. When it was realised that he was an asylum seeker, he was taken to Pentonville prison where he remained for three weeks. Becoming increasingly agitated at his imprisonment, he rebelled and refused an order that had been given to him to return to his cell. He was taken to the segregation unit of the prison where six to eight officers ordered him to lie on the floor of a cell, pinned his arms, legs and head down and stripped him of his clothes using scissors. By the time a doctor, who had been called to apply a tranquilliser, arrived in the cell, Omasase was dead. An inquest recorded a verdict of unlawful killing as a result of 'improper methods of excessive force'.[16]

The fear of deportation haunted refugee and migrant communities, particularly as the brutality and violence deployed by police officers (and private security officers involved in deportations) became known. A specialist squad at Scotland Yard, known as SO1(3), deployed an armoury of restraining gags, belts and tapes against those they were seeking to deport. On the morning of 1 August 1993, officers from SO1(3) entered the home of Joy Gardner, a 40-year-old Jamaican woman whose visa had expired. They disconnected her phone so that she could not ring her solicitor, cuffed her and forced her to the floor. Then two officers held her legs and one officer sat on top of her. Another officer placed a body-belt around her waist, bound her wrists to handcuffs attached to the belt, and tied her thighs and ankles with leather belts. Her head was then wrapped in thirteen feet of adhesive tape. Shortly afterwards, Joy Gardner stopped moving and she was later pronounced dead. All this was witnessed by her five-year-old son.[17] Following Joy's death, SO1(3) was disbanded but the climate of fear it had helped create remained. Three people are known to have died in London over the next three years as a result of falling from the balcony of their flats while attempting to hide from what they thought were immigration officers calling at their flat to deport them.[18]

In 1996, with a general election expected and John Major's popularity flagging, another Asylum Act was passed targeting asylum seekers' access to state support. It proposed to cut central government funding for housing and supporting asylum seekers who had not applied quickly enough after arriving in Britain, or those whose claims had been rejected, even if they were still mounting an appeal. The result was chaos, as what had quickly become seen as the 'burden' of supporting asylum seekers was passed from central government to cash-strapped local authorities in London, which, in spite of the new Act, were still bound by law to provide support 'in kind' to the destitute.[19] In order to provide this support as cheaply as possible, some London local authorities now began to 'disperse' asylum seekers out to other parts of the country, such as the Kent coast, where they could be put up in the cheapest possible accommodation. And, instead of providing cash support, a scheme of food vouchers was introduced. A policy more suited to fostering resentment could not have been devised. Around 750 asylum seekers, mainly Roma (Gypsies) fleeing persecution in Slovakia and the Czech Republic, were housed in Dover. Some had ended up there as a result of cost-saving schemes by London local authorities. Others were there because they had claimed asylum after arriving in the UK at Dover. Local newspapers, particularly the *Dover Express* and the *Folkestone Express*, both edited at the time by Nick Hudson (a former editor of the *Sunday Sport*), referred to thousands of asylum seekers flooding the area and, by sheer dint of numbers, running down the welfare state. Under an editorial headed 'We want to wash the dross down drain', asylum seekers were described as 'scroungers', 'bootleggers' and 'scum of the earth', targeting 'our beloved coastline'. Finally, Hudson told his readers that the 'backdraft of a nation's human sewage', which had been dumped on Dover, needed to be washed 'down the drain'.[20] The national press soon joined in. In October 1997, the *Sun* labelled the Roma asylum seekers 'Giro Czechs' and 'Slovak Spongers', and suggested 'teaching the gipsies two words, the second one being off'.[21] Even the more liberal *Independent* ran on its front page the headline 'Gypsies invade Dover hoping for a handout'.[22] The Roma were described in the press as 'dossers', 'scroungers', 'chancers', 'lazy', 'dishonest', 'wily', 'bogus', 'thieving', 'illegal'.[23] Petitions were organised by parents at two Dover primary schools in a bid to exclude Roma children from being admitted.[24] And in November, the National Front party held protests in Dover against the Roma.[25]

The stereotype of the 'Gypsy beggar' provided the perfect vehicle for a demand for action against 'foreign scroungers' accessing the welfare state. The familiar sight, from the mid-1990s, of Roma asylum seekers begging in London's underground stations provided an easy reference point. Since the Home Office had claimed that 'there is absolutely no reason for any asylum seeker to be begging on the streets – they are provided with enough to live on',[26] any who did beg were immediately seen as dishonest, feeding into long-standing prejudices against Gypsies as wily, deceitful parasites. The *Sun* launched a campaign against the 'scrounging Romanian gipsies'[27] under the headline 'Britain has had enough'. Leading commentators denounced the beggars as undeserving. Previous 'immigrants gained acceptance by working harder than the locals', wrote popular novelist Tony Parsons in the *Mirror*. 'That's why the rash of baby-toting Romanian beggars rubs the nation up the wrong way. Britain became a successful multi-racial country because the newcomers were ready to graft.'[28] (Unlike previous generations of immigrants, asylum seekers were banned from working and thereby encouraged by the system into begging.) The theme of 'Gypsy scroungers' would be revisited in 2004 when newspapers singled out the fear of Roma coming to Britain from the eight countries in eastern and central Europe that were set to join the European Union. Among the swarm of racist coverage, the *Daily Express* ran the headline '1.6 million gipsies ready to flood in' on its front cover, accompanied by graphics depicting a foreign invasion. An editorial comment stated that Gypsies were 'heading to Britain to leech on us'. If such a metaphor (literally, suck blood) were used of Jews, there would have been an outrage and demands for resignation.[29]

The reality in the 1990s was that Roma were fleeing systematic racist persecution, which their governments were doing nothing to prevent and in which the police were often directly involved – only to find in Britain the same combination of state racism, media bullying and neo-nazis on the streets. During the 1940s, between a half and one and a half million Roma were killed in the Nazis' 'final solution' to Europe's 'race problem'.[30] After the Second World War, Communist states in eastern Europe had pursued an assimilation policy, denying Roma their language and lifestyle in the hope of making of them good sedentary citizens. At least they benefited, though, from the social provisions of the Soviet system. In the 1990s, with the Communist system gone, Roma became outcasts and easy scapegoats for the failures of the 'transition' period, even as they suffered worst from the closure of state enterprises and rising joblessness. Violence against them sprung up across eastern Europe: their settlements were attacked, burned and looted, often with active police complicity, while the media explained away the racist violence as the result of 'provocation' by 'Gypsy thieves'.[31] In Poland, Hungary, the Czech Republic and Slovakia, the policy of segregating the majority of Roma children into 'special needs' schools continued.[32] In Slovakia, there were reports that Roma women had been forcibly sterilised in government-run health facilities in the east of the country.[33]

Ladislav Balaz, for example, a town councillor in his home town of Orlova in the Czech Republic, was forced to leave after he campaigned against police involvement in a neo-nazi skinhead attack on his friend. The police and the government offered him no protection against the death threats he was receiving from skinhead gangs. 'The police, judiciary, councils and government alike do not care about attacks on the Roma people,' he said. 'And the Czech media do not report these attacks for fear of jeopardising EU entry.' While in London, waiting for his asylum claim to be decided on, he set up the community organisation Europe-Roma, after noticing two Czech Roma families sleeping rough in Finsbury Park station and deciding to take them in. The temporary accommodation his family had been given soon became a makeshift community centre and refuge, while Ladislav spent his days visiting hundreds of Roma in the places where they had been marooned: Dover, Folkestone, Margate, Southend, Newcastle, Nelson (Lancashire) and the detention centres and prisons where they were often incarcerated while their asylum claims were processed. When his family began to suffer racist abuse, arson attacks and death threats, his local authority housing department refused to take action. How it must all have reminded him of home.

The problem for Roma asylum seekers was that their persecution in eastern Europe was not considered by the British Home Office to be state persecution; therefore their asylum claims were rejected. In 1997, the number of 'invading' Czech and Slovak Roma was no more than 400, along with 580 dependants – across the UK as a whole.[34] Only one of these was given permission to stay by the Home Office – and only for six months. The following year, the 'crisis' had not subsided. A mighty total of 385 Czechs, 810 Slovaks and 940 Romanians applied for asylum in Britain.[35] The *Daily Mail* published an 'investigation into Britain's immigration crisis', headed 'The good life on asylum alley'.[36] Dover was presented as a town under siege, swamped by a massive 'influx' of asylum seekers, who were 'playing the asylum appeals process' as a tactic to milk state benefits. According to the reports, a threshold of tolerance had been crossed: a violent reaction was the natural and understandable, though regrettable, response. Hoax letters were sent to addresses on the Kent coast, purporting to be from the 'Worldwide Asylum Seekers Association' instructing the recipient that their home had been selected to accommodate a family of five from Slovakia for six months. The recipients were advised that they should reorganise their 'home and personal habits to make the transaction as pleasant as possible' and occasionally give the family some 'pocket money'.[37] Violence against asylum seekers in Dover became an almost daily occurrence. As one local commented: 'It's starting to feel like Montgomery, Alabama, down here.'[38]

The significance of what had happened in Dover over these three years went far beyond the boundaries of that town. Whereas before, asylum had mainly been an issue for London local authorities, the way in which newspapers had dramatised events in Dover thrust asylum seekers on the national stage. Dover was not just any town; its white cliffs symbolised the point where Britain came closest to the world beyond its borders and it still resonated as the first place that invading forces would strike. Its apparent occupation by 'foreign hordes' was thus a sign of what might be in store for the rest of the country. With the violence that had flared up in Dover, there was also a potent demonstration of the virulent passions that were felt on the issue. It was obvious now that asylum was a major political issue in Blair's Britain. That the government's response was to institutionalise the *ad hoc* dispersal schemes introduced by London local authorities into a national dispersal programme only underlined this conclusion. Now, as ministers spoke of the need to 'spread the burden', every town in the country feared that what had happened in Dover would be repeated there. Dispersal was a policy that had been tried before, notably in the case of Vietnamese refugees who arrived in the 1970s and 1980s. Less of them in any one place would make integration easier, it was thought, echoing the consensus that lower numbers reduced racism. Unsurprisingly, dispersing Vietnamese around the country was also an attack on their own strategies for supporting each other as a community. According to a Home Affairs Committee report, the policy was 'universally regarded as mistaken'. By 1985, the government agreed that it would 'try to adopt a different approach if a similar situation arose in the future'. [39] But in 1999, the same argument was being used to justify a dispersal policy again: lower numbers of asylum seekers in any one place would ease their integration. The Home Office first suggested that an acceptable number of asylum seekers was one for every 200 local residents. Then it was upped to one for every 500.[40] But, by talking of 'quotas by locality', the implication was that it was the supposedly large numbers of asylum seekers arriving that were to blame for the violence in Dover, not the stigmatising logic of the government's own asylum system. The 'dispersal' solution, therefore, rather than solve the problem of anti-asylum violence, led to the Dover experience being duplicated across the country, as asylum seekers were sent out to deprived parts of northern cities where accommodation was cheapest. With the 1999 Immigration and Asylum Act, the government created the National Asylum Support Service (NASS), a whole new apparatus of second-class support for asylum seekers. NASS would contract with local authorities and private companies around the country to accommodate asylum seekers and provide subsistence. The aim of the system was not just to 'spread the burden' but also to discourage 'economic migrants' from exploiting the asylum process – hence the introduction of a national voucher system for paying benefits. Even though the Home Office acknowledged that the voucher system was more expensive to run than a system of ordinary benefits for asylum seekers,[41] vouchers were preferred because they were thought to be less attractive to the mythical armies of 'scroungers' coming to milk cash benefits. Without the right to work, asylum seekers were forced to scrape together whatever extra money they could from charity, begging or work in the undocumented economy. The message was sent out that asylum seekers were more likely to be 'scroungers' than genuine refugees. They were thus sent to the poorest communities in Britain labelled as a group of people whose aim was to make Britain poorer.

The result was predictable. In the Sighthill area of Glasgow, asylum-seeker children were followed to and from school by threatening gangs.[42] In one incident, a six-year-old girl had to have all her hair shaved off after a noxious liquid was poured over her head. In another incident, thugs armed with baseball bats attacked a five-year-old African boy in the playground. Asylum-seeker accommodation was marked out for attack by graffiti. In one high-rise block in Glasgow, thugs could easily identify where asylum seekers lived because they were all provided with the same yellow-flowered curtains. Doors were kicked in, excrement was pushed through letter boxes, abuse and harassment were routine. When 22-year-old Kurdish asylum seeker Firsat Dag was stabbed to death on the Sighthill estate in a racist attack in August 2001, pundits appeared on television to explain that the murder had been provoked by the delivery of new furniture to asylum seekers' homes. Having a new sofa now counted as 'provocation' for murder. But no matter: if British racism against the Roma, Kurds and Kosovans was as bad as Slovak, Turkish or Serbian racism, then the original incentive to seek asylum would be removed. Racial violence, too, could serve as another plank in the deterrence strategy.

In Leicester, the 'International Hotel', a dilapidated building that had once been a viable hotel business, was turned into a ramshackle hostel for 400 desperate asylum seekers. The body of Shokrolah 'Ramin' Khaleghi, a 26-year-old Iranian, was discovered there on 18 January 2001. Ramin had been a conscientious objector, who was jailed for refusing to serve in an army that would later be described as part of an 'axis of evil'. A medical report compiled in Leicester corroborated Ramin's account of the torture and beatings he had experienced in an Iranian prison, including acid thrown in his face by guards. According to his uncle, who lived in north London, Ramin had suffered 'every hell imaginable'.[43] The Home Office rejected his asylum claim, without interviewing him, writing to him that the secretary of state 'considers the findings in this case to be inconclusive'. After receiving the letter, Ramin told friends that he 'would not go back to Iran alive'. A week later, he was found dead in what appeared to be a deliberate overdosing of heroin. Ramin Khaleghi was not the only asylum seeker who seemed to choose suicide as the only way to find peace. From 2000 to 2002, Saeed Alaei (Iranian), Nasser Ahmed (Eritrean), Souleyman Diallo (Guinean), Shiraz Pir (Pakistani), Nariman Tahamasbi (Iranian), Mohsen Amri (Iranian) and Sirous Khajeh (Iranian) all took their own lives in circumstances that suggested that the combination of a hostile local environment, separation from one's community and the threat of deportation was making life unbearable.[44] Many others simply chose to move away from the accommodation that had been allocated to them by the dispersal system, forfeiting their right to benefits, preferring a friend's floor in London, or even sleeping rough.

Meanwhile the dispersal system turned an issue that had affected only one or two regions into an issue that infected the entire nation. Dispersal produced its own anti-dispersal: a not-in-my-back-yard mobilisation, in which each locality fought to have asylum seekers moved on somewhere else. Soon enough, Home Office planners were appeasing these campaigns and drawing up lists of towns where the racism had reached such a pitch that no more asylum seekers could be sent there. A Home Office spokesperson explained that, 'the whole point is to avoid any tension by not putting a burden on any one particular area'.[45] The point was, though, that it was less the (relatively small) numbers coming to an area that caused the tension and more the fact that the system had presented all asylum seekers as a 'burden' and a threat. In this way, the dispersal system inevitably achieved the exact opposite of what was intended. Rather than ease tensions, they were only made worse while, as a deterrent to further claims, dispersal made no difference. It was only logical that the dispersal programme would also provoke calls for asylum seekers to be removed entirely from the community and placed in detention centres. As early as February 2000, with the dispersal machinery about to roll out across the country, shadow home secretary Ann Widdecombe had called for all asylum seekers from 'safe countries' to be detained on arrival.

The Labour government rejected the proposal but the following month implemented its own plans to automatically detain asylum seekers from specified countries at Oakington detention centre, near Cambridge. By March, with local elections approaching, Conservative leader William Hague announced that his party would detain every asylum seeker on arrival, no matter what the cost. In April 2000, immigration minister Barbara Roche responded by announcing that the number of asylum seekers held in detention was to be greatly increased. The cost of detaining an asylum seeker was estimated to be £1,300 per week but, as we have seen, while any amount of money spent on supporting asylum seekers was too much, cost was not an issue when it came to deterrence, or at least, the appearance of deterrence.[46]

By the summer of 2001, the government was facing what David Blunkett referred to as an 'avalanche of criticism' over its dispersal policy.[47] His solution was to redesign the whole asylum process so that asylum seekers would be carefully tracked through a conveyor belt of induction centres, accommodation centres and removal centres, a model that was legislated for with the 2002 Nationality, Immigration and Asylum Act. Asylum seekers would be housed in specialist accommodation centres outside cities, where they would be cut off from communities and out of view and from where their eventual deportation would be all the easier. Blunkett argued that it would also prevent asylum seekers from 'swamping' local public services.[48] Except that, by now, the hostility towards asylum seekers had progressed to such a degree that nobody wanted an asylum accommodation centre in their locality. A wave of mass protests against plans for accommodation centres in Kent, Sussex, Oxfordshire, Hampshire, Dorset and Lincolnshire was fuelled by an explosive mix of prejudices, often verging on paranoia. It was the most significant grassroots anti-immigrant mobilisation since the dockers marched in support of Enoch Powell in 1968, except that this time anti-immigrant protests sprung up from the shires of middle England rather than from pockets of the working class. In Sittingbourne, Kent, vigils were held outside the Coniston Hotel, which was expected to be turned into a centre for 111 asylum seekers. Similar protests took place in Portland, Dorset, where a former naval base, on an island accessible only by a single road, was being considered as a site for an accommodation block to house 750 asylum seekers. Campaigners in Saltdean, Sussex, successfully fought plans to house sixty asylum seekers in a nearby hotel. At Caythorpe, in Lincolnshire, villagers protested at plans to convert a former agricultural college into accommodation for asylum seekers. A proposed accommodation centre for 750 asylum seekers to be built near Bicester, Oxfordshire, met with widespread protest. And a local campaign against plans to build an accommodation centre near Pershore, Worcestershire, won support from fashion designer Stella McCartney, who had a £1.3m farmhouse in the village, and *Songs of Praise* presenter Toyah Wilcox. The Home Office cancelled its plans after hundreds demonstrated at the proposed site. Similarly, a demonstration against the conversion of a former naval airbase at Lee-on-the-Solent, Hampshire, into housing for 400 asylum seekers was supported by the borough council and attended by an estimated 8,000 people. It also persuaded the Home Office to drop its plans. Just as the dispersal scheme had foundered on the rock of local resentments, so too had plans for accommodation centres.

RECASTING WELFARE

Ten years on from the first piece of asylum support legislation in 1993, and after three major pieces of legislation in the interim, all of which sought in various ways to restrict the access that asylum seekers had to state support, the issue was more fraught than ever. Every attempt at reform of the system had sought to reassure the public that its fears of foreign 'abuse' were being acted on through a clampdown of one sort or another but, in so doing, they implicitly gave official endorsement to the mythology of 'bogus asylum seekers'. And policies based on this mythology necessarily failed to solve the 'problems' they had misrepresented and tended to manufacture ever larger difficulties. Removing various categories of asylum claimants from access to state support had the effect of fuelling homelessness, illegal working and social disintegration, which in turn became pretexts for further media campaigns. The serious outbreak of street violence that had been witnessed in Dover was repeated in Wrexham, Peterborough and Derby. Legitimated by political action and media opportunism, the public's appetite for reassurance was never satisfied. Faced with daily images of asylum-seeking 'scroungers', confidence in the welfare state declined and a new national mood was shaped, in which earlier principles of the welfare state gave way to calls for new forms of coercion and surveillance to protect against 'abusive' claimants. One indicator of this new mood was the introduction of ID cards as a solution to the problem of identifying who was entitled to access public services.

It fell to the pundits and commentators around New Labour to rationalise this process as an expression of what they regarded as an underlying contradiction between diversity and the welfare state. David Goodhart's widely read article for *Prospect* magazine, 'Too diverse?', argued that entitlement to welfare should be clearly aligned with belonging to a shared British culture and that the survival of the welfare state depended on denying access to those who did not sit on the right side of a cultural dividing line between 'them' and 'us'.[49] People are only willing to pay in to a welfare state, he argued, if they believe that those receiving benefits share the same values as themselves. For this reason, welfare support to immigrants of a different ethnicity undermines the welfare state by fracturing the collective identity that it requires. Liberals, he concluded, must choose between the welfare state and diversity. Of course, this argument ignored the fact that the welfare state survived decades without cultural homogeneity. The whole history of the welfare state in Britain demonstrates that there is no trade-off between diversity and welfare provision: throughout its life, the welfare state has been essentially dependent on the contribution of workers from Asian, African and Caribbean backgrounds, who took up posts as nurses, doctors, drivers and cleaners, often on lower pay than their white colleagues. These workers and others from those backgrounds knew that the imperial exploitation of their countries had generated the wealth that made the welfare state possible; it was in this that their 'contribution' also lay.

While these workers had diverse cultures, most tended to share with the white working class the values of mutual aid and support that the welfare state embodied. At its inception, the welfare state was associated with a new sense of citizenship that was thought of by some as arising simply from residence in Britain while, on other accounts, it was regarded as a privilege to be earned or acquired through active contribution to the nation. In either case, it implied that the state no longer had the right to divide the poor into the deserving and undeserving on the basis of moral judgements. But today's rhetoric of substituting responsibilities for rights and demanding shared values among recipients returns the welfare state to neo-Victorian surveillance and compulsion in the administering of social provision. This is the direction that arguments such as Goodhart's lead even as they present themselves as defences of the traditional welfare state. The market-state rhetoric of 'rights and responsibility' points towards a future in which access to public services is conditional on values and lifestyle, and ID cards and electronic databases are used to police entitlements not just of asylum seekers and other foreign nationals but of sections of the British population too. The same political culture that produces the 'shop an illegal immigrant hotline' also creates the 'shop a benefit cheat' hotline. The real meaning of such arguments is an attempt to legitimise neoliberal 'reforms' by scapegoating ethnic diversity and wrapping the shift to the market-state in the pretence that reforms are necessary to reassure an aggrieved majority that the welfare state is safe from abusive immigrants.

6

The Dialectics of Terror

This is a moment to seize. The Kaleidoscope has been shaken. The pieces are in flux. Soon they will settle again. Before they do, let us re-order this world around us. – Tony Blair, October 2001[1]

The blurring of sovereignty that globalisation had brought about meant the blurring, also, of the right to military intervention. According to the United Nations Charter, one state can only use force against another if it is authorised to do so by the UN Security Council, or in self-defence against an attack. This was the principle of the equal sovereignty of all nations. But the US, whose military strength was, by the 1990s, vastly superior to all its nearest rivals combined, declared itself guardian of the 'new world order', implicitly assuming for itself a global military sovereignty, to complement the global reach of US corporations. The globalisation of capitalism needed a globalisation of military power, in order to ensure the security of the now universal system. As the *New York Times* columnist Thomas Friedman famously put it:

The hidden hand of the market will never work without a hidden fist – McDonald's cannot flourish without McDonnell-Douglas, the designer of the F-15. And the hidden fist that keeps the world safe for Silicon Valley's technologies is called the US Army, Air Force, Navy and Marine Corps.[2]

The façade of national sovereignty, which had masked the actual imperialism of the Cold War era, now fell away. In Africa and Asia, its thinness was already clear in the legacy of Western military intervention and covert action. And the collapse of the Communist system in eastern Europe, Russia and Central Asia showed, more than ever, how the national sovereignty system had been built on the tectonic plates of the Cold War. The fragility of national borders that were once set in stone was exposed – most obviously in Yugoslavia. The failure of the United Nations to prevent the slaughter of Bosnian Muslims and the genocide of the Tutsi population of Rwanda,[3] in 1994, gave a pretext for the new doctrines of military intervention that would replace the post-Second World War nation-state system and its discredited compartmentalism.

Unilateral 'humanitarian intervention' was to fill the gap that the UN was being pushed out of. 'Humanitarian intervention' implied an entirely new justification for war in which the most powerful states of the world assumed the right to unilaterally intervene wherever they wanted. The justness of the 'ends' – removing the leaders of 'rogue states' or providing humanitarian protection – was supposed to legitimate the 'means', which was the inevitable killing of thousands of civilians whose deaths were deemed to be no more than 'collateral damage'. The implication was that a powerful state could fight just wars against sovereign nations in the name of 'humanitarian intervention', even if its adversaries did not present a clear threat to its own security. It followed that no nation could any longer rely on its own sovereignty as a protection against attack. In the past, Western governments had intervened surreptitiously – backing a favoured autocrat here, sponsoring coups there – but, with the passing of the principle of national sovereignty, they could now unseat regimes and occupy nations openly and autonomously, all in the name of human rights. If wars could be legitimated in this way, it was the death, not only of the principle of equal national sovereignty, but also of the United Nations itself, an organisation that enshrined that principle in its constitution. Yet, with the United Nations marginalised, there was no process by which these wars could be made accountable to the world community on whose behalf they were, nominally, being fought.

Following the 9/11 terrorist attacks and the subsequent launch of a 'war on terror', a completely open-ended prospectus for war was enshrined in the Bush doctrine of pre-emptive strikes, regime change and full-spectrum dominance. It was 9/11 that provided the 'catastrophic and catalysing event – like a new Pearl Harbor', which, a year earlier, the Project for the New American Century, a major artery of neoconservative thinking in Washington, had suggested would be needed to achieve the massive militarisation programme necessary for the consolidation of a global US-led empire.[4] The 'war on terror' with its themes of unknown threats, global reach and open-ended conflict provided the perfect justification for a planned increase in military spending to US$470 billion in 2007 (more than the combined military spending of the rest of the world) and the establishment of over 700 overseas bases around the globe.[5] With the occupations of Afghanistan (2001) and Iraq (2003), the pretence of national sovereignty as a protection against foreign military intervention had become untenable. Instead, there was effective *global* sovereignty in the hands of the US, with the UK as a junior partner. The United States' network of allies across the world would still be used as regional policemen where appropriate – and have US troops stationed locally – but 'humanitarian intervention' provided another option for dealing with those 'failed states' that had got out of hand. A new age of empire was identified by writers like Robert Cooper (an erstwhile advisor to Tony Blair) who divided the world into pre-modern, modern and post-modern states: the pre-modern states were the 'failed states' that would be subjected to Western military intervention; the modern states were the nations that the West could rely on as allies; the post-modern states were the ones that led and controlled the global system.[6] It was this new imperialism that millions of people implicitly rejected in worldwide demonstrations against the war on Iraq on 15 February 2003.

THE AFGHAN *JIHAD*

The roots of 9/11 were complex and multi-faceted. They ran through the legacy of political repression in Egypt and Saudi Arabia, the occupation of Palestine and the failure in those countries of various forms of nationalist politics, coupled with the emergence of new movements that justified violence through a combination of religious and political arguments. They ran through the legacy of the proxy war that the West had sponsored in Afghanistan in the last decade of the Cold War, a war that first made it possible for a new global *jihadi* movement to emerge and establish itself. And they ran through the injustices of America's attempts to establish a 'new world order' in the aftermath of the Cold War – injustices that meant that those carrying out terrorist attacks could rely on a backdrop of support. Yet, 9/11 prompted little enthusiasm in the US and UK to comprehend these various causes. Not only was an examination of the causes mistakenly thought to justify the action; it was also that there was a gulf between the concerns of Western societies and those of the rest. While the Cold War meant peace in Europe, in the Third World it involved the systematic deployment of assassinations, bombings, missile strikes, proxy wars, covert wars and full-scale invasions, carried out by either the Soviet Union or the United States.

It was in regard to Afghanistan that this gulf of understanding was at its greatest. King Zahir Shah had reigned in Afghanistan since 1933 and, from the mid-1950s, had relied on the Soviet Union for purchases of arms and assistance with development projects.[7] Then, in 1973, Zahir Shah was deposed in a palace coup and Afghanistan entered a period of uncertainty that lasted until the 'April Revolution' of 1978 when the left-wing People's Democratic Party of Afghanistan (PDPA) took power. The PDPA was wracked with internal feuds and vendettas and had little understanding of the needs of the majority of the population residing outside Kabul, where literacy was low and access to healthcare and education were hard to come by.[8] But in Washington, the PDPA was viewed with suspicion for an entirely different reason: it was regarded as a conduit for Soviet ambitions. In July 1979, the CIA began a programme of covert action, which aimed at installing a pro-American government in its place. Half a year later, the Soviet army entered Kabul to prop up the PDPA regime and began a brutal military occupation of the country.[9] The US backed various groups of local and foreign fighters to battle the Soviets in Afghanistan. It secured the support of its three key regional allies: Pakistan (which provided training), Saudi Arabia (which provided funding) and Egypt (which provided arms). By joining the US in a war that was sold to Muslims as a *jihad* against the 'godless' Soviet invaders, these governments hoped to establish their own Islamist movement to rival that which had seized power in Iran in 1979. Soon, a billion dollars a year was going into funding the war against the PDPA government and its Soviet allies, with much of the weaponry purchased being British-made.[10] In Pakistan, *mujahedin* training camps, through which passed future al-Qa'ida and Taliban fighters, were run by the CIA.

Vast financial resources were available not only for military hardware but also for the ideological dimension of the Afghan conflict. In order to mobilise for the war against the Soviets, propaganda material, including school textbooks that continued to be used years later,[11] promoted a militarised notion of *jihad* that had been influenced by the writings of Sayyid Qutb. Qutb was an Egyptian intellectual whose involvement in the Muslim Brotherhood led to his being detained in a military prison in the early 1960s. Qutb's writings were wide-ranging but it was his 1964 *Milestones of the Road* that proved most influential. The *Milestones* argued that military *jihad* was not a collective duty to be fulfilled only when the Muslim community was subjected to aggression, but a permanent and individually binding religious duty to struggle politically and militarily against regimes deemed to be *jahili* – that is, regimes, such as the then existing Egyptian state, which were seen as presiding over 'pagan' societies analogous to pre-Islamic Arabia. A vanguard minority was necessary that could see beyond the decadence of contemporary society and traverse the milestones on the road to an ideal Islamic polity, in which Allah's sovereignty on earth would replace the authoritarianism of contemporary governments.[12] The *Milestones* established the conceptual framework of modern *jihadi* politico-religious movements: the idea that an ideal Islamic state was possible and necessary to overcome the sorry state of contemporary society; the division of society into a *jahili* majority who were trapped in a 'false consciousness' and an epistemologically privileged vanguard minority; and the requirement of struggle as a permanent religious duty. Ironically, these ideas had more of an affinity with the revolutionary politics of the European ultra-Left in the 1960s than with the ways in which Islam had traditionally been understood and practised. After Qutb's execution in 1966, the ideology of the *Milestones* circulated clandestinely among Egyptian radicals and on Saudi campuses, until the Afghan conflict of the 1980s, when the chief ideologue of the *mujahedin*, Abdullah Azzam, a native of the Palestinian West Bank, adopted Qutb's concepts and combined them with an emphasis on the need for Islamists to overcome their national divisions and form a unified movement.[13] The result was that the ideology of Qutb's *Milestones* was globalised, funded and armed, gaining influence in Algeria, Pakistan and Saudi Arabia.[14]

After a decade of bloody conflict, the Soviet army withdrew in defeat from Afghanistan in 1989. While the CIA celebrated its victory, however, no thought was given to the reconstruction of a country where the West's Cold War showdown had been acted out. While in the West there was talk of a post-Cold War 'peace dividend', Afghanistan became a cauldron of violence in the 1990s. The vast quantities of arms that had flooded the country fuelled an internecine war between the various armed groups that the US and its allies had trained and funded. About four million people – over half the country's population – fled the violence to neighbouring Pakistan, Iran or elsewhere. In 1996, Kabul fell to the ultraconserv-ative Taliban, who emerged out of the refugee camps in Pakistan and were encouraged by Pakistan's intelligence services. Under the Taliban regime, music was proscribed, girls were banned from school, women forbidden from working outside the home and children's games, such as kite-flying or playing ball, were outlawed. The anti-imperialist writer Eqbal Ahmad described it as a 'most distorted and uniquely repugnant visage of Islam'.[15] Around 20,000 Afghans sought asylum in Britain during the 1990s, many fleeing the brutality of the Taliban.[16] While these asylum seekers were initially recognised as genuine – Afghan asylum seekers were granted permission to remain in Britain in 800 out of 805 cases in 1999[17] – the Home Office soon responded to domestic political pressure and began treating Afghanistan as a country where few suffered oppression; by June 2000, roughly three-quarters of Afghan asylum seekers were being rejected.[18] Yet the following year, the bombing of Afghanistan by British and American forces was justified by the need to remove a deeply oppressive regime.

Meanwhile, the fighters who had come from the Middle East and North Africa to join the *jihad* in Afghanistan during the 1980s returned to their home countries with the CIA training manuals they had acquired, access to private funding networks for terrorism and experience of waging a successful guerrilla war against the Soviet superpower. Until the Afghan *jihad*, Islamist political movements had operated within diverse national contexts, often using conventional party structures and working through existing institutions. The target of their struggles was the governments of their own nation or, in the case of Palestine, the Israeli occupation. But with the end of the Cold War, a new kind of global *jihad* emerged, which dislodged itself from particular national causes and began to see each of these as a different aspect of the same millenarian global struggle against what the US had called its 'new world order'. The 1991 Gulf War was the first of several attempts by the US in the 1990s to consolidate a post-Cold War position of global dominance. In Egypt, Saudi Arabia and Algeria, autocratic regimes aligned their interests with those of Western governments rather than their own people, while Islamist opposition groups faced torture, detention without trial and execution in domestic 'wars on terror'. In Chechnya, Palestine and Kashmir, liberation movements were increasingly coalescing around groups that comprehended their struggle in terms of a global *jihad*. The links in a global chain of radical *jihadis* were now becoming apparent. Mirroring the 'clash of civilisations' thesis that Huntington was speaking of in the US, Osama Bin Laden, interviewed on the al-Jazeera network in 1998, announced that 'there are two sides in the struggle: one side is the global Crusader alliance with the Zionist Jews, led by America, Britain, and Israel, and the other side is the Islamic world'. Yet this Manichaean worldview was combined with the rhetoric of anti-imperialism:

It is not acceptable in such a struggle as this that he [the Crusader] should attack and enter my land and holy sanctuaries, and plunder Muslims' oil, and then when he encounters any resistance from Muslims, to label them terrorists. This is stupidity, or considering others stupid. We believe that it is our legal duty to resist this occupation with all our might, and punish it in the same way as it punishes us.[19]

Soon, Bin Laden's followers would prove that they knew no limits to the violence they were prepared to unleash as part of this struggle. The 'collateral killing' of first non-Muslims and then Muslims, too, became legitimised and mass, indiscriminate killing of civilians became as much a feature of their warfare as it was of their enemies in Washington.[20] While this desperate and deluded discourse is radically different from the Third World revolutionary nationalism of an earlier time, its ultimate referent remains the same: the injustice and immorality of Western imperialism. As numerous writers have pointed out, it is frustration at this that gives Bin Laden his reservoir of popular support, even among people who do not 'endorse either his extreme violence or the kind of *shari'ah* governance [he] would like them to live under'.[21]

AN 'EVIL IDEOLOGY'

It is this relationship between a set of linked political grievances and a millenarian ideology that is at the heart of *jihadi* terrorism. Yet the US and UK governments have consistently sought to sever the role of political grievances from acts of terrorism, and thereby avoid making connections to Western injustices. Terrorists must be represented as having no motive except pathology and no cause except evil. In the absence of an honest acknowledgement of the wider political context, it becomes necessary for politicians to focus all the more on an 'evil ideology' as the sole driving force of *jihadi* terrorism. Thus, the more that those political grievances are downplayed, the more that terrorism is understood simply as the result of a new ideology of absolutism that is at odds with modern, open societies: they hate our freedoms, they hate our democracy and they hate our way of life. Usually, there is the proviso that the majority of Muslims reject this ideology. But, without any political context, it becomes impossible to explain why this ideology has come into existence. By default, then, it comes to be seen as a problem of Muslim 'backwardness', and the causes of terrorism are reduced to a specifically Islamic failure to adapt to modern values, not only in the Middle East and Asia but also among Muslim communities in Europe. The upshot of this is a revival of older prejudices against Muslims as followers of a uniquely fanatical and anti-modern religion. In addition, there is the attempt to fill the void left by evacuating global injustice from any explanation of terrorism with simplified forms of psychopathology. According to a number of writers and politicians, including Conservative Party leader David Cameron, suicide bombers are driven to commit their acts of violence by the humiliation of living in a declining Islamic civilisation. For Cameron, 'Islamist thinking ... like other totalitarianisms, such as Nazism and Communism, offers its followers a form of redemption through violence.'[22] Others agree with the view, endorsed in a 2005 pamphlet published by the New Labour thinktank Demos, that suicide bombers are driven to violence by 'pent-up sexual frustration, which is a common characteristic in sexually segregated societies'.[23] Similarly, websites and talk radio programmes regularly invoke the supposed sexual gratification of the seventy-two *houris* (inaccurately characterised as 'virgins') that await Muslim suicide bombers,[24] a theme also of the cartoons of the Prophet Muhammad published in the Danish *Jyllands-Posten* newspaper in October 2005. None of these explanations can be reconciled with the fact that suicide bombings are not only carried out by Muslim men but are a tactic used also by women and by secular groups attempting to compel democracies to withdraw from what they regard as military occupations.[25]

The strength of the anti-war movement in Britain is one of the reasons why large sections of the public reject all of these explanations and believe that the 7/7 terrorist attacks were, indeed, partly a consequence of Britain's involvement in the occupation of Iraq. In support of this view, there was the testimony of the Joint Intelligence Committee, which had concluded prior to the war on Iraq in 2003 that the threat of terrorism against the West 'would be heightened by military action against Iraq'.[26] Moreover, the leader of the 7/7 suicide bombers, Mohammad Sidique Khan, had himself explained his actions by criticising governments that 'continuously perpetuate atrocities against my people all over the world', and warned that 'until you stop the bombing, gassing, imprisonment and torture of my people we will not stop this fight'.[27] Nevertheless, the government and its supporters in the media have sought to impose a different interpretation on 7/7. Tony Blair spoke of an 'evil ideology' that was not in any way linked to actual injustices committed by Israel or Western states: 'Their cause is not founded on an injustice. It is founded on a belief, one whose fanaticism is such it can't be moderated.'[28] Elaborating on this view in speeches the following year, Blair argued that 'whereas the economics of globalisation are well matured, the politics of globalisation are not', and that Western governments need a 'global policy based on common values'[29] to be promoted worldwide by interventions 'military and otherwise' that 'were not just about changing regimes but changing the value systems governing the nations concerned'.[30] It was these common values of democracy and free markets that were being opposed by a reactionary and violent ideology of extremism, shared not only by al-Qa'ida and the Taliban but also by Hizbullah, Hamas and the government of Iran. In fighting this ideology, he added, it was essential that 'we must reject the thought that somehow we are the authors of our own distress'.[31]

This approach, crudely lumping together very different Islamist movements, some of which clearly have their historical roots in Israel's occupations of Palestine and Lebanon, has been echoed across the press. A fanatical and totalitarian ideology, analogous to fascism or communism, is presented as a wide-ranging existential threat to the life of the West.[32] To assist in this process, a virtual industry of academic and journalistic discourse has emerged, which serves mainly to evade the political context underlying global terrorism. Criminologists Dave Whyte and Johnny Burnett refer to the role of 'embedded experts', academics with close relationships to military establishments, whose research is driven not by objective standards of scholarship but 'upon technocratic assessments that are of use to powerful state and corporate agents'.[33] The principal function of this expertise is to abstract terrorism from its socio-economic and political roots, which, when discussed and understood, pose 'too many awkward questions about Western state terror'.[34] Moreover, it serves to camouflage the fact that, in the Middle East, it is interventions by Western states and their support for autocratic regimes and military occupations that have done as much to prevent democracy as ideologies of 'Islamic extremism'. For example, whereas the Islamic Republic of Iran is vilified as part of an 'arc of extremism',[35] the Saudi regime is supported by Washington and Westminster, even though it is as authoritarian and undemocratic as Iran's, if not more so. The British and US governments argue that they are trying to bring democratic values to the Muslim world. But their allies in the House of Al Saud rule with no parliament and no independent judiciary. King Fahd of Saudi Arabia even argued that democracy is incompatible with Islam: 'The democratic system prevalent in the world is not appropriate for us in this region ... The elections system has no place in the Islamic creed.'[36] Yet this self-interested attempt to give an Islamic justification for the authoritarianism of his kingdom and his family's monopoly of its oil wealth does not feature in Blair's account of 'Islamic extremism' because it does not suit the interests of US and UK foreign policy: not just the need for Saudi oil but also the £1 billion a year that the Saudis spend on purchases from Britain's arms industry.[37] Democracy is as valued by Muslims as those of other faiths, but the American and British governments are selective in where and when democracy should prevail – it is on the basis of narrow strategic and economic interests that they choose which forms of Islamic politics to support or denounce.[38]

To gloss over such double standards, it is necessary for the US and UK governments to use the concept of terrorism in a wholly inconsistent way. As the writer Eqbal Ahmad pointed out, the only consistent definition of terrorism is one that includes not only the violence of non-state armed groups but also the violence that states themselves use to influence behaviour for their political, religious or ideological causes.[39] State terrorism is responsible for far more deaths than the non-state terrorism that is usually focused on, and includes torture, mass displacement and genocide. When states themselves are able to present non-state terrorists as the embodiment of absolute evil, they gain the perfect justification for the use of absolute power without question; in the face of absolute evil, all other evil, particularly one's own, can be faded into the background. Thus the lack of democracy in Saudi Arabia, Egypt or Pakistan can be presented by regimes there, and their supporters in Washington and London, as preferable to 'Islamic extremism'. These regimes can then be herded into a common front against terror ('You are either with us or against us'), and the giving up of freedoms at home and abroad is justified in this permanent state of emergency. 'Our safety must not play second fiddle to their supposed "rights".'[40] Torture, detention without trial and mass surveillance can all be openly legitimised in the name of 'national security'. The inevitable effect is to create a closer identification with Western states claiming to operate in the name of the civilised world. Significantly, it provides Western states with the means to monopolise the definition of legitimate violence – ruling any political violence not carried out by them as 'terrorism'. Thus armed groups that seek to mobilise their people against dictatorships that have Anglo-American backing are 'terrorists', while the invasion of Iraq is a legitimate use of force. The then British home secretary Charles Clarke inadvertently highlighted this inconsistency when he said in the aftermath of 7/7 that 'there is nowhere in the world today where violence can be justified as a means of bringing about political change'.[41] By 'violence', he must have meant violence not carried out by Western states because at the time that he spoke British and US forces were using extreme violence to bring about political change in Afghanistan and Iraq. The same inconsistency runs through the legal definition of terrorism used by most states, including Britain. Under the UK's Terrorism Act of 2000, terrorism is defined as the use of violence against people or property that is designed to influence any government anywhere in the world for political, religious or ideological causes. This definition means that throwing stones at tanks as part of a national liberation movement against a military occupation is equivalent in law to an indiscriminate bomb attack against a democratic and peaceful nation. Both are deemed to be 'terrorism'. The law does not, however, allow for states themselves to be guilty of terrorism. According to this logic, a US missile attack against a Pakistani village, killing eighteen villagers, including four children, carried out because it is suspected that somewhere in the village are terrorists, *is not* a terrorist attack because it is done by the US state.[42] Whereas the same attack carried out by 'Islamic extremists' *is* considered a terrorist act under anti-terrorist legislation. The killing of innocent civilians is reprehensible and unlawful irrespective of who carries it out, but the 'war on terror' has its own racist logic in which Islamic violence is considered inherently more evil than Western violence. That such perverse logic is acceptable to Western governments does not change the fact that across the world it provokes widespread anger and delivers a constant stream of new recruits to the global *jihadi* movement.

UNHOLY ALLIANCES

Franklin D. Roosevelt's famous comment on the Nicaraguan dictator Somoza, that 'he may be a son of a bitch but he's our son of a bitch', epitomised the foreign policy thinking of the Cold War, in which strategic support was given to authoritarian regimes in the name of fighting communism. The result of such short-sighted policies was always human devastation, violence and displacement that scarred societies for decades afterwards and sowed the seeds of lasting resentment. Yet the lessons of the Cold War have not been learnt. The 'war on terror' revolves around the return of the same Cold War mechanisms of sponsoring 'strategic allies' and backing their authoritarianism, torture and violence – this time in the name of freedom from 'Islamic extremism' rather than communism. Regimes that can present themselves as friends of the US-led *jihad* against *jihad* find an easy route to military assistance, economic aid, political support and *carte blanche* to suppress dissent, internal critics and minority groups – particularly if these regimes can offer strategic advantages in the quest to secure natural resources, such as oil and gas, or serve other interests of multinational corporations. Social groups and their organisations that oppose an autocratic regime can now be portrayed as having 'links to global terrorism', in order to justify arbitrary detention, secret trials and extraction of 'evidence' by torture.[43] Whereas today's refugees are, largely, a legacy of the Cold War era and its disintegration, tomorrow's refugees will be casualties of a 'war on terror' that has entrenched a new global acceptability of torture. After 9/11, regimes across the world, from the Philippines to India to Tunisia, tried to label their opponents as linked to al-Qa'ida in order to receive Western backing for the suppression of dissidents.[44] Regimes can also find new justifications for buying arms. The 'war on terror' has given a huge boost to Britain's arms industry, which in 2002 was subsidised by the UK government with £760m of public money.[45] Pakistan, for example, as a key ally in the 'war on terror', has collaborated in joint military exercises and training with the British army. Licences for British arms exports to Pakistan increased from £15m in 2002 to £40.5m in 2004.[46] The military dictatorship of Pervaiz Musharraf has been given financial and ideological support by the West despite the fact that his rule depends on increasing suppression of what remains of Pakistan's democratic institutions, while the military hardware supplied by the West is used to carry out the indiscriminate bombing of civilians in Baluchistan in response to separatist insurgency.[47]

Britain and the US might make occasional noises about human rights abuses but autocracies around the world know that these concerns will quickly be set to one side if they can offer themselves up as a strategic asset in the 'war on terror'. They also understand that, after 9/11, it is a case of 'do as I do' rather than 'do as I say': Britain and the United States' own practices at Guantanamo Bay, Abu Ghraib and Belmarsh prison, and the fact that British intelligence services are willing to accept information extracted from torture,[48] all indicate to autocratic regimes what is expected of them. For the Egyptian President Hosni Mubarak, speaking in December 2001, the US decision to try detainees in military courts 'proves that we were right from the beginning in using all means, including military tribunals'.[49] Furthermore, when refugees from these 'partner' regimes in the 'war on terror' seek asylum in Britain, the label of terrorist sticks and they face castigation rather than sanctuary, and deportation back to the very torturers they hoped to escape. On the other hand, for the so-called 'failed states' and regimes that refuse to be pulled into the 'war on terror', there is the prospect of military 'humanitarian intervention', leading to more war, displacement, occupation and plunder of resources. The US-led occupation of Afghanistan in October 2001 presaged not only a huge increase in refugees seeking to escape the bombing, but subsequently the wholesale capture of the economy by foreign corporations. Healthcare, water, electricity, oil, gas and mining were all privatised, making key services too expensive for ordinary people in a country that already had one of the highest infant mortality rates in the world.[50] Meanwhile, those Afghans who fled to Britain during the 1990s were pressured to return home through enforced destitution policies, with the then home secretary telling Afghan asylum seekers to 'get back home' and rebuild the country.[51]

In neighbouring Uzbekistan, the government of president Islam Karimov found that, after 9/11, it had a new strategic importance in the 'war on terror'. In return for support of the occupation of Afghanistan, and unfettered access through the country by the US military, the government received half a billion dollars in aid; $79m went to the security forces and law enforcement agencies that were responsible for torturing and killing dissidents. The then British ambassador Craig Murray broke with Foreign Office etiquette to speak out against these practices, stating that torture 'includes homosexual and heterosexual rape of close relatives in front of the victim; rape with objects such as broken bottles; asphyxiation; pulling out of fingernails; smashing of limbs with blunt objects; and use of boiling liquids including complete immersion of the body'.[52] Murray's account was confirmed by Human Rights Watch, which documented more than one hundred cases of torture, including five deaths resulting from torture in 2002 alone.[53] After making these revelations, Murray faced disciplinary charges at the Foreign Office and was replaced, while the British government proceeded to give military training to the Uzbek army.[54] In May 2005, hundreds of unarmed anti-Karimov demonstrators were massacred by Uzbek troops in the town of Andijan, prompting refugees to flee to neighbouring Kyrgyzstan. The Uzbek military sought to justify the crackdown to Western audiences by casting the civilian protestors as Islamic 'terrorists'.[55] By October 2005, the UK government had added the Uzbek Islamic Jihad Union to its list of proscribed terrorist organisations, even though the organisation appears to have been concocted by the Uzbek state itself to legitimise suppression of domestic opposition.[56]

In Azerbaijan, there is a similar relationship between Western governments and a state that tortures political dissidents. Its troops are trained by US military advisors and its annual military aid package has doubled to nearly £13m.[57] Bordering Iran and Chechnya, it is a country that US officials believe has a key strategic role to play in the 'war on terror'. Azerbaijan is also the starting point for a £2 billion pipeline bringing oil from the Caspian sea to the Mediterranean coast and on to Western markets. BP, Britain's largest company and one of its most profitable, has built this thousand-mile pipeline, supported by UK public money. Georgia, the second country through which the pipeline passes, has already forged an 'anti-terrorist' alliance with the US, based on a campaign against the Chechen refugees who have fled to Georgia's Pankisi Gorge, following Russia's renewal of conflict in Chechnya in 1999. These refugees, according to the US, provide a haven for al-Qa'ida terrorists and the US has established a $64m training programme for Georgia's army to clamp down on the area. According to Human Rights Watch:

Georgian operations in the Pankisi Gorge at times have been arbitrary and brutal. Georgian forces have committed at least one extrajudicial execution, several 'disappearances', summary extraditions [to the US], arbitrary detentions, and discrimination on the basis of racial and ethnic identity.[58]

In Turkey, the third country involved in the pipeline, it is through Kurdish areas, where people have been driven from their villages by the Turkish army, that the pipeline passes. That same army protects the pipeline in a specially created high-security militarised corridor. BP has been given virtual sovereignty over this stretch of land and is exempt from the usual social and environmental regulations of Turkish law.[59] An indication of what may be in store for Azerbaijan, Georgia and Turkey might be gleaned from the experience of BP's pipeline in Colombia. There, the company has faced allegations that it recruited paramilitaries and a secret army unit to provide security for its pipeline and that these carried out atrocities against civilians, including driving farmers from their land.[60] Colombians have sought asylum in the UK to escape the mass political killings carried out by the country's right-wing paramilitary organisations, which are widely regarded as controlled by the state's own security services. At least one former asylum seeker is known to have been killed by paramilitaries after his claim was rejected by Britain and he was deported.[61] Britain is the second largest supplier of arms and military equipment to the Colombian government and a strong supporter of its domestic 'war on terror' against left-wing guerrillas.

Another regime that has benefited from a new alliance in the 'war on terror' is that of Colonel Muammar Qaddafi in Libya, long considered an enemy of the West. According to MI5 whistleblower David Shayler, in 1996, one of the main opposition groups in Libya, the Islamic Fighting Group, which then reportedly had a close connection to al-Qa'ida, was paid tens of thousands of pounds of British public money to assassinate Qaddafi. The assassination failed but six Libyan civilians were killed.[62] Since 2001, however, Qaddafi has forged a fledgling partnership with Britain and the US.[63] By October 2005, the same Islamic Fighting Group was added to the UK list of proscribed terrorist organisations and five of its alleged members who had sought asylum in the UK were arrested. They face deportation to Libya where there is a serious risk of torture or execution – a Memorandum of Understanding that Britain has signed with Qaddafi is meant to ensure they are treated without cruelty but will give little reassurance to refugees being returned.[64] Another consequence of Qaddafi's embrace of Western governments has been his co-operation in securing the Mediterranean underbelly of Fortress Europe. Libya's earlier 'open door' policy for African migrants had been seen as facilitating migration from Africa to the EU. In 2004, it was ended and, as if to prove his willingness to co-operate in defending Europe's borders, Qaddafi, with support from Italy, expelled 54,000 undocumented migrants into the Sahara desert, where at least a hundred died.[65]

It is Algeria, though, that provided the prototype 'war on terror' partnership between the West and a repressive regime, before such partnerships were globalised after 9/11. In 1992, the country's military junta cancelled the country's first multi-party general election once it became clear that the Islamic Salvation Front (FIS) – widely supported by the young, urban poor who had risen up against the state in mass rioting in 1988 – would win.[66] Thereafter, the military shrewdly exploited fears of 'Islamic terrorism' to engage Western, particularly French, support for its brutal counter-insurgency strategy. Hundreds of thousands died in the conflict between the Algerian military and Islamist insurgents, with both sides carrying out mass killings of men, women and children with unprecedented brutality. '[A] comprehensive circuit of misinformation was installed by the military junta, feeding directly upon western prejudice and hatred of Islam.'[67] This insulated the junta from Western criticism and allowed it to work closely with European governments, which denied the claims of Algerians seeking asylum and, by the end of the 1990s, increasingly targeted Algerians for arrest on the basis of 'intelligence' supplied by the torturers of the Algerian state.[68] After 9/11, Algeria presented its 'Islamic terrorists' as lieutenants of Osama Bin Laden in order to shore up its relations with Washington and obtain further military assistance. By providing Western intelligence agencies with what they wanted to hear about the threat to their countries of 'global terrorism', they were able to criminalise Algerian exile communities. At the same time, human rights abuses and authoritarianism in Algeria were justified to prevent Islamists from gaining control of an oil-rich country. The US, in return for its support for the Algerian government, was able to establish a military presence in what it sees as yet another strategically important region.[69]

7
The Halabja Generation

If the Kurds [in Iraq] hadn't learnt by our example to behave themselves in a civilized way, then we had to spank their bottoms. And this was done by bombs and guns. – RAF wing commander, 1923[1]

7 April 2004. There is a cold wind blowing down the Westminster street where a hundred or so protesters are gathered in front of the Home Office. It has been announced that, despite the awful situation in Iraq, one year after the UK/US invasion, the government plans to begin deportations of failed Iraqi asylum seekers, the very people in whose name Tony Blair justified a 'humanitarian' war. The men and women demonstrating outside the Home Office are some of those who would be affected. Among them is Sady Hussein, a 29-year-old asylum seeker whom I had met a few days earlier. He told me how each time he appeared at an immigration court, where his asylum claim was being heard, he would set alarm bells ringing as he passed through the security barrier. Worried officials would search him for weapons and bombs before realising that the metal detectors were being triggered by the forty pieces of shrapnel lodged in his skin. On another occasion, while walking along Ealing Broadway, west London, he was pushed up against a wall by police officers suspicious of the way his shirt sleeve was tucked into his trouser pocket. In 1991, Sady had lost most of his right arm when he opened a booby-trapped car door during fighting in Kurdistan. As a 'failed asylum seeker', Sady was caught in a legal limbo between destitution and deportation. To normal society, he was invisible, disallowed from working, claiming benefits or accessing medical treatment. Officially, his only status was that of a number in a Home Office file awaiting a removal order. While his asylum claim was still being processed, he was shunted around the country, living in bedsits in Portsmouth, Walsall and London. Then, two months before I met him, he was informed that he had to leave his accommodation. Effectively homeless, he was forced to survive on the charity of friends and organisations like the YMCA. While other Iraqis in Sady's situation eked out a living in the undocumented economy, Sady's disability closed off that option. The

operation to remove the shrapnel from his body, which doctors had promised would ease the pain of his injuries, was denied him now that, to the NHS, he no longer existed.

According to the Home Office, there was no reason why Sady should not go back to Iraq. The policy of withdrawing housing, benefits and medical assistance from people like Sady would encourage all but the most desperate of people to take up the option of 'voluntary return' if it were safe for them to do so. But it is not safe. Even to travel into Iraq requires a dangerous journey along 'Highway 10', the road linking Jordan to Baghdad, which is notorious for hijackings and killings and passes through Fallujah and Ramadi.[2] The International Organisation for Migration (IOM), which runs the 'voluntary returns' programme, requires participants to sign a waiver that reads: 'I acknowledge that IOM has no responsibility for me or my dependants once I return to Iraqi territory and I hereby release IOM from any liability in this respect.'[3] Unsurprisingly, only a small number of Iraqis have taken up this option. Despite the imposed destitution and the fact that Sady had not seen his wife and child for three years, he too was still fearful of returning home. 'I'm not going back unless they take my dead body,' he told me. It is not hard to understand why. When he arrived in Britain in September 2001, Sady Hussein was confident that his plight would be recognised and he would be granted refugee status. He even brought with him a videotape and 36 different documents as evidence. 'After my first Home Office interview I was really happy,' says Sady. 'I thought I would maybe get my refugee status. I didn't expect to receive a letter saying they had refused me.' His claim for asylum, however, came at a time when seven out of ten Iraqi cases were being rejected, and Sady's case did not fit the skewed parameters of Home Office decision-making.[4] As a young man in 1991, Sady had joined the Patriotic Union of Kurdistan (PUK), one of the factions then fighting for Kurdish autonomy from Saddam Hussein's Iraq. But he grew disillusioned with its narrow nationalist politics and left to work for a radio station and an independent magazine. After speaking publicly against the party at meetings, he was repeatedly arrested by the PUK (which by then controlled part of northern Iraq) and was beaten up in prison. After the fourth arrest, his family bribed prison guards to release him and arranged for his escape from Iraq. Sady told me that other members of his family had been killed by the PUK and, if he returned, his life would be in danger. He believes that the Home Office had already decided to reject his asylum claim before his interview, as part of a policy of blanket refusals. He hoped that they would reconsider his case. 'They know what is going on in northern Iraq but they don't want to admit the reality.'

Sady is one of the 'Halabja generation', that generation of Iraqi Kurds who came of age in the shadow of Saddam Hussein's brutal *Anfal* campaign of 1988 which, according to Human Rights Watch, reached 'genocidal proportions'.[5] A hundred thousand Kurds were killed by Saddam's forces. Between three and four thousand Kurdish villages and towns were destroyed. Hundreds of thousands of Kurds were forced to flee.[6] Iraqi Kurdistan has never recovered. The worst single atrocity in the *Anfal* campaign occurred at Halabja on 16 March 1988. A gas that smelt of sweet apples was dropped on the town in an air raid. Five thousand were killed in the space of a few hours and many thousands more fled the town's 'nightmarish scenes' of 'women, children and elderly people huddled inertly in the streets, or lying on their backs with mouths agape'.[7] Today, there are thousands of members of the Halabja generation living in Britain, like Sady, in conditions of utter despair. They have had their asylum claims rejected, been disallowed from working and been denied any support – save for a discretionary, workhouse-style 'hard cases' allowance for some. As a result, many have been forced into illegal work in order to survive; in at least one case, the risks involved have led to loss of life.[8] Others have been made homeless or suffer from mental health problems caused by their rejection from Britain. Still more suffer from racist violence and police harassment. At least one has taken his own life[9]; at least one has died of hypothermia while sleeping rough.[10] While they understandably celebrated the end of Saddam Hussein's government in 2003, many Iraqi Kurds objected to the means by which it was done. Then there is the legacy of two US-led wars, a decade of sanctions and bombing and the fact that Iraq remains under foreign occupation. Infant malnutrition has doubled since the beginning of the occupation in 2003, while the proceeds from the oil industry are being used to pay for a privatisation-cum-'reconstruction' of Iraq that is dominated by US corporations.[11] Iraq, like Afghanistan, has suffered from continuous war since 1980 and the current UK/US occupation is only prolonging the bloody catalogue of violence and torture. 'Daily life for most Iraqis', writes Iraqi-born novelist Haifa Zangana, 'is still a struggle for survival with human rights abuses engulfing them.'[12] By the end of 2005, 650,000 Iraqis had sought refuge from the country's violence in Jordan and Syria.[13] A decade ago, those fleeing Saddam's torturers in Abu Ghraib prison still looked to Britain as a place where they could seek sanctuary.

Today, the thousands of Iraqis displaced by the US military's laying siege to Fallujah or Haditha no longer see Britain as a bastion of freedom and human rights but as an occupying power.

ROGUE STATES

Until 2001, most Iraqi asylum seekers had, in fact, been accepted in Britain as genuine. In July 2000, for example, only 14 per cent were classified as not in need of asylum or temporary protection. But, by February 2001, 78 per cent of Iraqis were being refused all forms of protection.[14] What had changed in the meantime was not the validity of the asylum applications themselves but Home Office policy. In this period, more asylum seekers were coming to Britain from Iraq than from any other country. With a general election looming and accusations flying that the government was a 'soft touch' on asylum, the proportion of Iraqi asylum seekers that were accepted was dramatically reduced. The result was that the victims of Saddam's regime, for whom Blair's government would later, supposedly, go to war, were denied the sanctuary they needed. When they arrived in the UK asking for help, they were met with an efficient indifference. An Iraqi power plant engineer, for example, who had disobeyed an order from Saddam's government to cut power to Kurdish areas, was arrested by Saddam's militia and tortured with electric shocks, beatings and a mock execution. In a letter from the Home Office refusing his application for asylum, he was told that the 'Secretary of State [Jack Straw] considers your claim to be an example of prosecution not persecution' and that his arrest had a 'valid cause'.[15] During 2002, as false claims of weapons of mass destruction were being used to ready the public for war, nearly 15,000 Iraqis came to Britain in the hope of being recognised as refugees. Only 700 were accepted by the Home Office as being genuinely in danger. Clearly the Home Office was acting as if the majority of Iraqis were quite safe in their own country.

It was an irony that was forcefully illustrated on the eve of the Anglo-American invasion of Iraq. In February 2003, with millions of people around the world marching against the war, unwilling to believe that Iraq represented a threat to the West, Tony Blair unveiled a new attempt to justify the war. While George W. Bush allowed the American people to believe that the war on Iraq was retaliation for the 9/11 terrorist attacks, Blair painted the war in the moral veneer of a 'humanitarian intervention'. Even if you did not believe that Iraq was a threat, and even if the UN Security Council did not approve it, Blair argued, war was nevertheless justified for humanitarian reasons, for the sake of the Iraqi people themselves. In making his 'humanitarian' case for invading Iraq, Blair quoted from those whom he described as Iraqi 'exiles'. He described their experience of Saddam's Iraq: the arbitrary imprisonment, the mass torture, the execution of political opponents. 'You will be hard pressed', he said, 'to find a family in Iraq who have not had a son, father, brother killed, imprisoned, tortured and/or "disappeared" due to Saddam's regime.'[16] At the very time Blair was using the persecution experienced by Iraqi refugees to validate his 'moral' case for war, his government was invalidating the claims of thousands of other Iraqis who had fled to Britain for the self-same reasons. Their claims to be at risk of torture or political persecution in Iraq were assumed to be unfounded by the same ministers who were so eager to describe the brutalities of Saddam's regime.

In the same week that he had spoken of the 'humanitarian' basis for invading Iraq, Blair was interviewed on the BBC's *Newsnight* programme about asylum seekers. He gave a pledge that he would halve the number of people claiming asylum in the UK within six months.[17] It was an odd thing to promise. Common sense would suggest that, at least in part, the number of asylum seekers in Britain would depend on the human rights situation in the countries from which they fled, not something that could be easily predicted. But Blair was basing his pledge on changes to domestic asylum policy. It was this that he claimed would bring about the reduction in numbers. New measures, such as the withdrawal of accommodation and subsistence for asylum seekers who did not claim 'as soon as reasonably practicable' after arriving in the UK, were meant to be the instruments for delivering the pledge.[18] What Blair's government was proposing was that Britain would remain a signatory to the Geneva Convention but, in practice, everything would be done to make it as hard as possible for any asylum seeker to find safety in the UK. After all, Blair had not pledged to reduce only 'bogus' asylum claims but all asylum claims.

To reinforce this point, Blair promised, in another television interview shortly afterwards, that, if the number of claims did not fall sufficiently, his government would also withdraw the UK from Article 3 of the European Convention on Human Rights.[19] Article 3 obliges states not to deport someone to another country if they could be at risk there of torture or inhuman treatment. By proposing that Britain might withdraw from this commitment, Blair finally abandoned any pretence of wanting to protect genuine refugees. Almost by definition, someone who might be tortured were they to be sent back to their home country is genuinely in need of protection. Since Article 3 is considered such a fundamental part of the human rights framework of Europe, there is no opt-out clause that allows for 'emergency' periods, as there is for some other clauses. Britain would therefore have had to withdraw from the entire European Convention on Human Rights. Tony Blair had spoken in February 2003 of countries that did not 'operate within any international treaties' and did not 'conform to any rules'.[20] They were 'rogue states' like Saddam's Iraq. If Britain, on the other hand, considered withdrawing from international treaties, such as the Geneva Convention or the European Convention on Human Rights, this was a necessary and reasonable response to the grave threat posed to Britain by asylum seekers.

DIVIDE AND RULE

Both Saddam and Iraqi refugees from his regime had been used by Britain and the United States for their own 'strategic' objectives when it suited them and then dropped when these alliances proved untenable. During the 1980s, it was around the need to control Iraq's vast oil resources and those of the surrounding states that an alliance between Saddam and the West was forged. Unfortunately for the Kurds, who mainly lived in Iraq's oil-rich north, when it was convenient for the West to do so, their safety was sacrificed. But to fully understand the story of the Halabja generation, one needs to go back even further than the West's temporary alliance with Saddam Hussein during the 1980s.

Britain first occupied Iraq during the First World War, using Indian troops to drive out the Ottomans who had previously ruled over the region.[21] After the war, the Middle East was divided up by Britain and France among themselves, leaving Turkey and Iran with parts of Kurdistan as compensation. The lines that were drawn across the Middle East at this time, and the 'divide and rule' strategies that were deployed to maintain European 'tutelage', left an inheritance of conflict that was to blight the region for years to come. Jordan, Palestine and Iraq – with a Kurdish region in the north – became British 'mandates'; Syria (also with a Kurdish minority) and Lebanon were handed to the French. For the Arabs, the promise made, during the First World War, that independence would be granted, was reneged on. For the Kurds – having a different history and language from the Arabs, Turks and Persians who were their neighbours – it left them permanently vulnerable to oppression by the nations in which they were now minorities. Soon the Kurdish language would be suppressed in both Iran and Turkey.

By instituting a pliant Arab monarch in Baghdad, drawn from the Sunni branch of Islam, which was a minority in Iraq, Britain found an efficient way of ruling. With autocratic powers granted by the British, the newly appointed King was willing to put down any rebellions that sprang from the Shi'ite Muslim majority, or from Kurds in the northern region. If these structures were unable to prevent trouble, direct military intervention could be applied. Winston Churchill, then secretary of state for war and air, proposed in 1920 that the Kurds 'could be cheaply policed by aircraft armed with gas bombs'[22] – the WMD of the day. In early 1923, the Royal Air Force (RAF) began a bombing campaign against Kurdish rebels camped in the mountains.[23] The RAF bombers would return in the 1990s and after. Yet another level to this 'divide and rule' strategy was developed when the Arab monarchy itself became defiant. For, then, the Kurds themselves could be given just enough British rope to rein in the government – but not enough to hang it. Although these sectarian divisions ran against the grain of Iraqi society, the general structures created by the British at this time for controlling Iraq's population remained intact for the rest of the century, even as different incumbents occupied the seat of power; and the formula of using the Iraqi Kurds as a check on Baghdad's power (but not a threat to it) would be used again by the West in the 1970s and in the 1990s against Saddam Hussein. Predictably, when the recolonisation of Iraq in 2003 met armed resistance, sectarian divisions between Shi'ite, Sunni and Kurd were once again instituted by the occupying powers in their bid to maintain control.[24]

Britain's post-First World War colonial mandate ended in 1932 but the British-backed monarchy lasted until 1958, when a nationalist revolution brought in the government of Abdul Karim Qassim. His takeover of power was widely welcomed by Iraqis – he was perhaps the only popular leader Iraq has ever had – but the British and American governments feared that Qassim, following Nasser in Egypt and Musaddaq in Iran, would nationalise the Iraq Petroleum Company, which was principally owned by US and British corporations. Initially, Qassim offered reassurance that the oil interests would be safe. But, in 1961, he annulled part of the concession to the foreign oil company, prompting concerns in the West that he would soon nationalise all oil production in Iraq – particularly as the Iraqi Communist Party was growing in influence.[25] Soon afterwards, in 1963, the CIA backed a coup by the Ba'ath ('renaissance') Party, which its operative in the region would later describe as a 'great victory'.[26] The CIA supplied to the Ba'athist plotters a list of names and addresses of Communist Party members, so that they could be arrested and executed. Over a thousand were killed, many after being tortured.[27] In the ruthlessness with which the US gave covert support to the bloodbath, the Ba'athist coup anticipated Pinochet's overthrow of Allende in Chile ten years later. Formerly secret Foreign Office files show how Britain also welcomed the coup despite knowing that thousands of people were being killed.[28] With Qassim gone, there followed a period of instability in which various groups competed for power and influence. By 1968, it was the Ba'athists who had become dominant and Saddam Hussein took up the post of vice-president (he was to become leader in 1979).

The nationalism of the revolutionary period had initially been inspired by Nasser and connected with the Third Worldism of the Bandung conference. By the late 1960s, however, Iraqi nationalism had ossified into a state ideology of narrow national identity. This involved 'both a recuperation of the past, sifted or even invented to suit present purposes, and the identification of what distinguished their own people or "nation" from others'.[29] Arab racism against the Kurds became a feature of Ba'athist propaganda and was institutionalised in education. The modernisation of Iraq, the impressive welfare state, the irrigation schemes and steadily rising living standards, which were then achieved, were dependent not only on oil wealth but also on the nationalist ideology that held these developments together while also demonising the Kurds.

A CYNICAL EXERCISE

The Ba'athists at this time were locked in a rivalry with their neighbour Iran. The dispute between the two countries centred on access to the Shatt-al-Arab waterway – a crucial thoroughfare for oil tankers passing into the Persian Gulf. Iran, then under the Shah, was a reliable ally of the West and, like Iraq, a major exporter of oil. The Ba'athists of Iraq, on the other hand, had aligned themselves with the Soviets. Caught in the middle of this rivalry were the Iraqi Kurds. US Secretary of State Henry Kissinger had encouraged the Kurds to resist the Baghdad government, and the CIA worked with Iran to support an insurgency by the Kurdistan Democratic Party (KDP), an armed faction based in Iraqi Kurdistan. However, in 1975, Kissinger brokered a deal between Iran and Iraq at Algiers, in which the waterway dispute was resolved and Iran agreed to end its backing for Kurdish factions in Iraq. The Algiers Agreement of 1975 effectively gave the Iraqi regime permission to destroy the Kurdish nationalist movement in the north, which the Americans had previously sponsored. The Ba'athists now embarked on the full-blown 'Arabisation' of the north: a massive programme of ethnic cleansing, in which at least a quarter of a million Kurdish men, women and children were driven from their homes and forced into desert settlements located on highways that the army patrolled or into camps on the outskirts of southern towns (which remain to this day). Arabs from outside the area were encouraged to resettle in the fertile land that had been vacated.[30] In 1976, the Pike Commission, which had been appointed by the US Congress to investigate the CIA, condemned the alliance of the US and Iran in first sponsoring and then abandoning the Iraqi Kurds, commenting that the CIA planners had not actually sought to resolve the question of Iraqi Kurdistan. 'They preferred instead that the insurgents simply continue a level of hostilities sufficient to sap the resources of [Iraq]... Even in the context of covert action ... ours was a cynical exercise.'[31]

The revolution in Iran in 1979, which brought the Islamist regime of Ayatollah Khomeini to power, gave Saddam Hussein, now in complete control of Iraq, the basis for an anti-Iranian alliance with the US. The following year he invaded Iran, beginning one of the longest and most devastating wars of the twentieth century. On one level, the conflict between Iran and Iraq had its roots in local disputes over land and sea borders and mutual nationalist antagonism. Superimposed on this, though, were Cold War alliances, with Iraq given support by the US and revolutionary Iran perceived in the West as a strategic threat. For the Americans, the war was doubly useful: first, it allowed 'containment' of the Iranian Islamist revolution, which they feared might spread across the Middle East to the oil-rich states of the Arabian peninsula; second, it tied up Iraq, the most developed nation in the Middle East and still regarded by the US as an ambiguous ally, in a costly war against a mutual enemy. As the balance of forces in the war settled into a brutal but unresolvable stalemate, both sides could be given support in kind by the West without having to worry about the consequences of an all-out victory by either one. Iraq and Iran were thus each secretly supplied with weapons by Western governments, including Britain, and both were, on occasion, supplied with intelligence information.[32] Nevertheless, Iraq remained the US's ally in the war and, towards its end, America intervened militarily on Iraq's side to ensure the free movement of tankers in the Persian Gulf.[33] Until Saddam's invasion of Kuwait in 1990, the United States and Britain continued to back Iraq with loans and supplies of military technology.[34]

Half a million lives had been lost in the Iran–Iraq war and untold damage done to both country's societies.[35] In each country, the war had served to consolidate dictatorship and repression. Yet again, the Kurds were caught between opposing camps. The logic of Ba'athist racism led to the *Anfal* campaign of 1988 in which a hundred thousand Kurds were killed. During this time, American support for Saddam was escalating and US corporations had been allowed by the government to supply Iraq with agents for manufacturing chemical and biological weapons.[36] Chemical weapons were used regularly against the Iranians and against Kurdish civilians, most notoriously at Halabja. As the full horror of the *Anfal* campaign was revealed to the world, the US Senate passed a resolution that would have imposed sanctions on Iraq, only for it to be blocked by President Reagan's administration on the grounds that it would be contrary to the United States' commercial interests.[37]

BETRAYED AGAIN

It was only with Iraq's invasion of Kuwait in 1990 that the US's favourable relationship with Saddam became untenable. After the Gulf War of 1991, though, President Bush senior chose not to remove Saddam from power and instead encouraged Shi'ites and Kurds 'to take matters into their own hands'.[38] However, fearing the influence of Iran on the Shi'ites and the possibility of escalating Kurdish unrest in Turkey, a close US ally, if the Iraqi Kurds achieved autonomy, the Americans stood by while Baghdad suppressed the uprisings. The counterattack against the Kurds in the north forced them to flee in their thousands to the mountains for safety, while the Turkish army amassed on the border to prevent refugees entering. Turkey had long been the United States' most reliable 'Muslim' ally, occupying a key strategic position overlooking the Middle East and Central Asia. Within Turkey itself, a policy of forced assimilation had been practised against the Kurds, along with a refusal to recognise the Kurdish language, despite it being spoken by twenty per cent of the population. In response to the armed uprising led by the Kurdish

Workers Party (PKK), martial law was introduced in the south-east, the Turkish military bombed Kurdish villages, people were driven from their homes and torture was used against imprisoned dissidents. Turkey also co-operated with Iraq during the 1980s against Kurdish activity in the region and, in 1983, its army, not for the first time, launched an operation inside Iraqi Kurdistan.[39]

With the Iraqi Kurds caught in the mountains, at the close of the 1991 Gulf War, between Saddam's army and hostile Turkish troops, there was pressure on the US to provide humanitarian relief. A 'safe haven' was created in the north-west corner of Iraq and a no-fly zone established. American and British aircraft continued to operate over Iraq in the 'no-fly zones' right up until the second Gulf War of 2003, ostensibly to defend the Kurds in the 'safe haven' from Saddam Hussein. The 'safe haven' itself was administered by the two Kurdish nationalist factions that had been sponsored by foreign allies over the years: the Patriotic Union of Kurdistan (PUK), which had been backed by the Islamic Republic of Iran during the Iran–Iraq war, and the Kurdish Democratic Party (KDP), which had been sponsored by the CIA prior to the Algiers Agreement of 1975. This would lead, during the 1990s, to a series of bitter conflicts between the two parties, the KDP siding with Saddam's army in cracking down on the PUK in 1996. Tens of thousands of people were driven from their homes as each party expelled the other's supporters from the areas it controlled. Iraqi Kurdistan became the crucible for another war by proxy, this time with backers in Tehran and Baghdad. The so-called 'safe haven' was also repeatedly invaded by the Turkish army between the close of the first Gulf War and the start of the second. Tens of thousands of Turkish troops entered each time, sometimes staying for months, destroying refugee camps and killing their inhabitants.[40] By the late 1990s, around three million refugees had been driven from their villages to live in encampments and slums on the edges of cities.[41]

It was largely in Turkey's interests that the 'safe haven' in northern Iraq had been formed. The British and American governments only wanted Saddam overthrown if they believed that they could control the process of 'regime change' so that, in the fall-out, there would not emerge an independent Kurdish state in the north or a Shi'ite state in the south, linked to Iran (outcomes that were, in fact, to be made more likely with the 2003 occupation).[42] While the RAF and US Air Force flew regular bombing missions over the region during the 1990s, their crews were quickly returned to base whenever the Turkish military wanted to bomb Kurdish villages in Iraq. Throughout this time, Turkey was a major purchaser of British arms and had become incorporated into the web of co-operating regimes to prevent the movement of refugees into Europe. The basis of the Kurdish policy during the 1990s had been driven by, on the one hand the interests of Turkey and, on the other, the need 'to keep [the Kurds] strong enough to cause trouble for Saddam Hussein while ensuring that Saddam Hussein is strong enough to keep repressing them'.[43] At the same time, economic sanctions were imposed on Iraq by the United Nations, at the behest of Britain and the US. The sanctions had a double impact in northern Iraq, as Saddam placed a blockade around the 'safe haven' leading to the collapse of the economy, with teachers, doctors and farmers alike forced to barter for their survival.[44] UNICEF estimated that, as a result of the sanctions, between 1991 and 1998, half a million children under the age of five died in Iraq.[45]

SEEKING SANCTUARY

A trail of refugees led from Iraq to camps in Iran and Turkey and, for some, from there to Western Europe. While the British media demonised these migrants as 'scroungers' coming to 'milk' the benefits system, the reality was a story of desperate people taking huge risks in order to flee real persecution or provide for their starving families. By 2001, Iraqi Kurdish asylum seekers who made it to the UK were being rejected *en masse* on the grounds that there was no risk for those in the 'safe haven' in northern Iraq. This was, as we have seen, untrue. In any case, many Iraqi Kurds were fleeing from parts of Iraq that were under Saddam's control, such as the town of Mosul. There, Kurds were still being driven from their homes as part of the Ba'athist 'Arabisation' policy. Since deportations back to Iraq were, in any case, nearly impossible, the policy of rejecting almost all Iraqi asylum seekers only had the effect of leaving them in limbo, not entitled to stay in Britain but unable to go anywhere else. They had neither the right to work nor support from the state, except in an emergency. Their only choice, until the situation was challenged in the High Court in 2002, was to survive by illegal working, begging or charity.[46] If they were forced to 'scrounge', it was because of Home Office policy.

Nevertheless, the newspapers focused on Iraqis as another dangerous 'horde' exploiting Britain as a 'soft touch', while failing to report any of the reasons why they might have good reason to flee their homes. When, on 18 February 2001, an overcrowded, dilapidated freighter carrying nine hundred Iraqi Kurds, of which more than half were children, ran aground on the French Riviera, the British popular press only worried that some might find their way across the Channel. On 21 February, the *Evening Standard* reported that the French Kurds were 'heading here' while the *Sun* headline shouted 'Stop France dumping the refugee Kurds on Britain'.[47] From the summer of 2001, the Red Cross centre at Sangatte, near Calais, which had opened in 1999 as a humanitarian shelter for those sleeping rough, many of whom were Iraqi Kurds, became the focus of an unrelenting media campaign.[48] The panic over asylum seekers reached a new pitch as television news began regular filming of young men attempting to enter Britain clandestinely through the Channel Tunnel.

One of those young men was Omid Jamil Ali. His parents lived in the village of Sharbarza, northern Iraq. In the late 1990s, they were desperate. Up till then, they had survived the turmoil and violence inflicted on Iraqi Kurdistan, making a living as farmers. However the double impact of economic sanctions imposed by the West and Saddam Hussein's economic siege of Kurdish areas had destroyed them. Like many other families in the area, where unemployment ran at seventy per cent, the only option left was to sell their land to pay for their eldest son to be sent to work in Europe. Omid, then aged 21, left his village in August 2001, carrying with him his family's hopes for future survival. He crossed first into Iran and then travelled through Turkey. Two weeks later he had reached Italy. He then made his way to Calais, hoping to enter the UK without permission. But Omid never saw Britain. Desperate not to disappoint his family, he risked everything by leaping on to a moving train from a bridge at the French end of the Channel Tunnel. In the fall, he injured himself severely. The train reportedly did not stop till it arrived in England. Only then was Omid retrieved and taken to hospital where he was pronounced dead.

Omid joined the long list of those who have died making dangerous attempts to enter the UK.[49] An inquest verdict of 'accidental death' was recorded. Having invested all their possessions and savings in paying for his journey to Britain, Omid's family in Iraq had no money to pay for his body to be returned for burial. Ironically, if Omid had still been alive, the Home Office would have been all too eager to arrange for his repatriation. In death, however, the state refused to pay the cost of his return. As a result, Omid's body remained frozen in a Kent mortuary for three years while the family, unable to put their grief behind them, struggled to raise the money to return the body.

SEGREGATION

If Omid had survived, he would have joined the thousands of other Iraqi Kurds driven to work in Britain's undocumented economy. Most are asylum seekers whose claims for refugee status have been denied by a Home Office that has, since 2001, rejected almost every application from Iraqi Kurds and then left them homeless and penniless. Others are migrant workers, hoping, like Omid, to support their families back home. As a result of the 'dispersal' policy operated by the Home Office since 2000, many Iraqi Kurdish asylum seekers have settled in Hull. There, they work forty hours a week at around £2.50 an hour in chicken-packing factories and pizza take-aways. Almost all are members of the 'Halabja generation', young men aged between 18 and 26. Those whose asylum claims are still being considered can have little hope of their claims being recognised. Without a solicitor, the already slender chance of a fair hearing for an asylum claim is reduced to nil, and there have been no solicitors in Hull willing to take on asylum cases since cutbacks in legal aid in April 2004.[50] Those whose claims have been rejected and who have exhausted the appeals process are effectively destitute. In October 2004, a local church in Hull estimated that 200 asylum seekers were sleeping rough in the city.[51] Others survive by sleeping on friends' floors.

Karzam is one of those asylum seekers in Hull who depends on friends who are willing to provide him with a floor to sleep on. His application for asylum had been rejected two years before I met him in April 2004. Then, he was sharing a one-bedroom council flat with two other destitute asylum seekers and the official tenant, one of the few Iraqi Kurds in Hull whose claim for refugee status had been successful. Karzam had been in Hull for five years and was now working in a bakery where the entire workforce was drawn from the Iraqi Kurdish community. He told me that he longs to return home and escape the hostility he finds in Hull – but he knows that northern Iraq is not a safe place. Although he has picked up the local dialect of English well enough, greeting people with the words 'alright, mate', he tells me he cannot go to pubs, clubs or football matches because of the abuse he gets as an asylum seeker. Like most other Iraqi Kurds, Karzam expected and wanted to socialise with British people but this proved difficult. Taking their cue from the national press, people accused him of being a scrounger and getting everything for free – a prejudice that is difficult for asylum seekers to correct because those that work do so illegally and must therefore keep their employment secretive. Furthermore, because Iraqi Kurds are segregated into the undocumented economy, it is difficult for them to meet British people in the workplace. For those that do not yet speak any English, things are even harder. There are reported to be 150 people waiting for places on English language courses in Hull. Others want to attend university to convert their existing degrees and skills to make them suitable for work in Britain but are unable to get places – even though they are happy to pay the fees with a loan.

It is no surprise, then, that the Iraqi Kurds in Hull have turned in on themselves, creating a separate community centred on the cafés where most spend their free time. The cafés themselves have, in turn, been targeted for racist attacks. In the summer of 2003, a local gang known as the Hull Cruise Club began a campaign of violence against asylum seekers in which cars would be rammed at Iraqi Kurds as they walked the streets around the cafés. In the worst single attack, Salar Mohammed, 32, was run over, breaking one leg and fracturing another.[52] Hundreds of Iraqi Kurds responded by gathering in Hull's Pearson Park to protest against the attacks and demand a stronger response from Humberside police. Other Iraqi Kurds chose to meet violence with violence, and a city centre car park became the scene for a street battle involving fifty Iraqi Kurds and locals armed with baseball bats and lead pipes.[53] No doubt, in a few years' time, when politicians notice that Iraqi Kurds in Britain tend to be cut off from other communities, Iraqi Kurds, like British Pakistanis in northern towns today, will be accused of 'not wanting to mix'. For the moment, talk of 'community cohesion' in towns like Hull is a cruel joke while the system does everything it can to drive Iraqi Kurds to the margins of society, in the vain hope that they might just disappear.

8
Integrationism:
The Politics of Anti-Muslim Racism

To demonize and dehumanise a whole culture on the grounds that it is 'enraged' at modernity is to turn Muslims into the objects of a therapeutic, punitive attention.
– Edward Said, 1997[1]

Speaking at a Fabian Society conference in January 2006, Gordon Brown announced that he would make the rearticulation of 'Britishness' the guiding idea of any future premiership. In the past, he argued, Britishness could be taken for granted as an authentic feeling of belonging. But now it needed the state to intervene to positively produce a new sense of nationhood. Being sure about what it meant to be British would help the nation 'champion democracy' globally and be a 'beacon' for freedom, while domestically it would allow a better response to the issues of asylum and immigration and improve community relations. The 7/7 terrorist attacks, Brown added, highlighted the need for more integration in British society. Britain, therefore, needed to rediscover from history the 'golden thread' of shared values that binds it together: liberty, responsibility and fairness.[2] There needed to be a new emphasis on this national story in the teaching of history in schools, and a Britishness day should be introduced in which these shared values should be celebrated. Behind the podium from which Brown delivered his speech, a flag pole held up the Union Jack.

Of course, an enthusiasm for symbols of Britishness has certain advantages for a Scottish politician looking for support in middle England, but Brown's speech reflected a far wider concern. The noun 'Britishness' has only entered the political lexicon relatively recently but it has come to be seen as central to the future of the centre Left, a fact reflected in the Fabian Society's decision to dedicate a conference to the subject. British nationality had historically been complicated both by the absence of a clear idea of what it meant to be a citizen of the British state and by the fact that it was a state made up of multiple nations (England, Scotland and Wales). The English resolved these difficulties by conflating an emotional belonging to

England as a nation with contractual belonging to Britain as a state; the myth of an ancient English *ethnos* thereby filled the space where a British constitution ought to have existed, while the Scottish and Welsh were left on the margins. But New Labour's politics of national identity harboured no ambition for genuine reform of Britain's obscure sense of citizenship through the introduction of a codified framework of rights and obligations. Neither could national identity any longer be, as conservatives had traditionally held, a reflection of a singular unchanging ethnicity. Rather, the new conventional wisdom is that a set of 'core values' is the glue that must hold Britishness together. According to this 'third way on identity', it was now vital that a 'national story' be developed by the state to bind the nation together.[3] That national story had to show how a set of core values were embedded in what it meant to be British while new symbols were needed with which the state could celebrate Britishness defined in this way. These core values would also be the mechanism by which limits could be set on multiculturalism, while allegiance to these values would be a factor in assessing the merits of different categories of migration as well as a necessary condition for the settlement of immigrants.

THE RISE OF INTEGRATIONISM

It has long been the contention of those on the right of British politics that cultural diversity is a threat to national cohesion and security. For the New Right ideologues of the 1980s, a non-white presence in Britain was conditional on its assimilating to a national culture, which these ideologies took to be an unchanging set of norms running through the history of English political life (see Chapter 3). It was no surprise to find right-wing newspaper columnists advocating a new emphasis on assimilation after 7/7, calling on the government to 'tear into those Muslim ghettos'[4] and to 'acculturate' Muslims to 'our way of life'.[5] Like many others, Melanie Phillips in the *Daily Mail* blamed a 'lethally divisive' multiculturalism,[6] while Anthony Browne of *The Times* thought that political correctness had 'allowed the creation of alienated Muslim ghettoes which produce young men who commit mass murder against their fellow citizens'.[7]

However, since the riots in Oldham, Burnley and Bradford in the summer of 2001 and the 9/11 terrorist attacks shortly afterwards, cultural diversity has been attacked equally vigorously by liberals and by those on the centre Left. They have argued that an over-tolerance of cultural diversity has allowed Asians in northern towns to 'self-segregate', resulting in violent tensions on the streets of Britain. They have argued that public confidence in the welfare state is being undermined by the presence in Britain of immigrants of a different culture. And they have argued that multiculturalism has encouraged Muslims to separate themselves and live by their own values, resulting in extremism and, ultimately, the fostering of a mortal home-grown terrorist threat. As leading liberal commentator Hugo Young wrote, soon after 9/11, multiculturalism 'can now be seen as a useful bible for any Muslim who insists that his religio-cultural priorities, including the defence of jihad against America, override his civic duties of loyalty, tolerance, justice and respect for democracy'.[8]

Since 2001, therefore, the existing right-wing critics of multiculturalism have found new allies from the centre and left of the political spectrum; all agree that 'managing' cultural diversity is at the root of many of the key problems facing British society. Furthermore, in the cacophony of voices that make up this new media-driven 'integration debate', it is Muslims who are routinely singled out: it is their cultural difference that needs limits placed on it; it is they who must subsume their cultural heritage within 'Britishness'; it is they who must declare their allegiance to (ill-defined) British values. By 2004, the liberal intelligentsia as a whole seemed to have abandoned its earlier tolerance of cultural diversity and adopted this new 'integrationism', which redefined integration as, effectively, assimilation to British values rather than, as Roy Jenkins had stated in 1966, 'equal opportunity accompanied by cultural diversity, in an atmosphere of mutual tolerance'.[9] A coterie of New Labour-friendly intellectuals and commentators – such as David Goodhart of *Prospect* magazine and Trevor Phillips, the then chair of the Commission for Racial Equality – acted as outriders for this new position.[10] After 7/7, integrationist demands reached a new intensity. Trevor Phillips spoke of Britain as 'sleepwalking to segregation'. Tolerance of diversity, he argued, had led to isolated communities, 'in which some people think special separate values ought to apply'. The response to 7/7, he added, ought to be a reminder of 'what being British is about'.[11]

It mattered little that segregation, in those parts of Britain where it existed, such as Oldham, Burnley and Bradford, was not the result of a liberal over-emphasis on diversity but an interaction between industrial decline, 'white flight' and institutional racism (see Chapter 3). After 2001, that history had been forgotten and its causality reversed so that it was 'Muslims' who were held responsible for refusing to mix, while 'multiculturalism' was blamed for allowing their 'self-segregation'. A new doctrine of 'community cohesion' was introduced, focusing on the need to integrate Muslims. Thereafter, individual and institutional racisms, which remained the principal barriers to the creation of a genuinely cohesive society, received little attention.[12] The integrationists made much of the need to correct the errors of an earlier politics of ethnic difference. But rather than challenging the underlying assumptions of that politics, they merely reversed its one-sidedness. Whereas the politics of ethnic difference held that any kind of solidarity automatically diluted ethnic identity, the politics of integrationism held that any kind of ethnic identity undermined solidarity.[13] Both shared the dystopian and dangerous New Right assumption that there was a necessary trade-off between solidarity and diversity, and neither could imagine how solidarity and diversity could co-exist.

The same assumption encouraged the thesis of a slippery slope from segregation to extremism to terrorism, which was widely accepted, despite its inconsistency with the actual biographies of terrorists. Of those involved in terrorism who grew up in Britain, most have lived lives that involved a large degree of interaction with people from other backgrounds and seemed to have been comfortable in the mixed neighbourhoods where they lived. Mohammad Sidique Khan, the leader of the 7/7 bombers, was a graduate who mixed freely with fellow teachers and students from all backgrounds at the primary school in Leeds where he worked; friends described him as 'Anglicised'.[14] Khan's accomplice, Shehzhad Tanweer, used to help his father in his fish and chip shop in a mixed area of Leeds. Omar Khan Sharif, who attempted to detonate a bomb in a Tel Aviv bar in 2003, was educated at a private school in Derbyshire. The most plausible explanation for these individuals' actions is a sense of injustice that morphed into an apocalyptic and pathological form through the ideology of global *jihad*. There is no doubt that part of the appeal of that ideology is its Manichaean vision of a 'them and us' militancy. However, those whose lives are rigidly divided on racial or religious lines do not seem to be any more or less susceptible to it than those whose lives are more mixed. There is no reason to believe that the reach of this ideology is somehow linked to ethnic segregation.

The assumption that the nation could only be held together by a core of cultural sameness also led to a normalisation of the anti-immigrant racisms that emerged in the 1990s. Integrationists, such as the influential New Labour pundit David Goodhart, saw in the hostility directed at asylum seekers a legitimate concern with the dangerous presence of alien cultures that threatened the homogeneity of British values (see Chapter 5).[15] Resentment towards asylum seekers was regarded not as an expression of a new form of racism but as a natural psychological reaction against 'strangers'. It was not a reflection of a social system of exclusion but a normal part of human nature. Cultural similarity, then, was taken to count for more than formal membership of the nation. When British subjects from the Indian Ocean island of Diego Garcia came to Gatwick Airport, having been exiled by the British government in the 1960s to make space for an American military base, they were left homeless and destitute as if they were 'illegal immigrants'.[16] They were what Goodhart was later to call 'stranger citizens'; their Britishness only existed on paper. On the other hand, foreign citizens from Australia and the US, who came to Britain to work, did not induce the same 'fears'. The whole language of 'bogus' and 'illegal' was not applied to the large numbers of Australians working without proper documents in London (or for that matter the large number of Londoners working without documents in Australia). Conversely, whatever their skin colour, asylum seekers were never really 'white' in a cultural sense; the perceived alien cultures of Roma, Kurdish and Kosovan asylum seekers meant that their presence was regarded as threatening. They were only deemed white when their whiteness was needed as an alibi for racism, at which point it provided a convenient means of denial. But was it possible to separate this concept of cultural belonging from a more general racism? Hostility to 'asylum seekers' tended to merge with racisms against established non-white communities, and the label 'asylum seeker' – which came to mean no more than 'unwanted foreigner' – was the means by which a whole host of immigrant groups that had long been the object of racial ideas in the British mind, such as Africans, Asians, Roma and Arabs, were demonised.[17]

In short, a whole raft of problems to do with segregation, immigration and terrorism are lumped together and misdiagnosed by the integrationists as resulting from an 'excess' of cultural diversity. This integrationist agenda is now increasingly not only a preoccupation of New Labour but also of David Cameron's Conservative Party. 'We need to reassert faith in our shared British values which help guarantee stability, tolerance and civility,' Cameron said in 2005. He added that history teaching, especially in relation to empire, should avoid politically correct criticisms of empire so that all children are taught to be proud of British history and values.[18]

The fault-line of this new agenda is the perceived incompat-ibility between British society and Muslim communities in which supposedly alien values are embedded. While the anti-terrorist legislation of the 'war on terror' institutionalised anti-Muslim racism in the structures of the state (see Chapter 11), integrationism has normalised an anti-Muslim political culture. This anti-Muslim discourse in Britain preceded 9/11 and emerged, in particular, in the wake of the Salman Rushdie affair. It was the same discourse that Edward Said spoke of as based on 'an unquestioned assumption that Islam can be characterized limitlessly by means of a handful of recklessly general and repeatedly deployed clichés'.[19] Since 9/11, however, it has become a regular refrain from high-profile 'muscular liberal' columnists such as Rod Liddle, Niall Ferguson and Melanie Phillips, who harangue Muslims for a supposed failure to share in the values around which Britishness is thought to coalesce: sexual equality, tolerance, freedom of speech and the rule of law. Unless this fact is faced up to, they suggest, Europe faces a gradual 'Islamicisation' as increasing Muslim immigration creates Islamic ghettoes across the continent.[20] The new integrationists of the Left rarely challenge such views and start from the same point – the perception that there is a threat from Muslim values embedded in 'alien' communities. Their only difference with the Right is that, whereas the Right is pessimistic about the possibilities of absorbing this alien population into modern Britain, the Left integrationists feel that Muslims can be assimilated through suitably aggressive policies.

This anti-Muslim political culture has very little to do with the ways in which Muslims actually live their lives or practise their faith. The complexity of faith identity and the different levels on which it operates, comprising belief, practice and affiliation, tend to be erased. Nor is there a recognition of the multi-faceted identity that a British Muslim citizen of Pakistani heritage, for example, holds, in which faith, heritage and cultures are separable and potentially conflicting. Instead, to be 'Muslim' in the 'war on terror' is to belong to a group with common origins, a shared culture and a monolithic identity that can be held collectively responsible for terrorism, segregation and the failure of multicultural Britain. The 'Muslim community' becomes, effectively, an ethnicity rather than a group sharing a religion.[21] Politicians and journalists often confuse religious and ethnic categories by referring to relations between 'Muslims' and 'whites', as if one is the opposite of the other. At the same time, anti-Muslim sentiment rationalises itself as no more than criticism of an 'alien' belief system – hostility to religious beliefs rather than to a racial group – and therefore entirely distinct from racism. But such distinctions are undermined by the fact that religious belonging has come to act as a symbol of racial difference. The new official language of 'faith communities' largely takes faith to be, like race, a destiny set at birth and something that someone can observe about you from your appearance. There is a truth to this, of course: faith is not just a matter of private contemplation but also to do with belonging to a community, which, more often than not, one joins at birth, and which one can identify with through distinctive forms of dress. But, in blurring the distinction between faith and ethnicity, the already impoverished language for describing racial, ethnic and cultural differences is further deprived of substance.

The model for this kind of racial ideology is modern European anti-Semitism. The anti-Semites of twentieth-century Europe hated Jews, not because of their lack of Christian religious beliefs, but because they were, like Muslims today, regarded as an alien intrusion into the national homogeneity that modern Europeans sought. No matter how much they integrated themselves into gentile society, they were still perceived as a threat to a cohesive national identity because their affiliation to a transnational religious identity had become the marker of a racial difference. Today, a similarly exaggerated dividing line between an 'alien' Islamic identity and modern Britishness serves as the basis for dividing communities into fixed, immutable 'natural' identities – the hallmarks of a process of racism.[22] Those who were once abused as 'Pakis' are now also abused as 'Muslims'. What had before been interpreted as a problem of Asians living in separate *cultures* has, since 9/11, been taken to be a problem of Muslims living by separate *values*. That the solution to these problematic values is always found to lie in the use of coercive force by the state, indicates that they have been made into symbols of racial difference and that those groups who are perceived as holding them are not being accorded their own rationality and citizenship.

The role of the state's own policies and pronouncements under the banner of the 'war on terror' is crucial in legitimising this anti-Muslim racism. While the state's official language of race relations prohibits hostility to persons defined by their (say, Pakistani) ethnicity, the language of the 'war on terror' legitimises hostility to the same persons defined by their Muslim faith. Similarly, the official discourse against asylum seekers legitimises hostility to the same persons in another way, if they are labelled 'asylum seeker'.[23] What is being produced in these ways are new stigmatising discourses that bypass and undermine existing strictures of official acceptability. The shift in perceptions brought about by this process has been felt intensely and immediately by British Muslims in their everyday interactions, not just in terms of an increase in physical and verbal abuse but also in the way that a whole set of mistaken integrationist assumptions about their very presence in Britain is now aired publicly.[24] People who had been British citizens, occasionally labelled 'coloured' or 'black' or 'Pakistani', are now an 'enemy within'. Every Muslim in Britain has come to be perceived as a potential terrorist and has had to explain themselves to the rest of the country, as if what happened on 9/11 was somehow their doing. Ultimately, the impact of this stigmatising discourse is to be measured in the numbers of racially motivated attacks. Reported racist attacks on Muslims and those perceived to be Muslim increased sixfold in the weeks after 7/7[25] and, in all, up to April 2006, eight Muslim men have been killed in racist attacks in Britain since 9/11.[26] The anti-Muslim dimension to such attacks is often overt: the gang of youths who murdered a Pakistani man, Kamal Raza Butt, in Nottingham just days after 7/7 taunted him with the word 'Taliban' during the attack.

ATTACKING CULTURAL DIVERSITY

The origins of integrationism lie in the government's response to the riots in northern towns in the summer of 2001 and to 9/11. The White Paper *Secure Borders, Safe Haven: integration with diversity in modern Britain*, published at the beginning of 2002, first indicated that integrationism was to be the new framework of race and immigration policy, with community cohesion and managed migration as the goals.[27] The death knell of the old consensus of cultural diversity and zero immigration had been sounded. In the foreword to the White Paper, then Home Secretary David Blunkett argued that 'the tensions ... which flow from the inward migration of those arriving on our often wet and windy shores, must be understood, debated and addressed'; it is 'confidence, security and trust' that 'make all the difference' in this process; and 'we need to be secure within our sense of belonging and identity'.[28] In order to create this sense of identity, the government was to promote a set of shared values that made up Britishness; citizenship tests, language tests and ceremonial oaths of allegiance to the Queen for those becoming British citizens would symbolise this new focus on national identity. So, too, would the unprecedented power to strip UK citizenship from people with dual nationality if they acted in a way that was 'seriously prejudicial' to the UK's 'vital interests'.[29] This, along with tough new asylum and immigration measures, was meant to provide the necessary 'confidence' among the public that their fears were being understood and addressed. At the same time, and within the limits set by the need to maintain a core of shared values and identity, 'managed migration' policies made a significant break with the earlier aim of maintaining zero immigration (see Chapter 9).

The White Paper shattered the framework of official tolerance of cultural diversity that Roy Jenkins had inspired with his 1966 definition of integration. The Jenkins formula had been based on a balancing act between integration (defined as equal opportunity and cultural diversity) and immigration, in which the existing non-white population was to be peacefully integrated while potential new 'coloured immigrants' were to be excluded (see Chapter 1).[30] For most of its life, this formula had been made to work by not allowing the official endorsement of tolerance for 'ethnic minorities' to get in the way of the barely concealed racism that underlay immigration controls against non-whites. With a degree of separation introduced between race and immigration, an important concept of being black British or British Asian could emerge. In the normal course of events, race policy was discussed as a separate area from immigration policy; home secretaries could be outspoken in their tough lines on immigration and, at the same time, adopt a tone of multicultural tolerance with regard to settled non-white communities. Of course, that contradiction was always precarious – it was family members of the existing non-white population who bore the brunt of state racism in immigration controls – but, nevertheless, it made possible a multicultural society in which it was unlawful to exclude Asians and blacks from pubs but essential to exclude them from the country. The state licensed one form of racism while nominally outlawing the other.

However, the 2002 White Paper blurred the separation between race and immigration policies, and with it the distinction between unwanted immigrants and tolerated 'ethnic minorities'. Thereafter, immigrants were themselves to be divided into categories of wanted and unwanted according to market needs (managed migration) while 'ethnic minorities' were to be ranked – and expelled – according to their perceived assimilation to British values (community cohesion). The response to the rioting of young British-born Asians in northern towns (a 'race' issue) was to be found in immigration and nationality policies, such as 'citizenship tests', oaths of allegiance and English language tests, that were normally directed at integrating new settlers, as if a lack of controls on who could become a British citizen was responsible for the violence in Oldham, Burnley and Bradford. Young people, who had been born and bred in Britain and spoke English with broad Yorkshire and Lancashire accents, were implicitly addressed as 'aliens' in need of assimilation. Practices such as forced marriage and female genital mutilation, Blunkett argued, had been tolerated in Britain because of an over-emphasis on 'cultural difference' and 'moral relativism', arising from the *laissez-faire* multiculturalism of the past.[31] Asians, Muslims in particular, became a specific target for a series of public pronouncements demanding they make greater efforts at conforming to 'British values'. In the days after the July 2001 Bradford riot, Keighley MP Ann Cryer had already claimed that the principal cause of the disturbances was the practice of arranging marriages with foreign spouses (as it led, she thought, to poor levels of English and consequent underachievement).[32] The White Paper repeated the call for the number of arranged marriages with overseas spouses to be reduced.[33] Later in 2002, Blunkett argued that if Asians spoke English at home, it would help them 'overcome the schizophrenia' they experienced.[34] It was, of course, true that forced marriages and genital mutilation could not be permitted under the guise of multicultural tolerance and that a knowledge of English would be an advantage in British society. But what was being implied now was that not just new settlers but also British Muslims would be scrutinised for their allegiance to a set of 'core values' and their acceptance as fellow citizens was conditional on their satisfying a 'British values' test. A fragile sense of belonging to Britain, which had been built up in previous years, was unseated.

Only three years before the White Paper appeared, a very different portrayal of non-white communities had briefly gained currency. The report of the public inquiry into the murder of Stephen Lawrence, chaired by Sir William Macpherson and published in February 1999, had, for the first time, given official recognition to the existence of institutional racism in Britain.[35] The outcome of years of campaigning by the Lawrence family and their supporters, the inquiry hearings were turned into a genuine public forum where evidence was accumulated of widespread racial violence and a police force that, by virtue of its own racism, compounded the problem. Crucially, the inquiry had the effect of broadening discussion of race relations from questions of managing cultural differences between communities to questions of the political relationships between non-white communities and the state. The implication was that the fight against racism was not just against personal prejudices but for human rights, justice and accountability. It was this that made the inquiry so troubling to right-wing columnists, who hoped, with Stephen Glover of the *Spectator*, that its recommendations would be emasculated so that 'race relations will stumble on, gradually getting better, sometimes suffering setbacks, and the politically motivated Macpherson report will be remembered as an ill-conceived piece of sophistry that, for a week or two, drove us crazy'.[36] They would soon find the concept of institutional racism, which they so objected to, being replaced by the new language of integration, community cohesion and diversity management. Indeed, the rejection of 'institutional racism' by government was already under way at the time of the report's publication. David Blunkett, the then education secretary, called it a 'slogan' that 'missed the point'.[37] The Macpherson report had recommended that a programme of anti-racist education be introduced, but Blunkett felt that such an approach would undermine national culture: 'We have tended to downplay our culture and we need to reinforce pride in what we have.'[38] From the summer of 2001, when Blunkett became home secretary, he rarely attended meetings of the steering group set up to monitor the implementation of the Macpherson report, even though he was its chair.[39] By then, Home Office schemes to tackle institutional racism were playing second fiddle to the new integrationism with its emphasis on reinvigorating national identity. The focus had shifted from the state's upholding of human rights to the responsibility of 'Muslims' to integrate themselves into the shared values of Britishness.

The concept of racism was turned on its head. It was no longer a question of the ways in which society systematically excluded particular groups and thus set in train a process of ghettoisation. It was supposed, instead, that non-white groups themselves refused to integrate and thus made themselves strange to whites, some of whom then became hostile. Racism was no longer 'institutional' but defined instead as a prejudice arising from unfamiliarity. It was to be understood as an outcome of segregation, not its cause. Not only did integrationism reverse the causality of racism, it also implied a fatalistic depoliticisation of the processes by which racism came into being. The often-hostile reaction of what was now being termed the 'host community' to those with 'alien' values (Muslims and asylum seekers) was taken to be an inevitable outcome of the rate at which the cultural make-up of Britain was changing. The House of Commons Home Affairs Committee, for example, suggested in 2003 that it was the numbers of asylum seekers coming in that led 'inevitably to social unrest' rather than the way in which those numbers were interpreted by a racist society.[40] Similarly, the government's panel of advisors on community cohesion wrote in its 2004 report that the 'pace of change' was too great and that the 'identity of the host community' was being challenged.[41] The role of the state and the media in creating a climate of racism was ignored and hostility was normalised as a natural reaction to the excessive mixing of different cultures. The state itself was seen as playing a benevolent role in making possible new national identities based on assimilation to core values. After 9/11, a number of centre-Left academics offered rationales for this approach, all of whom started from the position that diversity was threatening to social stability. One was the Harvard political scientist Robert Putnam, who was repeatedly invited by Downing Street to give seminars to civil servants on diversity. Putnam argued that there was an inevitable trade-off between ethnic diversity and strong communities. He regarded the correlation of higher levels of diversity with lower levels of 'social capital' (a measure of community spirit, or the degree to which there are networks of co-operation based on shared norms or trust) as a social law, which he illustrated in his presentations with a series of startling graphs. The responsibility of the state, he suggested, was to establish shared values that could ameliorate to some extent the flaws of a diverse society. Putnam's reliance on surveys and seemingly rigorous quantitative methods gave the impression of an evidence-based approach. But what his methods avoided tackling was cause and effect. His survey work showed that ethnically diverse communities in the US seemed to have high levels of untrusting, uneasy individuals. Whether this is caused by the fact of diversity itself, or whether it was a particular way in which people think about the diversity of their community in societies marred by racism, is a question Putnam avoids. In doing so, he leaves the impression that the presence of people from different ethnic backgrounds is itself the cause of social disharmony.[42]

BURYING ANTI-RACISM

To argue that there is a mechanical relationship between diversity and social disharmony is also to airbrush over the possibility of an anti-racist politics that comes out of communities that are themselves experiencing racism. Instead, 'anti-racism' is reduced to a conflict-management exercise carried out by the state, which does not grasp the underlying causes of racism and leaves existing power relationships in place. Integrationists consider the essential problem to be those with 'alien values' living separate lives; the solution at a community level is therefore direct encouragement of more contact between different groups. In this, there is a revival of the belief that racism and prejudice are mainly to do with mutual ignorance. It is this 'contact thesis' that increasingly dominates the new 'community cohesion' agenda. In mixed areas where cohesion policies are implemented, schools with large numbers of non-white students are 'twinned' with schools that have large numbers of whites, and youth groups are encouraged to meet up with their counterparts across the colour lines of divided cities. There is also a return to the idea of the 'community relations' work associated with the Community Relations Councils in the late 1960s. The 'community relations' approach encourages greater interaction between different communities by 'providing a meeting place for the exchange of views, and social intermingling'.[43] This kind of attempt to facilitate mixing is, of course, of some value but, on its own, it does not amount to a programme for challenging racism or overcoming division, which is why it was left behind by the anti-racist politics of the 1970s. Moreover, it is a notion of integration that is effectively one-sided, as it makes no efforts to encourage 'mixing' in the majority of schools in Britain that are almost exclusively white. Rather, the hope seems to be that social mixing will dissolve 'alien cultures' into a monolithic Britishness.

What is also at stake in the return to 'community relations' is the rolling back of the gains made by an anti-racist movement that traces its roots to the late 1960s: a politics that, influenced by Black Power and anti-colonialism, made black into a political colour. The network of grassroots community organisations produced by this movement provided the infrastructure for campaigns, such as that of Stephen Lawrence's family, which culminated in the Macpherson report. Whatever genuine community cohesion exists in Britain is largely the result of campaigns and movements such as these. But the integrationists feel little affinity for this legacy. Even the limited infrastructure of anti-racism associated with the Commission for Racial Equality (CRE) has been swept aside. Its taking up of discrimination cases under the 1976 Race Relations Act has been reduced in favour of the duty in that Act to 'promote good race relations' – which is now seen increasingly in terms of encouraging social mixing. It seems unlikely that the merger of the CRE into a new Commission for Equality and Human Rights will revive anti-discrimination casework. At the same time, the integrationist agenda has been boosted with the formation of a Commission on Integration and Cohesion. Equally, the integrationist agenda is hostile to independent community organising and grassroots campaigns for racial justice. With the new integrationism encompassing the entirety of the government's race relations strategy, the landmark recognition of institutional racism in the Macpherson report has been diluted and police racism has not been examined as a factor in the 2001 riots. In another significant example, the Home Office did all it could to block the attempts of the Mubarek family to obtain a public inquiry into the circumstances that led up to the racist murder of Zahid Mubarek in Feltham Young Offenders Institute in March 2000. In the new climate of the 'war on terror', notions of justice and accountability are treated as impediments to state control of the criminal justice system. That Blunkett as home secretary was eventually forced, after a defeat in the House of Lords, into initiating a judicial inquiry into racism in prisons, is testimony to the tenacity of the Mubarek family's years of campaigning and the importance of direct community-led challenges to racism.

Yet the integrationists claim that it is the promotion of a national story of British values, 'the reshaping of a civic British national mythology', to which Muslims and immigrants ought to be assimilated, that is the best way of combating racism.[44] They argue that, without such a national story based on values, it will be impossible to create 'public confidence' in the secure sense of identity necessary to forestall racism. What underlies this strategy of reassurance is the New Right myth that Britain is facing a national moral crisis caused by multiculturalism – an idea that is now deeply entrenched in Britain's political culture.[45] Prior to immigration, it is argued, there was an unspoken ethical base to British society that provided for its social stability. That moral consensus is thought to be shattered by multiculturalism and the diversity of values it introduces. The possibility that the saliency of this narrative in political discourse might itself normalise new forms of racism is ignored by the integrationists. They tend to equate racism solely with support for the extreme-Right British National Party (BNP) and believe that racism is being combated by offering potential BNP voters an alternative, even if that alternative shares the same New Right assumptions about national identity and therefore serves to legitimise an anti-Muslim, anti-immigrant political culture. With David Blunkett at the Home Office from 2001 to 2004, this strategy of reassuring whites that their identity was intact was raised to the level of a veritable philosophy. While the emphasis on values as the basis of national identity was new, there is a long and dishonourable history of similar strategies in the Labour Party's approach to race and immigration. Often, the Labour Party has protested strongly against racist policies when not in government, only to endorse those same policies, or worse, when in office and confronted with opposition.[46] Its failure to maintain a principled opposition to racism was always justified on the grounds that a small amount of pandering to prejudice in the short term was necessary to clear the ground for a progressive future. On every occasion, the strategy has failed and served only to encourage a worsening climate of racism.[47]

The result of New Labour's strategy of nationalist reassurance has been effectively to narrow the gap between its message and that of the BNP. The BNP's anti-Islam and anti-immigrant programme has been implicitly legitimised and its ambition to be seen as a 'legitimate' political party now seems close to being realised. The threat from far Right politics in Britain has reached an unprecedented level. The BNP's open pursuit of an 'all-white' Britain garnered 800,000 votes in the 2004 European elections; in the 2005 general election, it won 4.3 per cent of the vote across the 116 seats that it contested. At the time of writing, the party has around fifty councillors. In Labour's traditional heartlands, it presents itself as the true representative of the white working class and its message, if not the party itself, appeals to a significant number of voters in 'white flight' areas, for whom immigration and asylum have become symbols for failures in housing and education.[48] The sense of shame that once attached itself to support for the BNP has eroded and the party's near control of a local authority today provokes little outrage. Compare this to the situation in 1993, when Derek Beackon became the BNP's first elected official, winning a council by-election on the Isle of Dogs in east London. His victory prompted a massive united campaign against the BNP that removed him from office within a few months. Today, the situation is entirely different. That is hardly surprising given the shortening distance between the far Right and the centre Left on issues of immigration and diversity. At its most effective, campaigning against the far Right has targeted not just far-Right parties but also the wider racism from which they drew support. But nowadays that wider racism, in an updated form, is widely accepted. Official reports endorse the view that there is a rationality to the 'blame the immigrant' sentiment. Amid a conformist and populist political culture, few are willing to say loud and clear that Britain's housing problems, for example, cannot be blamed on immigration. And still fewer attempt to build unity in working-class areas by tackling shared problems of deprivation. At the same time, the Labour Party has little to offer the working-class voters whom it has left behind, except empty words about choice, respect and responsibility.

MODERNISING VALUES

The belief that, before multiculturalism, British civility rested on a set of core values implies that conflicts between incommensurable values are a recent social problem. But core values, such as freedom, are 'essentially contested concepts' that have always been battled over by divergent political interests. For some, freedom means freedom from the interference of the state, even at the expense of other values, such as fairness. For others, freedom is the absence of restraints imposed by poverty or by empire. Values that are today thought of as defining British society, such as freedom of speech and gender equality, had to be fought for (and still are) and often conflict with one another. How values are expressed, how they are balanced with one another in a specific framework of social norms and how they are organised into a 'story' that gives them shape have always been mediated by a range of political, cultural and class differences. This means that there will always be significant disagreement about social norms and that there cannot be one national story in a democracy.

By the same token, values such as freedom and fairness have an element of universalism that allows them also to be the basis for uniting culturally diverse communities, even where those communities have different 'stories' about the meaning of those values. This cannot be done unless shared values are found through an equal dialogue across the cultural horizons of different groups. Commonalities cannot be imposed artificially by demanding that a minority deemed 'backward' be absorbed into the professed values of a 'progressive' majority in what is regarded as a process of modernisation. Nor can one group claim ownership of a set of shared values and arrogate to itself the right to interpret what the meaning of those values is. Moreover, the idea of a shared set of core values that all do or ought to subscribe to is misguided unless it is accompanied by institutions that attempt to codify those values and provide formal mechanisms for their elaboration in particular contexts and cases. In doing so, the existence of conflicts over the meaning of values is not eliminated but methods are established for their negotiation. It is only in this way that values can be universalised so that their meaning is clear enough to be the basis of a consensus. The primary institution for codifying values at a national level – and thereby sharing them across society – is the law and an open and accountable system of justice.

However, the integrationist pursuit of shared values is nothing to do with seeking common values across the cultures of different groups. The domestic logic is the same as the global logic – that Muslim societies need to be forced to abandon 'their values' in what Tony Blair calls wars of 'values change'.[49] For integrationists, the values of Muslims are not only sealed off from modernity but have nothing to contribute of their own. Nowhere in this picture is there anything that resembles a genuine development of mutual integration on a level playing field. There is no sense here of an equal exchange across different cultural horizons.[50] The necessarily contested nature of values is reduced to a simple dichotomy between the superiority of (supposedly homogeneous) British values and the alien threat of Muslim values. Rather than allowing all citizens to participate demo-cratically in a debate about values, acceptance of Muslims as fellow citizens is taken to be conditional on their prior acceptance of British values. Integrationists argue that Muslims forfeit their citizenship if they call into question the basic tenets of British society. Trevor Phillips's declaration on the *Jonathan Dimbleby* television programme on 26 February 2006 that, if Muslims advocate alternatives to the British parliamentary system, they should live somewhere else, was typical of this attitude. Such comments are no longer idle threats. With the Immigration, Asylum and Nationality Act 2006, the state accrued to itself the power to strip British citizenship from individuals even if they were born in Britain. This new power allows the home secretary to remove British citizenship from dual nationals if it is considered by him to be 'conducive to the public good'.[51]

The new meaning of citizenship can also be gleaned from the naturalisation process that is required of would-be British nationals. The handbook that the Home Office has published to assist those preparing for citizenship ceremonies makes it clear that Britishness remains inseparable from imperialism. The 'national story' it regards as essential to being British includes an account of the British Empire in which it is related how 'for many indigenous peoples in Africa, the Indian subcontinent, and elsewhere, the British Empire often brought more regular, acceptable and impartial systems of law and order'. Furthermore, 'disparate tribal areas' were united through the spread of the English language and public health and access to education introduced.[52] There was nothing in this 'British national mythology' of the countless massacres and abuses committed under British colonialism, some of which would be living memories for those seeking naturalisation.[53] After all, Gordon Brown had announced in March 2005 that Britain should not apologise for its history of empire.[54] What is meant to be symbolised during the citizenship ceremony is not an equal exchange of one nationality for another but initiation into a superior civilisation.

Such thinking sets up a hierarchy in which different communities are ranked according to their inherent distance from British norms of civility. While that distance is perceived as greatest in the case of Muslims, all groups seen as 'alien' by virtue of their culture are caught up in it. The clearest example of this is the way that Islam has been singled out for its negative treatment of women. British values with regard to women are construed as exclusively 'modern' while 'Muslim values' are essentially backward. The fixation on the veil as an inherent symbol of women's oppression reflects this dichotomy. What is striking here is the confidence with which this 'integrationist feminism' obliterates any complexity to these issues in an effort to present British society as naturally liberal and Muslims as naturally sexist. The very sexism that is still widely seen by British men as 'natural' is now regarded as part of 'their' Islamic nature in contrast to 'our' inherent liberalism.[55]

Thus, for example, the epidemic of domestic violence that infects all sectors of British society, and includes two women every week being killed by their partners, receives less media attention than the problem of 'honour killings' carried out by Muslims.[56] It is right that the specific justifications that Muslim men use to legitimise violence against women are exposed. But this should not be done in such a way that combating violence against Muslim women is seen as fighting against a culture, while combating violence against white women is seen as a fight for rights. Domestic violence is always a matter of human rights. Integrationists assume a simple correlation between the Islamic faith and the oppression of women, ignoring the complexities of culture, underdevelopment and migration. But there is no great sociological chasm between Muslim and non-Muslim women's oppression. And, indeed, to focus solely on Islam effectively allows other communities to conceal their own oppressive practices and hide the various forms that patriarchy can take.[57]

Additionally, integrationists have no sense that Muslim women have long been fighting for their rights within their own communities in struggles that have rarely received solidarity from mainstream liberals and the centre Left. Integrationists have no affinity with the myriad women's groups in Asian communities that have been dealing with issues like forced marriage for decades. In their rush to cast Muslim communities as reservoirs of alien values, 'internal' differences, conflicts and struggles are overridden. Nor were these groups welcomed as partners by New Labour when it began to invoke forced marriage as a target of its 'core values' campaign. Instead, solutions were sought in tightening up immigration controls; those trying to escape abusive marriages faced the threat of deportation rather than support and protection. As Hannana Siddiqui of Southall Black Sisters points out, immigration controls have been 'blown out of proportion' as a solution to forced marriage and 'diverted attention from the real issues'.[58]

When values to do with women's rights are seen as inhering only in Western cultures, then their universal relevance is undermined; in this view, liberation for Muslim women means not autonomously transforming their own culture but assimilating into a different culture. Renunciation of one's identity becomes a prerequisite for emancipation, and a new kind of superiority is entrenched in the name of feminism. State coercion is then justified as a possible means for bringing about this 'emancipation'. Such thinking underlies not only the use of immigration controls to prevent transcontinental marriages but also attempts to justify war in the name of women's rights, as in Afghanistan. Behind this 'integrationist feminism' lies the tendency to regard the West as the sole bearer of enlightened progress and the European Enlightenment, not as one particular expression of universal values, but as the only possible expression for all time.

Human rights and democracy have roots in all cultures.[59] Yet, by rooting these values as unique to British history and making them the instrument of a particular identity, the British state can both obscure its own violations of these values (because we are British, we know when to ignore our values) and legitimise the exclusion of others from the nation (because they are not British, they are a threat to our values). The core values of human rights have been hugely undermined by New Labour in the 'war on terror' (see Chapter 11) at the same time as it uses 'British values' to legitimise war and racism. Crucially, as the executive seeks to bypass the courts and reach beyond the rule of law, disregarding principles of human rights in the process, the legal institutions that are a necessary part of sharing values across different communities are undermined. The market-state tends to prioritise the value of the market and the value of state violence. It is little wonder, then, that the government prefers to cast around for a mystical Britishness to bind society together, rather than find common denominators in values of human rights and democracy, codified by law. The effect of this is not only to trample over the rights of vulnerable communities but also to undermine the very process by which communities can come together with shared values enshrined in law and democracy.

What is being produced is the opposite of an integrated society as young Muslims, and others whose values are deemed 'alien', become disenchanted with national institutions that are all too mixed up with a culture of supremacy. With official thinking based on the assumption that alienation from Britishness is a sign of extremism and a step on the way to terrorism, this vicious circle looks set to worsen.[60] Yet, the more the state has degraded values of human rights and democracy, the more that young Muslims (and non-Muslims) have also sought to reclaim both human rights and democracy in their own political movements and see in them the basis of what connects them with global movements for radical political change. It is in such shared political struggles that the potential for true integration lies.

9
Migration and the Market-state

In the West there was panic when the migrants multiplied on the highways. Men of property were terrified for their property. Men who had never been hungry saw the eyes of the hungry. Men who had never wanted anything very much saw the flare of want in the eyes of the migrants. And the men of the towns and of the soft suburban country gathered to defend themselves; and they reassured themselves that they were good and the invaders bad, as a man must do before he fights. – John Steinbeck, The Grapes of Wrath[1]

Britain had moved from a period of post-Second World War reconstruction, during which a cheap Asian and African-Caribbean immigrant workforce was recruited through colonial connections, to the principle, established by the early 1970s, of zero immigration from outside the European Community bloc, on the assumption that free movement within 'Fortress Europe' would cater for all of Britain's labour needs. But, by the 1990s, the Fortress Europe system was failing to provide a sufficient supply of 'flexible' workers at the bottom levels of the British economy. As a result, capital turned to the growing underclass of Third World and eastern European migrants as a source of labour (see Chapter 4). This kind of migration to Britain was unplanned and undocumented – and, therefore, provided little guarantee for capital that incoming labour met its needs. In addition, globalisation increasingly depended on the relatively free movement of managers and professionals, particularly in the IT and finance sectors. Centre Left intellectuals had, for some time, been returning from visits to California's Silicon Valley with optimistic tales of a new kind of economy, based on a 'cosmopolitan openness' in which immigration was central to success.[2] The journalist Jonathan Freedland, witnessing the naturalisation ceremony performed by recent arrivals in the United States, commented: 'It was an extraordinary sight. Immigrants, elsewhere tolerated and often loathed, were being embraced by an official of the United States government. Dark-skinned foreigners were not being cast out, but ushered in.'[3] The implication was that, in a knowledge economy, national competitiveness was linked to skilled immigration. Silicon

Valley seemed to offer a model of growth in which a stream of entre-
preneurial immigrants added to the ability to innovate and generate
new ideas. Britain, it seemed, ought to reap the economic advantages
of following an American-style immigration policy.

It was not that US immigration policy was more liberal. Rather,
with the gradual evolution of a system of national origin quotas,
encouragement of overseas recruitment and minimal welfare provision
for new arrivals, it was more finely tuned to the developmental needs
of US corporations. The US IT industry, for example, was able to use
Indian computer programmers whose education had been paid for
by a poorer country. The Indian Institutes of Technology – Nehru's
hopeful springboards for an independent, scientific and prosperous
India – had become finishing schools for a life serving American
capitalism. In Britain, towards the end of the 1990s, corporate
interests with an eye on similar opportunities formed an alliance with
New Labour in favour of the introduction of legal routes for economic
migrants with key skills. Immigration was also thought to provide a
solution to the difficulty of an ageing population, in which the cost of
caring for those who had retired was set to outstrip the ability of those
in work to pay. Supplementing the workforce with young taxpayers
from abroad was to be one way out of the dilemma, albeit a temporary
one. New Labour began to talk of a 'positive' immigration policy, in
which 'a system of positive selection of those immigrants with most
to contribute' would be an alternative to the target of zero primary
immigration that had been promoted by both parties since 1971.[4]
Immigration policy would then be free to follow the requirements of
economic need, in a planned, rational and evidence-based manner,
with the 'invisible hand' of capitalism determining the entry and
exclusion of foreign labour. This new thinking led, first, to a revised
approach to the issuing of work permits – which allowed employers
to recruit outside the EU if no suitable applicants could be found in
Britain – to ensure that employers would be able to enlist workers from
abroad more easily. The numbers of work permits issued rose steadily,
reaching more than 100,000 in 2001.[5] This system allowed for the
migration of thousands of professionals, such as doctors, nurses,
teachers, IT workers and business managers. The NHS, in particular,
was becoming increasingly dependent on migrant workers. During
the 1990s, of the 16,000 new staff recruited to work in the NHS,
half had qualified abroad.[6] In addition, a Highly-Skilled Migrants
Programme was introduced that made it easier for people with key
skills to settle in Britain. These workers could now come without

first having to find a job that no British resident could do. Though the numbers in this category were small, it meant that, for the first time since the 1960s, a small number of migrants from outside the EU could come to Britain legally to look for work rather than have to wait until companies in Britain agreed to employ them.

MANAGED MIGRATION

The problem for the state was how to maximise the economic gains of a migrant workforce, while preventing that workforce from acquiring a social and political presence in Britain. With the 2002 White Paper *Secure Borders, Safe Haven: integration with diversity in modern Britain*, the clearest picture yet of what was truly distinctive about New Labour's approach to this problem emerged.[7] In the existing system, it was suggested, immigration was haphazard, *ad hoc* and irrational. Because of immigration laws inherited from the early 1970s, IT workers from India, for example, were forced to work illegally, even though there was demand for their skills. Following the prevailing prejudice, the White Paper also argued that almost all asylum seekers were coming to Britain to work rather than to flee persecution. By opening up legal routes for work migration at the same time as reducing provision for asylum seekers to the barest minimum, it was thought that 'economic migrants' would choose this route instead of the more costly asylum process. 'Our clear message', stated the White Paper, 'is if people want to come to the UK for economic reasons they must apply under the economic routes available to them.'[8] This 'managed migration' system thus effectively institutionalised the mythology that asylum seekers were disguised economic migrants and reflected the idea that migration is essentially an economic calculation. Each sector of the economy would be surveyed and, where appropriate, its needs met through tightly controlled routes into the British labour market. 'Bottlenecks' in the labour market would be avoided through 'efficient matching of employers and workers' at 'both the high and low end of the skill spectrum'.[9] Migration routes would be fine-tuned to the needs of capitalism. New Labour's market-state – an active, 'enabling' partner to the market – would reimagine immigration controls: borders would be managed by the state, not to prevent the entry of all potential migrants, but in order to enable the flow of whatever 'human capital' each sector needed – and to shut out the unwanted. Just as welfare-to-work, directed at the existing population, had sought to produce the kinds of cheap, 'flexible' workers that the new economy demanded, so too would New Labour's managed migration policy, directed at the floating population of migrant workers, seek to regulate the supply of workers according to the demands of low wages and disposability. Both constituted different sides of the same active labour market policy.

This new model was itself a reflection of the shift from industrial capitalism to post-industrial capitalism. Whereas the immigration of the 1950s and 1960s had been based on the idea of a one-off intake of permanent settlers, the new model was of an ongoing flow of temporary migrants. Since workers were no longer a long-term investment for their employers, so migrant workers were to be brought in 'just in time' for when they were needed: the 'rotating door' labour market implied a 'guest worker' system of immigration, in which workers were expelled at the end of their contract. This implied, also, that those migrating into this peripatetic underclass would be rightless and without a foothold in society, unable to wield any of the formal rights of citizenship that post-Second World War settlers enjoyed, and which enabled them, eventually, to challenge the indignities meted out to them.

If that, in brief, was how the 2002 White Paper proposed to reap economic advantages from the new migration, how did it intend to manage the potential social and political fall-out? One half of the answer was through a large-scale expansion of the apparatus of state control over migrant communities. This ensured that migrant workers were a throwaway population, denied the right to full participation in the society they were enriching, living half a life before being expelled on a market whim. The other half of the answer consisted in applying an integrationist racism (see Chapter 8) to migrant communities, in which the acceptability of different groups of migrant was to be measured by their imagined distance from British values. Implicitly, migrant communities would be held responsible for the social costs of their presence: if they provoked hostility, it was because of their refusal to adapt to norms of Britishness. Thus, the desirability of different groups of migrant was measured by, on the one hand, their economic value and, on the other, by their perceived assimilability to British values. The underlying principle of the managed migration system was to allocate or deny rights and entitlements to migrants in proportion to their desirability according to these measures. Those migrating into the higher economic strata of the labour market enjoyed the right to bring along family members, settle permanently after a number of years and switch jobs relatively easily. Those on the lowest-level migration schemes were to leave as soon as they were not needed, had no rights to have children or spouses join them and were indentured to their employers. Lower still, of course, were the undocumented migrant workers and destitute asylum seekers, working without any effective rights at all. The picture, then, was of a series of different routes into the labour market, each providing its own specific combination of immigration status, welfare rights, family union rights, protections in the workplace, length of stay in Britain, access to public services, and so on, along with an expanded state apparatus to police access to the labour market and public services at different levels of that hierarchy.[10] While the post-Second World War immigration was a 'reserve army' of manual workers, the new post-industrial migrant workforce was characterised by several distinct streams – reserve regiments of labour – each adapted to the specific needs of different sectors of the economy. The intricacies of this system would be kept subject to constant review and adjustment, so that the numbers, character and entitlements of workers entering the economy under different schemes could be changed as necessary. Each of these various routes provided employers with a different package of exploitation, while migrant workers faced a corresponding racial hierarchy that was matched to their perceived assimilability to Britishness and informed by the vagaries of a populist media.

By 2005, this system had been codified into a points system made up of five tiers.[11] Tier one was for the 'highly skilled migrants', a few thousand of whom had, since 2002, been arriving from India and the US, without the earlier restriction that they had first to secure a job that no British person could do.[12] Tier two was for skilled workers – IT professionals, nurses, teachers and doctors – who had a job offer in the UK; these workers were mainly from India, the Philippines, the United States, Australia and New Zealand.[13] In this tier, the migrant's right to be in Britain was tied to a particular job and was therefore temporary and dependent on the employer's willingness to continue the post. Tier three was for a limited number of 'low-skilled workers', who were to fill temporary shortages, for example in agriculture, food processing and catering. These 'guest-workers' had to be under thirty years old, were allowed fewer rights than those on tier two and only permitted to work in Britain for up to a year. Tier four was for foreign students, who were allowed to work for up to twenty hours per week during term-time. By 2003, over 300,000 foreign students a year were being admitted to the UK, and higher education in Britain was becoming increasingly dependent on the fees that foreign students were paying.[14] Tier five was for young people who wanted to work temporarily as part of a holiday. Under-30s from Commonwealth countries had, for some time, been allowed to enter Britain's labour market and work for up to two years on the condition that they only work half of the time and show that they had their own funds – which meant that the scheme was largely used by those from wealthy Commonwealth countries, such as Australia. After a small increase in applications from India and Pakistan in 2003, quotas were set for these countries.[15]

This arrangement was complicated further by the expansions of the EU in 2004 and 2007, which opened up the potential of new streams of migrant workers from eastern Europe. These workers had to be granted the rights to indefinite residence that came with EU citizenship. But beyond that basic entitlement, rights were allocated according to an integrationist logic of assimilability. Unlike pre-2004 EU citizens, Poles, Latvians, Lithuanians, Estonians, Hungarians, Czechs, Slovaks and Slovenians can only participate in the UK labour market subject to their enlisting on a registration scheme and paying a £50 administration charge. They, also, have to be self-supporting until they have established a twelve-month period of continuous work and residence. Romanians and Bulgarians, on the other hand, will not be allowed free access to the UK labour market for some years.

A policy of managed migration implied, also, that unplanned, undocumented and spontaneous migration, which did not come and go under the direction of the state, was to be curbed. The basis on which migration policy was implemented was shifting from a model defined – in theory if not in practice – by various rights (to asylum, to family union) to one that was determined by the interests of the market-state. Asylum seekers, whose claims to be in Britain were based on rights defined in the Geneva Convention and the European Convention on Human Rights rather than on market efficiency, were to be the first victims of this new set-up. In July 2002, the concession that allowed asylum seekers to work legally, if their claim took longer than six months to process, was removed. Their rights to support as asylum seekers and to a fair hearing for their case would also be gradually stripped away in the years to come. Britain would, for the sake of appearance, remain a signatory to the Geneva Convention on Refugees but, to all intents and purposes, it would be abandoned. In the managed migration model, potential migrants, whatever their reasons for coming to the UK, could only be accepted if they first converted themselves into 'economic migrants' – the very label that had earlier been used to vilify them. Moreover, the arrival of 'less alien' economic migrants from eastern Europe to take up jobs at the bottom of the economy meant also that asylum seekers and refugees from the Third World could be dispensed with.

A NEW HIERARCHY

For some, particularly those from eastern European countries that had joined the EU, there were potential benefits to the new model. Whereas before, Britain had forced them to work without permission and, as such, subjected them to a fear of detection and a higher risk of exploitation, the increased opportunities for legal migration meant that some of those dangers were removed and they became entitled to workplace rights, including the minimum wage. Yet conditions for migrants were not necessarily improved by the mere fact of their working legally, particularly as the terms on which the lower tiers of workers were admitted reinforced the dependence of workers on their employers. In Lincolnshire, for example, migrants from EU countries were recruited to work on local farms and given accommodation in houses that were often massively overcrowded and without any tenancy rights. On paper, the employer paid them the minimum wage that they were entitled to but, in fact, most of it was kept back to 'cover' the cost of accommodation and transport. Some workers were left with less than ten pounds a week to live on, but to give up their job would have made them homeless in an unfamiliar country.[16] Ukrainian agricultural workers on the third tier of the managed migration points system were similarly exploited. The accommodation they were provided with could be no more than a shared caravan and the hours on the fields, paid by yield rather than duration, were necessarily long when work was available. Complaints were met with dismissal – and effective loss of legal status in the UK.[17] Legalising the status of a migrant worker is important because it reduces the immediate fear of deportation but it does not by itself diminish their exploitation; it only does so if workers can go on to translate their status into enforceable rights.

For the thousands of asylum seekers, overstayers and victims of trafficking who were working without permission in Britain's migrant underclass, there was no attempt to survey the work they were carrying out and offer legal routes for these people out of the undocumented economy. The assumption of the managed migration system was that the unskilled work that had previously been taken up by some asylum seekers would now be carried out by legal migrants from eastern Europe and that this would diminish demand for asylum seekers to migrate to Britain. But it was not the presence of job vacancies that was driving the migration of the majority of asylum seekers. As such, forced migration from countries such as Iraq, Afghanistan, Somalia and Zimbabwe continued. Except that because the managed migration model had provided a pretext for further clampdowns on the right to asylum, it became increasingly pointless for people fleeing persecution or warfare to even claim asylum and involve themselves with the immigration authorities. Instead, they joined the thousands of workers who had already drifted into the dangerous, dirty and difficult work of the undocumented economy, without employment rights or access to public services.

The effect of the new managed migration policies was thus to institutionalise the new cheap, disposable, migrant workforce, rather than transform it. Managed migration meant that the hunger of neoliberal labour markets for cheap, docile workers was further encouraged, pitting different groups of worker against each other in a new climate of competitiveness. For groups at the lower levels of the labour market, including the white working class and established immigrant communities, it meant downward pressure on wages. The Home Office had seemed to believe, at first, that, in a flexible economy such as Britain's, increased migration would not generate wage stagnation for the existing workforce. Its 2001 report *Migration: an economic and social analysis* argued – as did many economists – that, if migrant workers were to be used to expand and complement the existing economy, rather than replace existing workers, there would be no impact on wage levels. This depended on ensuring that migrant workers could be hired and fired easily from jobs that the existing workforce did not want to do, and that their underclass status as labour market 'gap fillers' would be maintained until they returned home.[18] It left out of the picture the possibility that newcomers would want to improve their situation and were likely to demand jobs and wages that competed with the existing workforce, unless the system prevented them from doing so. Employers perceived Poles, a hundred thousand of whom had entered the labour market by 2005, as hard-working compared to workers from outside Europe, and they were regarded as possessing more of the 'British values' that were seen to be the basis for integration.[19] It was unlikely, then, that they would remain as 'fillers' in the labour market, especially in London, where there already existed a bottom rung of non-white immigrant workers. It was these earlier generations of non-white immigrant worker who now found themselves competing with the new generation of white immigrant workers from eastern Europe. The result was that immigrant workers as a whole faced mounting downward pressure on wages driven by intense competition. A 2005 study found that, of low-paid workers in London, 90 per cent were migrants, half of whom had tertiary-level qualifications acquired before moving to the UK; they earned on average £10,200 per year before tax and national insurance, which almost all paid even if they worked illegally.[20] With the low wages paid to migrant workers generally thought to be a significant factor in minimising inflation, these workers were therefore also subsidising the low-inflation, low-interest-rate lifestyles of middle England.

MECHANISMS OF CONTROL

Managed migration implied a change in the *modus operandi* of immigration controls. Border controls were now to be aimed at managing 'flows' of largely temporary migrants rather than preventing new settlement in Britain *per se*. Britain's borders were no longer directed at an absolute sealing off of its labour market from other countries. Instead, they were meant to filter out the wanted migrants from the unwanted, the temporary from the permanent and the privileged from the unprivileged and maintain, where necessary, the condition of deportability that allowed for migrant workers to be differentiated from non-migrant workers. The managed migration system thus required a large-scale expansion of the state's powers for managing and policing migrant populations. The new 'enabling' side of the market-state's immigration policy would have to be matched with a strong 'disabling' side – a necessary consequence of the need to regulate the supply of migrant labour in line with the needs of the market-state. This implied a step change in the policing of borders and increased surveillance of the lives of migrants, compared to earlier regimes of immigration: not just checks at ports but an entire network of policing and control that began with immigration officers stationed in 'sending countries' and military surveillance of migration routes, ran through the new high-tech detection systems at ports and the introduction of iris scans and fingerprinting in passports and culminated in the internal controls of ID cards, stops and searches at railway stations, workplaces, marriage registrars and public services.

In short, migrants were to face a new level of authoritarianism, with the ultimate sanction being expulsion.

At the centre of this transformation is the introduction of ID cards containing biometric information (fingerprints or iris scans), which the Home Office regards as its primary tool for policing the migrant population. In the ID cards legislation that was passed in 2006, cards are not initially compulsory for the majority of the British public. But migrants, refugees and other foreign nationals have to pay for biometric identification and register their details on the new national identity database, if they have been in Britain for longer than three months. By 2008, there will be biometric residence cards for foreign nationals – and these will be required prior to travel to Britain on certain 'high risk' routes. By 2011, all non-Europeans will have to have biometric identifiers before they are allowed to travel to Britain.[21] The ambition of this new approach is to create a system of total surveillance of foreign nationals, enabling the authorities to monitor and locate every non-citizen travelling through or resident in the UK. The introduction of ID cards will be accompanied by unprecedented levels of electronic checks – at airports, workplaces, social security offices, hospitals and police stations – against those suspected of being *sans plastique* (without ID cards). In hospitals and social security offices across Britain, electronic readers will connect scanned-in cards to the national identity database, to establish whether the bearer is entitled to access support or medical care. In this sense, the ID card will really be an 'exclusion card' that divides the population between those who are entitled to access services and those who are not. Already, access to all but emergency medical treatment is contingent on immigration status and, in 2004, the NHS regulations were revised to exclude failed asylum seekers from free primary and hospital healthcare. In a context in which there is growing pressure on the NHS to refuse treatment to foreign nationals, even if it puts them and wider society at severe medical risk, ID cards provide a means to enforce boundaries of access, with doctors and nurses expected to check ID cards for immigration status before registering new patients. This will lead not only to exclusion of certain groups of foreigners but also disproportionate suspicion falling on non-white communities in general, who will be more likely to be asked to prove their eligibility.

The police have not been granted any new powers to demand the production of ID cards. However, for particular communities, it may become virtually compulsory that they carry an ID card if police officers become suspicious of those who do not voluntarily produce a card, particularly if their skin colour or accent makes them seem more likely to be an 'illegal'. With growing pressure to step up the number of deportations of 'failed asylum seekers' and as refugee communities become increasingly stigmatised as breeding grounds for terrorism, police forces are likely to conduct more and more stop and search operations aimed at rounding up 'illegals'. Already, between May 2003 and July 2004, immigration and police officers participated in 235 such operations at underground stations and bus stops in London, where those suspected of being 'immigration offenders' were pulled out of lines of commuters and questioned.[22] The impact of such operations will be felt by non-white communities in general, not just by foreign nationals, as police officers on the street target particular communities for checks on immigration status. Similarly, the introduction of compulsory ID cards for foreign nationals is likely to be seen as providing a more efficient way for employers to test if someone is entitled to work. There will be increased pressure on employers to police illegal working by checking the immigration status of workers, especially those whose colour or ethnicity marks them out as 'suspicious'. This will continue the existing bias in the way that illegal working is policed, which targets foreign workers for punishment rather than their British employers. In 2003 and 2004, there were 1,488 successful 'operations' against illegal working and 5,111 illegal workers were 'detected' and presumably arrested and imprisoned or deported. Yet, over this period, just nine employers were prosecuted for employing persons not entitled to work.[23]

A decade ago, the American model of immigration policy seemed to offer Britain a positive alternative that could benefit the economy while, at the same time, break with the legacy of racist immigration controls. But the reality has been very different. Wage deflation, insecurity and potential social conflict between competing migrant and settled groups at the bottom of the labour market have been the hallmarks of the managed migration model. The racism that accompanied the policy of zero immigration from outside the EU from the early 1970s has been modernised and now consists of a hierarchy of entitlements and exclusions, driven by a notion of how well potential migrants assimilate to British values, as well as by their market value, while the expansion of mechanisms of controlling migrants introduces new layers of institutional racism to the police, public services and labour market. The new 'zero tolerance' approach to immigration offences is leading to the imprisonment and expulsion of vast numbers of people in Britain's poorest immigrant communities.

The lesson coming out of the US today is not that such a system offers a positive model but that it has the potential to explode into mass protest. On 1 May 2006, millions of predominantly Latino immigrant workers took to the streets in a national boycott and general strike. The immediate trigger was the passage of a bill that would criminalise undocumented immigrants, but the mass mobilisation reflected anger at the whole climate of insecurity that immigrant workers are subject to. In France and Belgium, there has also been a long struggle against 'disposable immigration', from the famous campaigns of the *sans papiers* in the mid-1990s to the mass demonstrations of immigrant workers in Paris in May 2006. Similar movements are likely to develop in the UK in coming years. They will be based on a range of migrant communities uniting against the state authoritarianism of managed migration, on the one hand, and the intense exploitation that migrant workers suffer in neoliberal labour markets, on the other. The demand will be for a living wage and an extension of a basic dignity to all workers who contribute to the British economy. In the end, this is a struggle against the whole culture of 'flexible' labour markets and the degradation they impose on British and foreign workers alike.

10
Here to Stay

If there is one rule, which more than another has been observed in modern times, by all independent States, both great and small, of the civilized world, it is the rule, not to deliver up refugees ... The laws of hospitality, the dictates of humanity, the general feelings of mankind, forbid such surrenders; and any independent government, which of its own free will were to make such a surrender, would be universally and deservedly stigmatised as degraded and dishonoured. – Lord Palmerston, 1848[1]

The plane lands at Ndjili airport, Kinshasa, Democratic Republic of Congo (DRC), in the dead of night – the better to avoid monitoring by journalists and human rights activists. Then the returning asylum seekers are led out on to the tarmac by their European escorts to be handed over to the Congolese authorities. Some will have suffered violence in the process of being deported or in the detention centre where they were held prior to the flight. Others will have been tied to the seats with scotch tape for the duration of the seven-hour journey. Most would have been prevented from using the toilet or eating. They are handed over to the offices of the Director-General of Migration (DGM), ostensibly the Congolese immigration service but, in reality, an arm of the government's security services. A file containing details of their claim for political asylum in Europe is also passed to the DGM. According to René Kabala Mushiya, an activist with the Congolese National Human Rights Observatory, this is the moment when European governments abandon those who have claimed asylum in their countries to a state that violates human rights with impunity.[2] He describes a trail of abuse that stretches from Europe's immigration detention centres to the brutality and violence of the notorious Makala Central Prison – nicknamed the 'morgue' in recognition of the numbers of people who have lost their lives there.

'According to reports that we have had from returning asylum seekers as well as from agents of the DGM,' says René Kabala, 'deportees are held by the DGM in small cells at the airport. There are no windows and there is no light. But you can see cockroaches and

153

rats. From these cells, they are called in one by one to the director of the DGM for an interrogation.' During the interrogation, deportees are sifted into different groups. Only those able to pay a bribe of between US $250 and $300 have a chance of immediate escape from detention. Since the officials of the DGM have not been paid for so long, accepting bribes is their only income. Yet few deportees have easy access to these sums of money; it would take a university professor six months to earn the required amount on local wages. Of those who cannot bribe their way out, many are handed over to the National Security Agency (ANR), which operates its own extra-judicial prisons where people are detained illegally for long periods of time. As individuals who have claimed asylum in Europe, deportees are automatically regarded by the ANR as threats to national security in Congo. Simply because they have claimed asylum in the West, the Congolese authorities consider them political dissidents. 'There are cases I have dealt with,' says René Kabala, 'in which somebody asks for asylum in Europe for humanitarian rather than political reasons. However, when they are returned to Ndjili airport, they are put in prison like all the others.' They may then stand trial under the national security legislation and, if convicted, find themselves imprisoned at Makala.

Makala is a place where political prisoners mingle with homeless children who have been rounded up off the streets of Kinshasa.[3] All depend on the support of outside relatives for food and medical care. The US State Department reported that sixty-nine people died there in 2003, some as a result of severe beatings, the others as a result of starvation and disease. Often the families of returned asylum seekers would have already fled Kinshasa to avoid persecution, meaning that deportees sent to Makala are less likely to have networks of outside support. According to René Kabala, there are lots of cases of political prisoners who were held at Makala by the Congolese authorities, then bribed their way out before fleeing to Europe to claim asylum. Because of Europe's failure to properly assess asylum claims, these asylum seekers were then sent back into the hands of the authorities from whom they fled and, in turn, found themselves back at Makala prison, the very place from which they had hoped to escape. Asylum hearings in Europe tended to treat stories of bribery with scepticism, further reducing the chances of sanctuary for refugees from places like Makala. The proportion of asylum seekers deported from Europe that end up in Makala or other forms of illegal detention in Kinshasa is not known. 'There are many cases which escape us,' he said. 'We can follow up those that we know about. Others disappear if we haven't got contact details for their families.' However, even those deportees who are released face insecurity. The DGM takes down details of all deportees' family members and, often, agents arrive on their doorsteps a few weeks later to make arrests. Some deportees have understandably chosen to disappear on their return to Kinshasa to avoid rearrest.

Evidence from organisations working with Congolese asylum seekers in the UK supports the account given by René Kabala. Bail for Immigration Detainees (BID), a charity that assists asylum seekers held in UK detention centres, discovered that, of three deportees who were removed to DRC between October 2003 and April 2004, two were able to pass information back to the UK revealing that they had ended up in Makala Central Prison. BID also documented abuses that occurred after thirteen Congolese asylum seekers were deported from the UK on a charter flight on 12 March 2002. According to the testimony of one of the deportees, who later returned to the UK, they were detained and beaten on a daily basis by three to six soldiers who accused them of being 'traitors'. The National Coalition of Anti-Deportation Campaigns (NCADC) says it is in touch with a number of asylum seekers who have been removed from the UK to DRC and who allege that they have since been held in detention there. For Congolese asylum seekers in Britain whose applications have been rejected and who have exhausted the appeals process, there is only a life of fear, destitution and detention while they struggle to avoid return. 'A' fled Kinshasa after being tortured and raped in a police detention centre but she was left homeless on the streets of Cardiff despite being pregnant.[4] 'H' fled to London after working in DRC as a trade unionist. His benefits and accommodation have been withdrawn and he lives a peripatetic existence, sleeping on friends' floors for a few days at a time. He has lost contact with his wife and two young children who also had to flee Kinshasa and had headed towards the border with Angola. Were he to be deported, 'H' would be unable to take any money with him, having had no entitlement to work. He would not therefore be able to bribe himself out of detention in Kinshasa. 'I would certainly be scared that I could end up in prison,' he said. 'I just hope it's not going to happen that way.'

Half of the population of Kinshasa lives on one meal per day and a quarter has to walk more than one kilometre to fetch water, work that is usually done by women and children.[5] Throughout the 1970s and 1980s, the resources of the country, then named Zaire, were plundered by the violent dictatorship of Mobutu Sese Seko, who for Washington was 'our man in Kinshasa'. Belgian colonialism had already established a brutal state apparatus directed at stripping Congo of its natural resources. Under the colonial system of collective punishment, men would be slaughtered, houses burned and women raped, if targets for the production of rubber were not met. The removal of the democratically elected left-wing leader Patrice Lumumba, in a Belgium-supported assassination carried out shortly after independence in 1960, paved the way for the assumption of power by Mobutu. The basis of the state remained the intertwining of natural resource extraction, personal enrichment and routine brutality, which had been inherited from Belgian colonialism. In spite of the natural wealth of minerals and diamonds presided over by Mobutu, by the mid-1980s mounting debts forced the introduction of structural adjustment programmes, leading to massive restrictions in the state provision of health and education. By the early 1990s, the public sector was bankrupt and surging prices led to riots in Kinshasa and heavy loss of life. The state was imploding and no longer commanded authority over much of the country. At the same time, the government was pressured by the World Bank to privatise the state mining companies and open up the industry to exploitation by multinational corporations.[6]

By 1997, the Mobutu regime had been ousted leaving behind foreign debts which, by the turn of the millennium, amounted to US$9 billion.[7] As Laurent Désiré Kabila assumed power, heading a coalition of insurgents that had removed Mobutu, the economy of diamond and mineral extraction became increasingly militarised. A variety of rebel armed groups, linked to neighbouring states, competed to control the sale of these natural resources to multinational mining corporations. Serious shortages of staple foods resulted from the abandonment of traditional agriculture in favour of the profits to be had from the extraction of minerals, such as coltan – used in the manufacture of mobile phones. As competition intensified and traditional social safety-nets disintegrated, militias tied to the mineral extraction economy became essential protection for everyday survival.[8] The rising revenue – diamond exports alone were thought to be worth hundreds of millions of dollars per year[9] – was poured back into further purchases of arms and an escalation of the bloodshed. In 1998, this rising tide of militarism exploded into a civil war, in which three million Congolese perished – the highest death toll of any war since the Second World War. In spring 2005, it was reported that one thousand people were continuing to die each day in this ongoing political and humanitarian crisis, in which sexual violence against women played an integral part.[10] As 'D', a Congolese asylum seeker in Britain, told me: 'In traditional Congolese culture, rape is considered one of the worst crimes and carries a death penalty but you cannot imagine how many cases of rapes are now being reported on a daily basis. There is nowhere in Congo right now where a woman can say that she will be safe.' Even the UN peacekeeping mission in Congo, which is supposed to provide security, has become mired in allegations of paedophilia.[11]

Only once has the Congolese war made the front page of a British newspaper. Yet eighteen British or British-based companies have contributed to the perpetuation of the conflict. According to an official UN investigation published in 2003, some entered directly into business relationships with the various armed groups by trading minerals or supplying arms, a direct violation of Organisation for Economic Co-operation and Development (OECD) guidelines.[12] The United Nations has called on the British government to investigate these companies and sent dossiers to the Department of Trade and Industry (DTI). At the time of writing, the DTI has taken no further substantive action. British arms traders, who were co-responsible for perpetuating a conflict that killed millions and forced 450,000 Congolese to seek refuge in neighbouring African countries, have faced no criminal prosecution.[13] Yet the small numbers of Congolese asylum seekers who have come to Britain fleeing that conflict have been imprisoned in detention centres and accused of being 'illegal immigrants' before being sent back.

DANGER

Stripped of their access to solicitors, subsistence and housing, rushed through a decision-making process that increasingly resembled a rubber-stamping of rejection letters, reduced to no more than illegal immigrants, scroungers and terrorists, asylum seekers were, by 2004, just numbers to be removed. In the same year, Tony Blair had set a 'personal target' to deport more people each month than the number of new 'unfounded' applications being made, in order to attempt to empty society of the thousands of remaining 'failed asylum seekers'. At the time that he announced the target, 3,000 asylum seekers were being rejected each month and 1,100 deported. The target would require an almost threefold increase in the number of deportations – an unprecedented mass repatriation operation that would induce a corresponding increase in detention centre capacity and a vast expansion of the state's ability to swoop on immigrant communities. To meet the target, large-scale deportations would have to begin to countries such as Afghanistan, DRC, Iraq, Somalia and Zimbabwe, which had not, till then, had many asylum seekers sent back to them from Britain, either because they were considered too dangerous or because they had no functioning state to receive back deportees. Now ingenious methods were found to return 'failed asylum seekers' even to these 'failed states'. Whereas before there had been several countries that were considered too dangerous to receive deportations, by the end of 2004 there were none left – Zimbabwe being the last. Worse still, there was no published policy stating which countries were deemed suitable to receive deportees or what the criteria were. DRC was therefore just one of many countries that was taken off the 'no returns' list and labelled 'safe for deportations' by the Home Office.

In April 2003, Britain had already begun the first deportations to Afghanistan in eight years. At an estimated cost of £120,000, twenty-one Afghan asylum seekers were placed on a specially chartered flight to Kabul. Some later complained that they were tied up and manhandled in order to force them on board the plane.[14] The following March, deportations to Somalia took place, although the exact details remained unclear. The Transitional National Government in Mogadishu was not recognised by the UK and only had authority over a small part of the city. Asylum seekers were thought to have been returned via Dubai, on uninsured flights to an old Soviet airbase at Bale Dougle which was controlled by the militia of one of Somalia's clans.[15] Then, in April, the Home Office announced it was to begin returns of Iraqi asylum seekers. By November, Zimbabweans too were being returned. According to the Zimbabwean Community Campaign to Defend Asylum Seekers, those returned to Harare were handed over to the authorities on arrival and detained for questioning. Their families had to pay bribes to have them released.[16] Not only were risks of torture, inhuman treatment or violence in the receiving countries tolerated, there was also widespread indifference to the violence used during the deportation itself and in the detention centres where asylum seekers were held beforehand. When Nick Sommerlad of the *Daily Mirror* carried out an undercover investigation at Yarl's Wood detention centre and discovered that brutal racism was prevalent on training courses, as trainee custody officers relished the prospect of being 'allowed to punch, kick and headbutt difficult detainees', there was little public concern.[17] Nor was there much outrage when a BBC undercover investigation demonstrated the violence that custody officers used in attempting to bundle detainees on to deportation flights.[18] The Medical Foundation for the Care of Victims of Torture documented the cases of fourteen individuals who had been subjected to excessive or gratuitous use of force during an attempt to remove them from the UK. In all these cases, doctors confirmed that their injuries were consistent with their account of the treatment suffered. Inappropriate and unsafe methods of force, which carry higher than acceptable risks of injury, had been used, often in the privacy of the back of vehicles.[19] According to the Chief Inspector of Prisons, Anne Owers, some custody staff at Haslar detention centre, near Portsmouth, routinely carried wooden staves as weapons.[20]

New Labour has vastly increased the numbers held in detention centres. In May 1997, when it took office, there were 733 individuals detained; by June 2006, there were 2,285 being held in detention centres, despite a lower rate of asylum claims than in 1997.[21] That more and more asylum seekers were being held in detention centres – prisons in all but name – reflected the extent to which to be an asylum seeker was increasingly perceived as akin to being a criminal. Yet it was precisely to escape from arbitrary detention without trial that many asylum seekers had fled their home countries. Some asylum seekers even find that the private companies running detention centres in Britain are themselves linked to the regimes they are fleeing from. Group 4 Falck, for example, which has run a number of UK detention centres, has also been active in providing private security services for prisons in occupied Iraq and for illegal settlements in the West Bank of Palestine.[22] The detention of asylum seekers and other migrants is part of the globally expanding industry in running prisons for private profit. In Bedfordshire, the government ordered the construction of Yarl's Wood, Europe's largest detention centre with 900 places, and contracted Group 4 Falck to run it. This centre was specifically built to hold entire families, including small children. Three lines of secure walls more than five metres high surrounded the building itself and, by using Ministry of Defence land, the project was subject to the vagaries of the Official Secrets Act, as well as the usual secrecy of 'commercial confidentiality' that private contractors enjoy when receiving public money. The security devices installed at Yarl's Wood included microwave detection units and pan-and-tilt dome cameras, of the kind normally found only in the highest-security prisons. The centre was also ringed by chain-link fences two and a half metres high, topped by three lines of barbed wire. According to the Home Office, this prison was not a prison. According to those inside, it was a disgrace and their anger exploded into rioting three months after it was built – when half of the centre was burned to the ground. In a rush to build the centre quickly enough for the government to meet its deportation targets, sprinklers had not been fitted.

The Home Office's media-directed deportation targets also led to the pursuit of 'soft targets', such as families and schoolchildren.[23] According to the grim logic of Home Office planners, an asylum-seeking family with children at school was an easier target to round up and remove from the country than a single individual. They were less likely to have absconded and could more easily be located using legal powers that required local authorities to pass to the Home Office information about students whose families' asylum claims have failed. Moreover to deport a family of four meant that four persons were counted as removed from the country, even though theirs was a single asylum claim. Since the government's target was aimed at raising the rate at which individuals were deported to the rate of fresh claims, families were of particular utility. Children were no longer children; they were just numbers. During 2005, more than 2,000 children were locked up in detention centres for some period of time, the majority at Yarl's Wood.[24] Although the rules stated that they were only meant to be held in detention centres for a few days before a deportation, there were no firm legal safeguards to prevent children from being held arbitrarily at the discretion of immigration officials. Thelma Konan, for example, was detained with her mother Jacqueline for over six months, after they fled to Britain from Ivory Coast. Jacqueline had suffered a miscarriage the day she was taken into custody, for which she received no medical attention while in Harmondsworth detention centre. They were finally granted bail on 23 December 2002, after 190 days in detention and repeated pleas to the Home Office that detention was having an adverse effect on the health of both mother and child. Jacqueline went on to be recognised as a genuine refugee.[25]

Around the country, there were thousands of families who lived in fear of being woken up in the early hours of the morning by immigration officers, ready to handcuff them and bundle them into the back of a van. The Home Office even produced a document advising immigration officers on what techniques to use to 'control and restrain' children during the deportation process.[26] One teenager subjected to such 'control and restraint' was Sebrin Thaha, who, until 24 February 2005, had been just another teenager at Notre Dame School for Girls in Plymouth. But in the early hours of the morning, her home was raided by an immigration 'snatch squad' and, along with her mother Ruir and 12-year-old sister Hannah, she was taken to Tinsley House Removal Centre near Gatwick Airport. Over the following weeks, the sisters were first separated from their distraught mother and put in foster care and then allowed to join her at Yarl's Wood. Sebrin's mother Ruir attempted to take her own life on three separate occasions during her detention. Then, three weeks later, the family were deported to Germany from where they faced being sent on to Iraq. Five officers – four male and one female – woke the family at two in the morning to escort them to the airport from Yarl's Wood. Sebrin says that an officer pulled her hair and threatened to punch her if she caused any problems.[27]

Then she grabbed me by my wrist and my arm and dragged me to the van. It was very disturbing and I was crying. When I tried to say something the woman put her hand over my mouth to stop me. She was swearing at me and pulled my hair and hit me in my body. I was pushed into the van and hit my head.

She says that her wrist and arm were sore and swollen and that her younger sister also had blue marks on her wrist. Their mother was cuffed to the seat all the way to the plane while Sebrin and Hannah were restrained during the van journey by escort officers. After the flight to Düsseldorf, the family was split by the German authorities, leaving Hannah twenty miles away from her older sister, while their mother was taken to a mental health clinic. Sebrin's greatest fear was that the family would be deported to Iraq. 'We want to live in Plymouth not die in Iraq,' she says. Hers was an ordeal that no teenager should have to endure.

In 2004, New Labour introduced a further measure that targeted asylum-seeking children in an even more cruel way. Under Section 9 of the Asylum and Immigration (Treatment of Claimants, etc.) Act 2004, the Home Office could withdraw benefits and accommodation from asylum-seeking families who did not leave voluntarily once their claims had been refused and their appeals rejected. What this meant was that local authorities would not be allowed to house families in this situation and they would be forced on to the streets. Except that, since local authorities had a legal duty to take homeless children into the care of social services, children in the family would have to be separated from the rest of their family. The aim of this measure was simple: to use the threat of starvation and separation to intimidate into leaving the country those families the Home Office had not yet deported. But, if the threat was actually carried out, it would mean taking children into care solely on the grounds of poverty, a practice that Britain stopped more than half a century ago. The British Association of Social Workers pointed out that to carry out such a policy would violate the professional ethics of its members and that such a policy could never be in the best interests of the child.[28] Generally, the effect of this clause has been to force families underground at the end of the asylum process, swelling the class of people forced to survive in the illegal economy, too frightened of being caught to seek healthcare or to send their children to school. But immigration minister Tony McNulty claimed that families in this position had brought it on themselves: 'All the talk about us making people destitute, us forcing people to choose between themselves and their children, isn't the case ... The choices are the families' involved in these cases.'[29] At the time, forty families had had their support withdrawn because they were failing to 'co-operate' in their own deportation.

One family who faced this threat was the Sukulas, who have become well-known in Bolton for their campaign against deportation. Daniel Sukula, at 15 the eldest son in the family, wrote to me at the beginning of 2005 speaking of his fears:

I am writing this because me and my family face deportation to Congo. I don't want to go back to Congo because there is a war there and, if I go back, my life will be finished. One of my mum's friends who was deported was killed in a prison in Congo. If we go back, we might also end up in prison, so please help us. And I am scared that if I go back, I will be forced to become a soldier. I don't want to be a soldier when I am older. I want to be a football player. I play for a local team and, when I am older, I want to play for England.

Having recently learned that an asylum appeal had been rejected, his mother had received a further letter warning that the family – including six children, aged from seven months old to 18 – might also be thrown out of their home. The greatest fear was that they might be sent back to the life-threatening dangers from which they had escaped three years before. Daniel's mother Ngiedi Lusukumu and her children came to Britain to seek sanctuary in 2002 after being forced to flee from Kinshasa, where she was badly beaten by government militia and threatened with further violence. The militia were looking for her husband, who had already been forced to leave the country as a suspected opponent of the government. The beating inflicted on Ngiedi left her with permanent scars but, after claiming asylum in Britain, the family were told by the Home Office that their claim was unfounded, and it was later also rejected by an appeals adjudicator. The fact that the family had only suffered one attack, it was argued, meant that this was not genuine persecution. As Daniel asked, 'if soldiers come to your house and beat your mother unconscious, would you wait to see if it happens again?' By the summer of 2005, the family's benefits had been withdrawn by the Home Office.

Because of the widespread hostility to asylum seekers, inspired by the newspapers and politicians, such abuses generally go unnoticed. But increasingly it is through networks of support established through schools, churches and community campaigns that the efforts of the Home Office to remove failed asylum seekers are being thwarted. In Daniel Sukula's case, it was a teacher at his school who managed to orchestrate a strong public campaign in Bolton, leading to over two thousand people signing a petition calling for the family to stay in Britain. Pressure on Bolton Council and strong support for the family from the *Bolton Evening News* has meant that they have been allowed to remain in their council house and the children have not been taken into the care of social services although, at the time of writing, they remain under threat of deportation. Across the country, school students have led other campaigns to prevent asylum seekers in their school from being removed. To students, the person they sit next to in class is not a number or the hate figure of the newspapers, but a friend and a member of the school community. It is only natural that they respond with anger to a government wanting to remove that person from their school. Lorin Sulaiman, 15, her mother, Amina Ibrahim, 51, and sister Eva, 16, were granted permission to stay in Britain for two years by the Home Office, after a campaign led by students at the Mayfield school in Portsmouth. Lorin was on her half-term holiday when police raided their home at five in the morning to take them into detention. 'I was in shock. I thought it was the Syrian police. I never expected the British police to behave like that.' Lorin went on hunger strike. When news broke that the campaign had won a two-year reprieve for the Syrian Kurdish family, Mayfield's headteacher Derek Trimmer said:

It is still the school holidays but all the pupils have been texting each other with the good news. This is not just good news for Lorin but for the rest of the pupils too. If she had been plucked away from her friends the effect on them doesn't bear thinking about.

Students at the school had been offered counselling when it first became apparent that the family might be deported.[30]

In 2002, the government attempted to respond to the strength of anti-deportation campaigns by considering the introduction of special accommodation centres where asylum-seeker children could be educated separately from mainstream schools. By segregating these children from other students, it was hoped that their eventual deportation would be all the easier. Defending this idea, David Blunkett said that '[t]he difficulty sometimes with families whose removal has been attempted is that their youngsters have become part of a school, making it virtually impossible in some circumstances to operate the managed system to which we should all sign up'.[31] He added that if asylum-seeker children were allowed to become a part of school communities, they were in danger of 'swamping' local schools.[32] Eventually, these plans for segregated education were dropped, but New Labour continues to argue that asylum-seeking children should not enjoy the same rights as other children. Speaking to the parliamentary select committee on education and skills in February 2005, Margaret Hodge said that to provide the same protections for asylum-seeking children as for others would introduce a 'loophole', which could be exploited by asylum-seeking families.[33]

11
The New Leviathan

This is the generation of that great Leviathan, or rather (to speak more reverently) of that Mortall God, *to which wee owe under the* Immortal God, *our peace and defence.* – Thomas Hobbes[1]

In Bradford, it is 'community cohesion' week. The Task Group charged with creating cohesion across the district is busy organising a series of seminars, exhibitions and conferences to explain what the concept of community cohesion is supposed to mean and publicise the 'huge inroads' it has made in promoting it. The Task Group's director says that community cohesion is 'about having shared values and shared understanding'. The Task Group's day-to-day work revolves around endless delivery plans, performance indicators and a series of branded initiatives: 'diversity exchange' is a website that provides training in community cohesion and 'safe spaces' for people to raise issues; the 'faith forum' provides for faith leaders to meet with each other; 'B-equal' is a project to identify 'barriers to getting employment'. 'It's about using different mediums, whether it's sport, art, culture or whatever, to bring people together.' During the previous winter, a ski slope was set up in Keighley town centre and a skating rink in Bradford, under the auspices of the community cohesion programme. They were part of the effort 'to break down parallel lives'. Another way of 'bringing people together' into a cohesive community is 'Spice', a combined shopping, restaurant and educational complex to be built in the centre of Bradford, around the theme of 'spices, herbs and aromatics'. Mirroring similar projects in Oldham and east London, the aim is to redefine the 'Bradford brand', turning its perceived association with a troublesome Pakistani community from a marketing liability to an asset. Such rebranding is aimed at Bradford's own citizens as much as potential visitors. In simple terms, curry becomes a vehicle to restore Bradford's civic pride. As the plan itself states: 'Today, hot spices are cool: they have dynamism, energy and variety.'

Shahid is a youth worker in Manningham, the centre of Bradford's Pakistani community.[2] For him, curry is 'the only thing this country wants from us'. His father arrived in Bradford in the 1960s to work in the textile mills, then the town's major industry. As soon as he got there, though, the mills began to close down. Instead, his father started a job making chappatis. 'I think my mum and dad made a big mistake coming to this country. I would have been happier living in Pakistan,' Shahid says. He knows that if he went now he would be a foreigner there too and would miss the comforts of living in a wealthier country. But events in Bradford have made Shahid angry. As a youth worker, he is often called on to mediate disputes. He believes strongly in what he calls 'people skills', the ability to resolve issues with a relaxed, respectful attitude to others. He dislikes the gangster image of gold chains and expensive cars that appeals to some young people in the area. In the past, he has persuaded youths to engage responsibly with the police rather than fall back on easy generalisations about their racist attitudes. On the night in July 2001 when riots broke out in Bradford, Shahid was away with police officers on a weekend trip that was designed to improve community relations. In short, Shahid is someone whom the police and the local authority should have on their side.

Yet the flurry of community cohesion projects designed to overcome the disaffection and divisions among young people in Bradford has largely passed Shahid by. Because of what has happened to his brother and to his friends, Shahid says that he now hates the police, every one of them, even the officers who he used to know personally through work. Like hundreds of others in Manningham, Shahid's family lost one of their sons to a criminal justice system that was out to discipline the entire community for its involvement in the 2001 riots. Judge Stephen Gullick, who issued exceptionally long sentences to most of the rioters, explicitly ruled out from consideration any causes or context to the rioting, telling them, 'I am not concerned with its origins'. Shahid's brother, aged eighteen at the time, was caught on CCTV throwing stones at the police. After pictures of him appeared in the local newspaper, he presented himself to the police and pleaded guilty. He was convicted of riot and sentenced to around four years in prison. Having never been involved in crime before and behaving himself while inside, he was released early from prison. However, his time spent inside taught him the art of stealing cars. As soon as his electronic tag was removed, he disappeared and went on a four-week crime spree that ended with him getting caught again and receiving a second prison sentence, this time of five years.

Like many young people in Manningham, though, what makes Shahid most angry is the way that the area is policed. He tells a story of a recent incident in which two officers stopped a couple of Asian men in a car, which the officers suspected was stolen. The men denied this and said that they had only been stopped because of their colour. One of the men was dragged into the police car and arrested. Meanwhile, an audience gathered and someone went into the arrested man's house to find the paperwork to prove the car was not stolen. The man's mother and brother also came out to ask the police what they were doing. By then, the police were not interested in whether the car was stolen or not. The officers called for assistance; a riot van, a dog patrol van and three other cars arrived on the scene. Within minutes, CS gas and batons were being deployed on the arrested man's brother, and his mother was also gassed and collapsed on the floor. It is an example of the kind of routine heavy-handedness that many working-class communities regularly face in Britain. Shahid believes it is just a matter of time before an incident like this erupts into yet another full-blown riot in the town. Yet with each month that passes, the powers available to the police, to the immigration officers, to the intelligence services, to the whole structure of the state, increases in the name of the 'war on terror', while thousands of Shahids across Britain become more and more enraged by the routine injustices they are expected to endure. The glossy 'community cohesion' projects designed to ameliorate such anger and overcome 'parallel lives' seem increasingly lost in a parallel universe of their own.

Never before has such a vast and rapidly expanding accumulation of state power confronted young Asians, Africans and African-Caribbeans, Muslim and non-Muslim, immigrant and British-born. Under anti-terrorist powers, they face mass stop and search without reasonable grounds for suspicion, the virtual return of the 'sus' tactics that so angered Brixton in 1981. They face new powers of arrest that dramatically extend the time held in police custody prior to any charges being brought. They face the threat of raids in the early hours, often on the flimsiest of suspicions of involvement in terrorism or 'immigration offences'. They face virtual house arrest without the right to defend themselves in a court. They face mass surveillance at places of worship, at train stations and at airports. They face the risk of armed police deploying shoot-to-kill tactics. They face prosecution for expressing unacceptable opinions, for protesting, for supporting foreign charities, for being members of political organisations deemed unacceptable to the government. Finally, they face the ultimate sanction of having their citizenship itself stripped away at the behest of the state. The picture is not one in which the state has tilted the balance between liberty and security in one or two areas. It is rather a dramatic alteration in the underlying relationship of state to citizen, such that the state reserves to itself the right to define the nature and gravity of the 'threat' it faces, while judicial checks on state authoritarianism are eroded. It is a scenario that takes us back to Thomas Hobbes's seventeenth-century vision of the state as a Leviathan that 'hath the use of so much Power and Strength conferred on him, that by terror thereof, he is inabled to conforme the wills of them all, to Peace at home, and mutuall ayd against their enemies abroad'.[3] In short, this is a state that fuses absolute power and absolute fear to create absolute conformity and absolute peace – or so it is hoped.

Tony Blair's decade in office has been marked by an ongoing sundering of the principles of liberalism – just as the previous decade had seen the party leadership abandon socialism. Thus, both halves of the party's historic alliance were dispensed with. The market-state that the New Labour government was building demanded a shift away from rights granted to citizens in favour of responsibilities owed to the state. Authoritarianism became its hallmark, from the illiberal approach to welfare provision to the vast array of new criminal justice legislation, typified by ASBOs, with all their arbitrary power over young people. The 'war on terror' required that tolerance of cultural diversity be eroded, along with *habeas corpus*, freedom of speech and the right to protest. New Labour politicians spoke of the need for a debate on where to draw the line between liberty and security, but this debate was conducted in such a way that security always trumped liberty. Moreover, what was never acknowledged was that it was specific communities, designated as 'suspect', that were having their liberties removed in order that other communities could be offered the pretence of security. If the cost of the 'war on terror' was a rebalancing of liberty and security, it was a cost that was unequally distributed between different groups. State powers that would be strongly resisted if used against the general population were allowed to come into existence on the tacit understanding that they would only be deployed against 'alien' communities: Asians, African-Caribbeans, asylum seekers and Muslims. In the case of anti-terrorist powers, anti-Muslim racism would determine the use of these powers as much as the attempts to justify their existence. In an age of media-driven fears and focus-group politics, democracy provided no obstacle to the removal of liberty and only assisted in what John Stuart Mill had anticipated as a tyranny of those who claim to speak for the majority.[4] The only limit was that set by the courts; the New Labour executive increasingly found itself locked in a battle with the judiciary over human rights violations.

A CLIMATE OF FEAR

It was precisely because of the long history of needless confrontations between the police and black communities that the Macpherson report had recommended reforms to the way that stop and search powers were used. Thereafter, stops and searches of all groups decreased as police forces were pressured into shifting to the use of 'intelligence-led' policing. But in a new climate dominated by the 'war on terror', the numbers of non-whites stopped and searched began to rise once more. The police's power to conduct stops and searches had been expanded by Section 44 of the 2000 Terrorism Act. Police chiefs claimed that new powers were necessary to disrupt potential terrorists, not just on the basis of 'reasonable suspicion' but in a much more arbitrary way. This meant that, uniquely under these powers, officers could cite someone's ethnic group as a valid reason for stopping and searching. 'Ethnic profiling', in which the sole reason to conduct a stop and search was that an individual's appearance matched a preset ethnic 'profile' of a particular category of crime, was relegitimised after 9/11 – leading to the widespread phenomenon of being stopped for 'driving while brown'. This, in turn, encouraged members of the public to engage in their own private vigilante 'profiling' – deciding, for example, that Asian passengers on flights were suspect. Africans, African-Caribbeans and Asians have been around four times more likely than whites to be stopped under Section 44 powers since they were introduced.[5] Home Office minister Hazel Blears even went so far as to state that Muslims should expect that these powers will be 'experienced disproportion-ately' by them.[6] By 2002, police in England and Wales were already stopping and searching an average of sixty people a day as suspected terrorists, the majority while driving. Over the whole year, only eighteen out of over 20,000 stops and searches led to an arrest of someone in connection with terrorism, and none of those eighteen arrests actually resulted in a conviction for terrorist offences.[7] Police forces themselves know that their use of anti-terrorist stop and search powers cannot be justified in terms of the convictions achieved. It is through in-depth extended investigations and intelligence work that terrorist plots have been intercepted, not random stops and searches on the basis of ethnicity. However, the police now offer the argument that the powers are justified because terrorists planning attacks may be deterred if they see police officers carrying out stops and searches.[8] Lord Carlile, who was appointed as an independent reviewer of the operation of anti-terrorist legislation, found this unconvincing: 'There is little or no evidence that the use of *section 44* has the potential to prevent an act of terrorism as compared with other statutory powers of stop and search.'[9] Given this lack of evidence, why are these powers in place? Perhaps the reason is to provide a sense of reassurance to the public, a feeling that tough action is being taken. If so, those communities considered to be 'suspect' are paying a substantial 'ethnic penalty' in order to provide the wider public with the confidence that something is being done.

Armed raids across the country, sometimes involving hundreds of officers, have led to children being held at gunpoint, a woman suffering a heart attack and a young man shot in the chest. The shoot-to-kill operation that led to the killing of Jean Charles de Menezes at Stockwell underground station in July 2005 reveals how brazenly the police resort to lethal force. Dawn raids of households, involving the rounding-up of family and friends of terrorist suspects, have become familiar. The statistics of those arrested and convicted speak of the often arbitrary nature of these round-ups: from 11 September 2001 to 30 September 2005, 895 people were arrested under the Terrorism Act, of which more than half were released without charge.[10] Only twenty-three were actually convicted of offences under the Terrorism Act, and many of those appear to be men convicted of wearing insignia associated with proscribed organisations in Northern Ireland.[11] The huge gap between the number of arrests and the number of convictions under anti-terrorist laws shows how arrests are now not simply a probable antecedent to an appearance in court but effectively a form of arbitrary punishment in itself – with the possibility of up to twenty-eight days in custody before any charges are brought. For those subsequently released and for the families of those in custody, the stigma remains, the fear of harassment, the ostracising by others who fear that they too will be criminalised. Those wrongfully arrested are also likely to remain on intelligence service 'watchlists', as will friends and family; these watchlists may, in turn, be exchanged with state security apparatuses in other countries.

In numerous cases, arrests have been accompanied by a great media fanfare based on selective police leaks heralding the capture of a so-called terrorist cell, only for the case to be quietly dropped days, weeks or months later. Often, there are what appear to be deliberate leaks to the press of spectacular revelations from the police and/or intelligence services at the time of the arrests. Not only may these prejudice any potential trial, they often also serve to damage the reputations of innocent individuals. The subsequent admission that those arrested had done nothing illegal hardly registers at all in the media. For example, Noureddine Mouleff, an Algerian, was arrested in November 2003 along with four other Algerians and charged with 'possession of items in connection with terrorism'. He later walked free from court after it emerged that the dangerous device in his possession was a rucksack containing batteries and wires. Four British Muslim men were arrested in Dudley, Walsall and Luton in December 2003 and charged with, among other things, receiving training in the making of chemical and biological weapons. A sum of money, thought by police to be funds for terrorist activity, was also seized from Dudley Central Mosque during a police raid. Four months later, all charges were dropped and the money returned. Then, there were the ten Iraqis and North Africans who were arrested in April 2004 during armed raids involving 400 police officers in Manchester, Staffordshire, Yorkshire and the West Midlands. The ten were suspected of involvement in a plot to bomb Old Trafford football ground. Details of the alleged attack plan were leaked to the media, making for extensive coverage. The men were held for eight days of questioning; yet no terrorism charges were brought. It later emerged that the so-called terrorists were ardent Manchester United fans and it was only their possession of used ticket stubs that had led police officers to suspect the plot. In other cases, Muslims who have been involved in crimes such as credit card fraud or forgery have also been charged as suspected terrorists. In this way, the police have used the extra powers available under terrorism legislation against ordinary criminal suspects. Thus, special powers granted by parliament to the police for tackling terrorism are extended to other spheres in a way that effectively subjects Muslims to a separate criminal law.[12]

Then, there are the attempts to recruit informers, as intelligence officers approach people in their homes or in the street and threaten them with deportation if they do not provide some sort of information.[13] Muslim organisations in the UK say that security services visited hundreds of mosques and Islamic organisations across the country after 9/11 and questioned imams vigorously about their attitudes towards al-Qa'ida and the Taliban.[14] One of the consequences has been that many Muslims no longer publicly discuss politics or attend public meetings and, when civil rights abuses do occur, few are willing to speak out. In 2003, a group of Muslim teenage boys from a youth club in east London were taken by youth workers for a weekend trip to Devon. On returning, one of the minibuses on which they were travelling broke down. While the group was waiting for the repair service to arrive, one of the teenagers was holding a rolled-up magazine and pointing it at passing cars. The driver of one of these passing cars called the police and reported that a group of Asians with guns had parked up on a Devon motorway. Soon both lanes of the motorway were closed off and helicopters hovered overhead as armed police descended the banks on both sides of the motorway. The teenagers were escorted off the minibuses at gunpoint and made to lie face down on the ground with guns pointed at their backs. They were held in this position for a full twenty minutes before the police realised that they were only dealing with a youth group. On returning to London, the group decided not to tell its story, for fear that their youth club would become associated with terrorism. Abuses such as this, and the trauma they cause, are too often brushed under the carpet as a result of the pervasive fear that anti-terrorism measures have produced.

Where this approach leads is illustrated by the history of the policing of Irish and African-Caribbean communities. When faced with the threat of terrorism from the Irish Republican Army, the British state adopted many of the same techniques of coercion that are being redeployed in today's 'war on terror': the use of special courts where the usual rules of scrutiny and due process do not apply; the use of extended indefinite detentions; the use of cruel and inhuman treatment during interrogations; the suppression of freedoms of speech and protest; and extra-judicial killings. The abuses and miscarriages of justice that flowed, from Bloody Sunday onwards, were entirely counter-productive and only encouraged young men to turn to violence. Similarly, in the history of the policing of African-Caribbean communities, decades of institutional racism interacting with poverty, bad housing and exclusions from school have produced a total ostracisation of young poor African-Caribbean men from British society. This, in turn, has fed the breakdown of human relationships and the manufacture of mental health problems. The relationship between the state and young Muslim men is now being pushed along this same path, as the 'war on terror' witch-hunt undercuts all other concerns.

PUNISHMENT WITHOUT TRIAL

Since the Terrorism Act 2000, there has been a concerted attempt to construct a shadow criminal justice system that bypasses the conventional judicial procedures of open hearings and trial by jury, while the ancient principle of *habeas corpus* (no detention without trial) has been undermined. Immigration laws, which have always been islands of legal unaccountability, offer particularly fertile soil on which to build such a system. The 1971 Immigration Act, for example, allows the home secretary to detain and deport any foreign national considered by him to be a threat to national security; it also allows bail conditions to be imposed on those awaiting deportation that are so restrictive as to resemble house arrests.[15] Immigration detainees also lack many of the rights of criminal prisoners: those arrested for criminal offences can only be held for ninety-six hours, while immigration detainees can be held indefinitely. By grafting anti-terrorist powers onto these existing powers in immigration law, a convenient way was found of targeting foreign nationals for indefinite detention without the need for any kind of proper criminal trial to hear the evidence against them. The only limit to the 1971 powers to detain and deport had been introduced in 1996, as a result of a test case involving Karamjit Singh Chahal, an Indian Sikh separatist living in Britain. The European Court of Human Rights ruled that deporting him to India would involve a real risk of 'inhuman and degrading treatment', because of the likelihood of his being tortured, contravening Article 3 of the European Convention on Human Rights (ECHR), and it ruled that the arbitrary detention of Chahal without the prospect of a trial or a legitimate deportation was a violation of Article 5 of the ECHR.[16] However, after 9/11, the government announced that Britain, uniquely in Europe, was facing a 'public emergency threatening the life of the nation'. This allowed for it to override Article 5 and commence the detention of foreign nationals as security risks under the 1971 Act. Through this convoluted legal route, the state had found a way of detaining foreign nationals indefinitely and without trial.

The only mechanism by which these detentions were to be scrutinised was the Special Immigration Appeals Commission (SIAC). In SIAC hearings, the suspicions that the intelligence services and

Special Branch had about a foreign national were brought before judges, while the suspect was 'represented' by a special advocate. But there was no presumption of innocence and no requirement that the case be proven beyond reasonable doubt. All that was necessary was some level of suspicion. Furthermore, what the detainee was suspected of, and why, was kept secret so that the suspect and his lawyer were unable to know the nature of the suspicions or argue that they were groundless. Over three years, from December 2001 onwards, sixteen Muslim men were detained – effectively interned – on this basis.[17] Belmarsh maximum security prison in south-east London and Woodhill prison, near Milton Keynes, became places where men were held without trial and without hope of release. As the human rights lawyer Gareth Peirce said of the allegations against these men:

These were assertions, unsupported by any evidence whatsoever; thus an individual would be said to have been certificated as being an international terrorist or person who was a supporter of international terrorism on the basis that he associated with groups which in turn had links with al Qaeda ... Of course the words 'link', 'associated with', 'extremists' are words lacking any definition.[18]

Once someone had been branded a terrorist in this way, there was no way of removing the suspicion; he would remain a terrorist suspect forever.

Effectively, the British state had created a new kind of court system in which men could face secret trials, be found 'guilty' of unspecified charges, according to unspecified evidence, and then be detained indefinitely. Little wonder, then, that the detainees went slowly mad or even suicidal. Mahmoud Abu-Rideh, a Palestinian who as a teenager had been tortured, suffered a mental breakdown as the trauma of what he had suffered in his teens was reactivated in Belmarsh prison. The reason that suspicion appeared to have been cast on him was his work raising money for schools, orphanages and wells in Afghanistan. In other cases, it appears that men were detained because of their raising funds for charitable work in Chechnya, or providing logistical support to those in Chechnya fighting for national independence from Russia. Support of whatever kind for the Chechen resistance had been turned into effective support for al-Qa'ida, even if that support was provided some time ago.[19] Most extraordinarily of all, from the moment of their arrest and throughout the duration of their internment, none of the detainees were questioned or interviewed by police officers, and at no point had the Crown Prosecution Service considered the possibility of bringing charges against any of these individuals.[20] Did this mean that their detention was not to prevent any actual threat to Britain but, rather, intended to send a signal of fear into refugee communities? Or, perhaps, it was to reassure Britain's foreign 'partners' in the 'war on terror' or to send a message of strength to a nervous public. If any of these were the case, then these men paid a terrible price for such 'symbolism'.

Eventually, three years after its introduction, the detention without trial of terror suspects at Belmarsh and Woodhill prisons was found by the Law Lords to be unlawful. Rather than release the men, the government changed tack once again. A new piece of legislation, the Prevention of Terrorism Act 2005, was rushed through parliament. This allowed for the men who had been detained to be put under virtual house arrest through the use of so-called control orders, another form of punishment without trial. Moreover, control orders were applicable to British as well as foreign nationals. Where the Home Office had 'reasonable grounds for suspicion' of involvement in 'terrorism-related activity', the state could issue 'control orders' that severely restricted all aspects of a person's life. At the time of writing, there are fourteen control orders in force, five on British citizens. These individuals are subject to an eighteen-hour curfew, electronic tagging, requirements to report by phone to a monitoring company twice a day, the restriction of visitors and meetings to those persons approved in advance by the Home Office, a requirement that police officers be allowed to enter one's home at any time and search and remove any item or install monitoring equipment, prohibitions on phones and internet access and restrictions on movement to within a defined area that might even ban the use of one's own garden. The result was the creation of a prison in one's own home with a regime of effective isolation from the outside world. Family life became severely restricted as children were unable to do ordinary things like access the internet or have friends round to visit. Things that could normally be taken for granted, like getting a plumber or chatting to neighbours over the fence, became potential violations of the order. If any of the control order conditions were broken, the subject of the order could be imprisoned for up to five years without there even needing to be a trial. None of those subjected to these frightening powers have been tried in a court of law or been able to see the 'evidence' against them.[21] The decision to issue a control order rests solely with the home secretary, after which the SIAC courts have the chance to 'confirm' the order but can only not do so if it is 'obviously flawed'. Yet the whole process is obviously flawed: since the evidence against a suspect is secret, it can never be challenged or disproved and, once the control order has been issued, the label of 'terrorist' attaches for the rest of the suspect's life, even if the control order is not renewed.[22] This is not any form of justice system at all. As the parliamentary Joint Committee on Human Rights has stated, there are significant concerns about whether 'this regime of control orders is compatible with the rule of law and with well established principles concerning the separation of powers between the executive and the judiciary'.[23]

The reason that the state has sought to avoid the use of the criminal courts in these cases is probably straightforward: the intelligence services do not want their allegations to be tested in open court and subjected to proper scrutiny. One reason for this may be that information identifying suspects comes from interrogations carried out by foreign security services using torture; evidence known to have come from torture is not accepted by courts in Britain. Eliza Manningham-Buller, the head of MI5, has defended the use of information that may have come from torture on the grounds that to ask foreign security services to confirm whether their information was obtained by torture or not would jeopardise relationships with 'partners' in the 'war on terror'.[24] UK intelligence agents have been present during interrogations in the US detention camps at Guantanamo Bay and at Bagram airbase in Afghanistan. It is likely that the British intelligence agencies have also made use of information obtained from the 'extraordinary renditions' that the US has carried out to outsource torture to a network of co-operating regimes in the 'war on terror'. A former CIA agent based in the Middle East has explained how the US co-operates with oppressive regimes in this way: 'If you want a serious interrogation, you send a prisoner to Jordan. If you want them to be tortured, you send them to Syria. If you want someone to disappear – never to see them again – you send them to Egypt.'[25] Refugees who have fled to the UK are particularly vulnerable to being arrested and imprisoned in Britain on the basis of 'evidence' from the security agencies in their home countries. Moreover, those refugees increasingly face the risk of being deported to the countries they fled from, as the British government seeks to use diplomatic 'memoranda of understanding' to bypass human rights concerns about returning foreign nationals to regimes that practise torture. By the summer of 2006, memoranda had been signed with Algeria, Libya, Jordan and Lebanon, in which these countries' governments agreed to treat those deported humanely. Since these governments publicly deny practising torture in any case, it was hard to see what extra guarantee these memoranda provided and, without any genuine mechanism for monitoring the treatment of deportees, they gave little reassurance to those being returned into the hands of the security agencies they had fled. What this amounts to is a system of 'outsourcing' torture, in which Britain can openly and under cover of diplomatic assurances hand persons over to torturing regimes and then make use of the 'information' so obtained. Whereas in the past, the British state attempted to conceal its own practice of torture in colonial settings such as Kenya and Northern Ireland, now it colludes in torture openly and without embarrassment and campaigns publicly for a softening of the absolute ban on torture in the European Convention on Human Rights.[26]

Not only was there a growing list of countries to which it was deemed safe to return foreign nationals. The grounds on which foreign nationals could be deported for national security reasons was also widened, to include not only activities related to terrorism but also activities perceived by the Home Office as being detrimental to community cohesion. In August 2005, the government published a new list of unacceptable behaviours for foreign nationals in Britain. It included such vague violations as 'distributing material, speaking publicly or running a website which fosters hatred which might lead to inter-community violence in the UK'.[27] This was a catch-all test, which meant that anyone who strongly criticised Western governments might be thought to have committed a violation. Without any proper court hearings to oversee how these criteria were interpreted, the Home Office could simply remove those it believed were expressing views it disliked. When this measure is combined with another new power, introduced in the Immigration, Asylum and Nationality Act 2006, which allows the Home Office to strip those with dual nationality of their British citizenship, the implications are still more frightening. This new power allows the home secretary to remove British citizenship from dual nationals, even if they were born in Britain, if it is considered 'conducive to the public good'.[28] What this means is that the same criteria of unacceptable behaviours that applies to foreign nationals also applies to British nationals with a second nationality – which is a common status for many non-white British citizens. Thus, anyone who is a British citizen and born in the UK but also has Jamaican, Pakistani or Indian nationality will be liable to be deprived of their citizenship if they have said something which, in the secretary of state's view, 'fosters hatred'. They would then be detained and deported to that country, perhaps arriving there for the first time in their lives and prevented from ever returning to Britain. Worst of all, there need not be objectively reasonable grounds for exercising this power – it is entirely arbitrary.

A further significant limitation on freedom of speech is the new crime of 'glorifying' terrorism, introduced under the Terrorism Act 2006. It makes it a criminal offence to glorify terrorist acts in such a way that, either intentionally or recklessly, others are indirectly encouraged to emulate those acts 'in existing circumstances'. The concept of 'glorification' is thus wider than the long-established offence of incitement, which involves directly encouraging or persuading a person to commit a criminal act. Abu Hamza, for example, was convicted under incitement legislation dating from the 1860s. The new concept of 'glorification', on the other hand, is intended to cover a wider series of acts that are more oblique than incitement. This is where the basic problem with the glorification clause lies: in cases where there is incitement, prosecutions can take place already under existing laws; and in cases where there is no incitement, to prosecute would be to limit freedom of speech on the grounds that the state finds the expression of an opinion unacceptable. What lies behind such legislation is an attempt to prevent the circulation of what is regarded as the ideology of terrorism (see Chapter 6). Indeed, at the UN Security Council meeting on 14 September 2005, Tony Blair tabled a call for such legislation to be introduced globally. Resolution 1624 declared its repudiation of attempts at the 'justification or glorification of terrorist acts' and called on states to take measures against such attempts. Blair argued that 'glorification' legislation was necessary because terrorism is 'a movement with an ideology and a strategy', which would only be defeated when 'the [Security] Council united not only in condemning acts of terrorism but also in fighting the poisonous propaganda that the root cause of terrorism lay with [us] and not them'. He went on: 'The root cause of terrorism was not a decision on foreign policy, however contentious, but was a doctrine of fanaticism.'[29]

The thinking here was clear: terrorism is a fanatical ideological movement; that ideology is defined by its view that the root causes of terrorism lie with powerful states; the war against terror must therefore involve also a criminalisation of those who attempt to describe root causes in this way. Because UK anti-terrorist legislation does not draw a distinction between terrorist actions against the British state and against other states, the new offence of glorification criminalises not just supporters of al-Qa'ida but anyone who argues in favour of the use of force against occupations in Palestine, Iraq and Afghanistan – or for that matter in Burma. Hundreds of thousands of people in the UK have thereby been placed in a position where expressing their political views might be a criminal offence. Of course, the number of prosecutions brought is likely to be small but the real impact will be found in the thousands of hidden acts of self-censorship and informal censorship that are likely to result, preventing the very discussions that need to be allowed if the causes of terrorism are to be honestly examined. When any kind of strong opposition to British foreign policy by Muslims becomes criminalised as 'extremism', one of the most fundamental democratic principles – that no state official should have the right to proscribe certain opinions as 'extreme' – has been weakened. The result is that legitimate discussion is outlawed and the threat of violence is increased rather than decreased. While liberals have agonised noisily about the threat to freedom of speech from protesters against cartoons of the Prophet Muhammad, the greater threat to freedom of speech that has been legislated for in the name of the 'war on terror' has been largely ignored.

12
Community: Theirs and Ours

I remind myself that the greatest threat of all is my own fear; that it is our fear, the fear of [those] who want a different future, that makes our opponents powerful.
– Shirin Ebadi[1]

The beginning of the 21st century marked the high point of progress against racism in Britain. Since then, multicultural Britain has been under attack by government policies and vitriolic press campaigns with an intensity unmatched by anything since at least the 1970s. New forms of racism – linked to a systematic failure to understand the causes of forced migration, global terrorism and social segregation – have spread. The result is a climate of hatred and fear, directed especially at Muslim and migrant communities, and the erosion of the human rights of those whose cultures and values are perceived as 'alien'. Communities are more fractured than ever. Yet the government presses ahead with flawed immigration and 'integration' policies and anti-terrorist legislation that creates further resentment, alienation and criminalisation. Behind it all lies a refusal to grasp the ways in which the world has been changed by neoliberal globalisation.

The worsening racial climate of Britain has only been encouraged by the absence of a coherent anti-racist politics. The anti-racist movement that emerged in the late 1960s, influenced by the politics of Black Power in the US and anti-imperialist movements in the Third World, had been the major factor in making it possible for Asian, African and African-Caribbean communities to gain a foothold in British society. But its original notion of a 'black' political identity had fragmented, by the 1980s, into the politics of ethnic difference (see Chapter 3). By the end of the decade, there was clearly no easy return to an earlier sense of collective struggle. The idea of uniting ethnically diverse communities into a singular 'black' struggle came to be seen as an artificially imposed commonality. What was less obvious at the time was that, in discarding this 'black' political identity, the ideal that it embodied, of anti-racist political solidarity combined with cultural diversity, was also lost. Indeed, any notion of solidarity was henceforth regarded as inherently dangerous.

At the same time, there was the rise, across all of Britain's poorest, non-white communities, of religious identity. In the absence of alternative ideologies of hope, the mushrooming of religious practice in the inner cities was one way of responding to the neoliberal breakdown of the social fabric and the resulting pathological cultures of violence, humiliation and ostracisation that gripped many of Britain's most deprived neighbourhoods. Moreover, many experienced religious identity as a way of moving beyond the narrowness of being perceived as an 'ethnic minority' and saw in scriptural and puritan versions of their faith a simple set of lifestyle prescripts that seemed to remove many of the confusions of a society based on untrammelled economic competition and racist victimisation.[2] In this context, fundamentalist groups, whether Christian evangelist, Islamist or Hindu nationalist, flourished.

The politics of ethnic difference gave a further fillip to politicised 'faith' identity, with the breaking down of secular categories such as 'Asian' into separate religious identities. As the anti-racist movements of the 1970s and 1980s withered, or became institutionalised in town hall multiculturalism, religious identity politics began to appear as an alternative at the community level. The Indian army's attack on the Golden Temple at Amritsar in 1984, for example, provoked one of the largest demonstrations of Asians in Britain and encouraged the formation of a distinctly Sikh political identity in Britain. The Rushdie affair (1989), the first US-led war on Iraq (1991) and the massacre of Bosnian Muslims (1994) had similar impacts on British Muslims, all seeming to indicate a worldwide structure of Muslim suffering, and clearly demonstrating a level of anti-Muslim racism in Britain: the 1991 Gulf War led to a wave of racist attacks against Muslims, while the UK government interned over a hundred Arabs wrongly suspected of being supporters of Saddam's regime.

The state has sought, increasingly, to manage the rise in a politicised religious identity through an updated version of the colonial-style strategies it had deployed in the name of multiculturalism since the 1980s – with the appointed community leaders now being defined by 'faith' as well as by ethnicity. The leaders that the state selects as partners in this project are chosen on the basis of their effectiveness in containing dissent and serving strategic interests, often as much linked to foreign policy as domestic affairs. Hence, in the 1980s, the Foreign Office backed Saudi-linked organisations in Britain as the official 'representatives' of UK Muslims. Then, following the Rushdie affair and the emergence, in the early 1990s, of influential

Iranian-linked radical groups, the state encouraged the formation of the Muslim Council of Britain (MCB), which was seen as a preferable alternative. Key figures in the MCB leadership were active in the fundamentalist Jamaat-i Islami[3] but they nevertheless saw advantages in seeking to work with the British state, which itself used them in its bid to 'manage' growing Muslim anger at the 'war on terror'. Gradually, though, grassroots pressure forced the MCB to be more critical and, by 2006, the organisation was no longer deemed by the government to be a reliable ally in the 'war on terror'. The state looked instead to the Sufi Muslim Council as a replacement, not because it represented the majority sect among British Muslims, but because it was perceived as supportive of the government's foreign policy. Of course, this double state strategy of seeking suitably compliant community leaders who can act as surrogate voices for their community, while, at the same time, demonising that community and systematically violating its civil rights, is the worst possible combination for creating a genuinely cohesive society. Its effect is to generate a permanent state of fear, anger and resentment among the 'suspect community', while suppressing any kind of constructive public expression of those feelings.

In Hindu communities, branches of the Vishwa Hindu Parishad (VHP, World Hindu Council) are often considered official community representatives, and the organisation and its affiliates are regularly given platforms in the mainstream media as the authentic voice of Hindus in Britain. The VHP is directly linked to India's Rashtriya Swayamsevak Sangh (RSS), the Hindu nationalist 'volunteers corps' that was formed in India in the 1920s on the model of Mussolini's Black Shirts.[4] The RSS is dedicated to turning India into an exclusively 'Hindu nation' by abandoning its secular and egalitarian constitution, rendering Indian Muslims and Christians into second-class citizens and resisting challenges to the power of India's upper-caste elites. The UK counterparts of the Indian RSS share the same ideology but, in the British context, focus on winning official recognition for their own version of 'Hindu' identity.[5] Yet, organisations which seem to promote a genteel identity politics in Newham can support violent chauvinisms in Nagpur. Globalisation has made untenable a rigid separation between domestic and foreign concerns as ideologies and funds flow freely across continents and events abroad impact directly on UK communities. In February and March 2002, VHP-led mobs massacred thousands of Muslims in Gujarat, among them three British Muslims on holiday in India; the weapons used to kill them were probably paid for by funds raised in the Hindu diaspora, although often donors are unaware of this.[6]

The committee circuits that operate around various UK government departments, and which aim to represent 'faith communities', tend to institutionalise these religio-political groups, which are seen by the state as useful allies in its efforts to manage 'community relations'. The thinking that lies behind this approach is that communities consist of ready-made identities, which need a layer of representative organisations to be imposed on them in order that dissent and unrest can be channelled away ineffectually. This creates a climate in which different faith-based organisations compete with each other for state patronage by attempting to establish themselves as the authentic representatives of particular communities. These organisations have little interest in mobilising at the grassroots in struggles for social justice or civil rights; it is rather the state that they aim to mobilise to intervene in the community on their behalf – for example, by funding educational and cultural activities that endorse their ideology. The result is, often, the closing down of spaces, particularly for the young and for women, where communities can come together to tackle the injustices they face. This whole process has led to the erosion of anti-racism and the emergence, in its place, of a highly compromised politics of communal identity, in which unrepresentative community organisations lobby for state favours through the promotion of their own inward-looking sense of victimisation, while, at the grassroots level, the demand for organisations that can mobilise, support and empower communities goes largely unmet.

One measure of the bankruptcy of this kind of communal politics is the lack of solidarity and support that has been extended to asylum seekers, refugees and other new migrants. These emerging new communities are both excluded from the existing structures of community representation and are effectively denied the means to construct their own. They have been at the sharp end of state racism for over a decade and have had to fight against the incarceration, expulsion and surveillance that have, more recently, been extended to Muslim communities in general. Yet they have had to carry out this struggle unsupported by most of the 'community leaders' of multicultural Britain, and with exceptionally limited resources. As Abbas Amini, who led protests against deportations to Iran by sewing his lips together and going on a hunger strike, pointed out to me:

Most refugees have to work long hours in slave-condition jobs in order to survive here and they are scared of being arrested and deported. Many think that, for the time being, they will keep their heads down and not fight for their rights.

Migrant workers are often in a similar situation, in which the personal risks of protesting are too high. In these circumstances, it has been difficult to build independent organisations, rooted in refugee and migrant communities, that can mobilise against the injustices of the asylum and immigration system. Those organisations, such as the National Coalition of Anti-Deportation Campaigns, that have supported refugee communities and fought against injustices have been subjected to vilification in national newspapers and had their funding withdrawn. Nevertheless, a common struggle has emerged in migrant communities against destitution and poverty, against the system of immigration detention and against deportations. Its message is that, in a globalised world, rights cannot stop at national borders: foreign nationals who come to Britain to work or seek humanitarian protection carry with them a set of core rights that can no longer be denied on the grounds that diversity threatens national cohesion.[7] The beginnings of new struggles against the increasing racism and authoritarianism of the immigration system and for minimum workplace standards and a living wage are emerging, such as the recent successful campaigns to organise cleaners at high-profile financial firms in London.[8] What role the existing institutions of the labour movement, including trade unions, will play in such community-based political movements remains to be seen. At present, though, those bearing the brunt of the immigration system are generally isolated politically and unable to make their voices heard.

Is there, then, any basis for overcoming the legacy of communal identity politics through building new alliances, not in the sense of paper coalitions but at the level of genuine solidarities rooted in community-based activism? In spite of all the obvious difficulties, the objective conditions for such an approach can, perhaps, be found in the structures of the market-state itself, which demonises the Muslim community for having 'alien' values, excludes the underclass for having no value and expels asylum seekers for being both valueless and alien. The political culture in which the market-state thrives is one of conformism and populism. Its circuits of fear and insecurity galvanise an ever greater authoritarianism from which, ultimately, no one is safe. The drive to minimise the rights of asylum seekers and foreign nationals only strengthens the state to remove the rights of its own citizens, whether in the name of the 'war on terror' or to prevent abuse of public services. It also provides a testing ground for new surveillance measures, such as ID cards, that end up being targeted at the whole population. Likewise, the exploitation of migrant workers rebounds on all workers by entrenching a casualised labour market. The racisms of the 'war on terror' and the 'war on asylum' are not just destructive of the human rights of Muslim and refugee communities but also serve to camouflage the transition to a globalised neoliberal economic order and a market-state model of politics. In the final analysis, as the state accrues to itself more and more power over people's lives, these racisms threaten the very possibility of a democratic Britain.

The grassroots anti-war movement that emerged after 9/11 demonstrated the possibilities and challenges of a politics of collective action that sought to make connections between war, racism and attacks on civil liberties. The 15 February 2003 anti-war demonstration represented the greatest expression of political solidarity in Britain in recent history and successfully conveyed the message that Muslims were not an isolated minority but part of a wider social movement against racism and imperialism. As the 'war on terror' has, more and more, led to the demonisation of Muslims, the networks that emerged through the anti-war movement have gradually turned to the issue of racism. Whether this willingness to focus on anti-racism will translate into a genuine community politics of solidarity remains to be seen. What is clear is that any alternative to the imposed and divisive communal politics of the state will have to grapple with the issue of faith-based politics.

In a context in which anti-Muslim racism is institutionalised by the 'war on terror', it is natural and necessary that Muslims organise *as Muslims* in fighting the specific racism they face. Confronted by an intensely anti-Muslim political culture, Muslims cannot be expected to leave their religious identity behind when they enter the public sphere. To do so would only reinforce the mistaken belief that there is an incompatibility between Islam and democracy. Many on the Left, however, reject any kind of religion-defined politics as inherently at odds with liberal secular principles. They argue that the creation of a secular public sphere in which religious arguments carry no weight is necessary because human progress requires the stripping away of religious falsehoods and their replacement with critical rationality. On this 'enlightenment' view of secularism, the restriction of religion to the private sphere is necessary, both because religious beliefs are false and because falsehoods impede social progress. It is a mistake, therefore, for a Left movement to make any kind of alliance with an organisation that defines itself by religion. Religious believers who want to work with the Left should leave their faith behind when they enter the political arena. For these 'enlightenment' secularists, religious belief will gradually disappear as societies develop and scientific values take hold, resulting in the eventual dissolution of religious difference into a universal rationality. It is this 'enlightenment' definition of secularism that lies behind the fact that, in common usage, 'secularism' is taken to mean an anti-religious viewpoint.

However, there are other ways to conceive of secularism. A secular state is not necessarily anti-religious or based on restricting religion to a private sphere. The separation between a non-religious public sphere and a religious private sphere might be justified if one accepts the downgrading of religion in favour of 'enlightenment' rationality. However, once the 'enlightenment' assumption of natural and inevitable progress to a single set of non-religious values is abandoned, secularism becomes more a matter of the political question of how different religious and non-religious values can peacefully coexist. In the US, for example, the secular state was established on the principle of a wall of separation between church and state, but the state is not anti-religious – far from it. Historically, the deeply religious society of the US found a secular state to be necessary because religious matters were thought too important to allow the state to intervene in them. State neutrality was seen as the best way of securing religious freedom. In India – also a deeply religious society – a secular constitution, adopted in 1950, encourages the state's active sponsorship of multiple religions, as long as it maintains a neutrality between them. Three principles underlie India's version of secularism: religious freedom; 'celebratory neutrality', in which the state assists in celebrating each religion but is neutral between them; and social reform, in which the state is entitled to intervene in religious practices to remove injustices, for example to do with gender or caste.[9] These examples point to an alternative definition of secularism as a form of pluralism based on the need to enable peaceful relationships between different value-systems, including those embedded in different religious communities. The example of India's secularism suggests that the creation of a neutral public sphere, in which no one religion is privileged, does not require that, within that domain, participants leave their faith behind. It recognises that, for religious people, faith is a central part of their identity and values, and informs their reasoning. Moreover, a 'pluralist' secularism does not imply that the enlightenment belief in critical rationality is misplaced. It merely acknowledges that not everyone is necessarily travelling on the same path towards an atheist worldview. What it does require is an acceptance of pluralism and common democratic values. Without this accompanying pluralism, secularism tends to involve discrimination against minorities. This is the case in Britain, where the state sponsorship of the Church of England (such as through the blasphemy law and the disproportionate state funding of Anglican schools) contradicts the reality of a largely secular society with significant non-Anglican minorities.

The danger of 'enlightenment' secularism is the exclusion from the public sphere of groups that define themselves by religion. The clearest example is France's ban on 'oversized religious symbols' in state schools – which was aimed at preventing Muslim girls from wearing the hijab. The danger of 'pluralist' secularism is patronisation, as unrepresentative 'community leaders' or organisations come to stand in for religious communities in the public sphere and, perhaps, exploit the politics of representation to impede social reform. The latter is the common criticism made of the leadership of the anti-war movement in Britain and the alliances it has forged with particular Muslim organisations. There has been resentment from some at the way in which some organisations have been made by the Left, effectively, into official representatives of Britain's Muslims, while deliberately ignoring what the political ambitions of these organisations are in Muslim communities. There is no simple formula for resolving such dilemmas, but the three principles of religious freedom, celebratory neutrality and social reform based on universal human rights do offer the Left a set of guiding principles to unite diverse religious and non-religious communities in a common political struggle, without falling into the twin traps of 'enlightenment' arrogance or pluralist tokenism.

In the final analysis, the test of a secular society is whether it is capable of safeguarding freedom of belief and eliminating racisms based on religious difference. Today, driven by the attempt to legitimise a deeply unequal global order, racism has taken on new forms, at present directed specifically at Muslims and others perceived as 'alien'. Ultimately, the struggle against these forms of racism is not a fight for a particular religion or culture but a fight for universal human rights and against the vast economic and political inequalities of our world. It must involve a battle of ideas, in which alternative narratives – rooted in the experiences of migrant and Muslim communities – of the origins of terrorism, segregation and migration are advanced. At the same time, it must involve the building up of independent community-based organisations that are capable of empowering victims of racism, taking up cases, raising issues and creating a movement for justice based on real solidarity, rather than imposed and divisive identities.[10] It is only through such a struggle that genuinely integrated and cohesive communities will emerge.

Notes to the Text

INTRODUCTION

1. Frantz Fanon, *The Wretched of the Earth* (New York, Grove Press, 1968), p20.
2. Samuel P. Huntington, 'The Clash of Civilisations?', *Foreign Affairs*, vol. 72, no. 3 (Summer 1993), pp22–49; Francis Fukuyama, *The End of History and the Last Man* (Harmondsworth, Penguin, 1992).
3. Edward Said, *Covering Islam: how the media and the experts determine how we see the rest of the world* (London, Vintage, 1997), p. xxii. Italics in original.
4. Liz Fekete, 'Anti-Muslim racism and the European security state', *Race & Class*, vol. 46, no. 1 (July 2004), p25; Liz Fekete, 'Enlightened fundamentalism: immigration, feminism and the Right', *Race & Class*, vol. 48, no. 2 (October 2006), p5.
5. 'Growing danger on roads', *Daily Express* (13 December 2003), p5; 'Now they're after our fish', *Sun* (5 July 2003), p1; 'Asylum seekers are pilfering our pike!', *Daily Star* (5 July 2003), p27; 'Swan bake – asylum seekers steal the Queen's birds for barbecues', *Sun* (4 July 2003), p1; 'Asylum-seekers ate our donkeys', *Daily Star* (21 August 2003), p1.
6. Ted Cantle, chair, *Community Cohesion: a report of the independent review team* (Home Office, 2001), p9.
7. Quoted in Verena Stolcke, 'Talking culture: new boundaries, new rhetorics of exclusion in Europe', *Current Anthropology*, vol. 36, no. 1 (February 1995), p3.
8. 'If we want social cohesion we need a sense of identity', interview with David Blunkett by Colin Brown, *Independent on Sunday* (9 December 2001), p4; David Blunkett, 'It's not about cricket tests', *Guardian* (14 December 2001).
9. Polly Toynbee, 'Why Trevor is right', *Guardian* (7 April 2004), p21; David Goodhart, 'Too diverse?', *Prospect* (February 2004); Tom Baldwin, '"I want an integrated society with a difference": interview with Trevor Phillips', *The Times* (3 April 2004), p1.
10. Gordon Brown, speech to Fabian Society, 14 January 2006, http://www.fabian-society.org.uk/press_office/news_latest_all.asp?pressid=520, last accessed 6 October 2006.
11. Jesse Norman and Janan Ganesh, *Compassionate Conservatism* (London, Policy Exchange, 2006), p67.
12. The British 'liberal tolerance' that was heralded by Roy Jenkins in his famous 1966 speech on race relations co-existed comfortably with various forms of racism (see Chapter 1). Indeed, the concept of tolerance can itself imply a paternal 'putting up with' that is very different from the mutual respect and equality that societies ought to aspire to. However, as Jürgen Habermas has argued, tolerance does have its own importance

in culturally pluralist societies and its loss has far-reaching negative consequences. See Jürgen Habermas, 'Religious tolerance – the pacemaker for cultural rights', in Lasse Thomassen, ed., *The Derrida–Habermas Reader* (Edinburgh, Edinburgh University Press, 2006).

13. *Secure Borders, Safe Haven: integration with diversity in modern Britain* (Home Office, CM 5387, 2002).
14. *Secure Borders, Safe Haven*, p3.
15. Thomas Hobbes, *Leviathan* (Cambridge, Cambridge University Press, 1996), pp120–1.

CHAPTER 1: ECHOES OF EMPIRE

1. Quoted in Philip Schlesinger, *Putting 'Reality' Together* (London, Routledge, 1978), p117.
2. Basil Davidson, 'Columbus: the bones and blood of racism', *Race & Class*, vol. 33, no. 3 (January–March 1992), p21.
3. Cedric J. Robinson, *Black Marxism: the making of the Black radical tradition* (London, Zed Books, 1983), p162; Peter Fryer, *Staying Power: the history of black people in Britain* (London, Pluto Press, 1984), p134.
4. Robinson, *Black Marxism*, p83.
5. Norman Cohn, *The Pursuit of the Millenium: revolutionary millenarians and mystical anarchists of the Middle Ages* (London, Paladin, 1970).
6. Marika Sherwood, 'Race, empire and education: teaching racism', *Race & Class*, vol. 42, no. 3 (January–March 2001), p1.
7. Sherwood, 'Race, empire and education: teaching racism', p10.
8. Alastair Bonnett, *White Identities: historical and international perspectives* (Harlow, Pearson Education, 2000), p33.
9. Robert Young, *Colonial Desire: hybridity in theory, culture and race* (London, Routledge, 1995), pp72–6.
10. Bonnett, *White Identities*, p38.
11. Bonnett, *White Identities*, p40.
12. Sherwood, 'Race, empire and education: teaching racism', p10.
13. Bernard Semmel, *Imperialism and Social Reform: English social-imperial thought, 1895–1914* (London, George Allen & Unwin, 1960), p51.
14. Jenny Clegg, *Fu Manchu and the 'Yellow Peril': the making of a racist myth* (Stoke-on-Trent, Trentham Books, 1994), pp30–3.
15. Ann Dummett and Andrew Nicol, *Subjects, Citizens, Aliens and Others: nationality and immigration law* (London, Weidenfeld & Nicolson, 1990), p107.
16. Mike Davis, *Late Victorian Holocausts: El Niño famines and the making of the Third World* (London, Verso, 2001), pp297–301.
17. John M. Hobson, *The Eastern Origins of Western Civilisation* (Cambridge, Cambridge University Press, 2004), p273; Clegg, *Fu Manchu and the 'Yellow Peril'*, pp13–17.
18. Andrew Blake, 'Foreign devils and moral panics: Britain, Asia and the opium trade', in Bill Schwarz, ed., *The Expansion of England: race, ethnicity and cultural history* (London, Routledge, 1996).
19. Karl Polanyi, *The Great Transformation: the political and economic origins of our time* (Beacon Press, Boston, 1957).

20. T. H. Marshall, 'Citizenship and social class', in *Citizenship and Social Class, and Other Essays* (Cambridge, Cambridge University Press, 1950).
21. Steve Cohen, *No One is Illegal: asylum and immigration control past and present* (Stoke-on-Trent, Trentham Books, 2003), pp100–1.
22. Dummett and Nicol, *Subjects, Citizens, Aliens and Others*, pp133–42; Kathleen Paul, *Whitewashing Britain: race and citizenship in the postwar era* (Ithaca, Cornell University Press, 1997).
23. Tom Nairn, *The Break-up of Britain: crisis and neo-nationalism* (London, New Left Books, 1977), p265.
24. Nairn, *The Break-up of Britain*, p269.
25. A. Sivanandan, 'Race, class and the state: the black experience in Britain', in *A Different Hunger: writings on black resistance* (London, Pluto Press, 1982), pp101–26.
26. Paul, *Whitewashing Britain*.
27. Bill Schwarz, '"The only white man in there": the re-racialisation of England, 1956–1968', *Race & Class*, vol. 38, no. 1 (July–September 1996).
28. Anthony Lester, ed., *Essays and Speeches by Roy Jenkins* (London, Collins, 1967), p267.
29. Andrew Sparrow, 'Howard's "liberal" defence of asylum policy', *Daily Telegraph* (23 April 2005).
30. Sivanandan, 'Race, class and the state', p109.
31. Conservative home secretary Reginald Maudling justified the 1971 Immigration Act by saying that stricter controls would improve community relations. Conservative home secretary Douglas Hurd, introducing the 1988 Immigration Act, reiterated that firm immigration controls were the best way to fight racism. Dummett and Nicol, *Subjects, Citizens, Aliens and Others*, p220; Cohen, *No One is Illegal*, p13.
32. Tony Kushner and Katharine Knox, *Refugees in an Age of Genocide* (London, Frank Cass, 2001), p172.
33. Steve Cohen, *From the Jews to the Tamils: Britain's mistreatment of refugees* (Manchester, South Manchester Law Centre, 1988), p18.
34. Anne Karpf, 'We've been here before', *Guardian Weekend* (8 June 2002), p23.
35. A Convention Relating to the International Status of Refugees had been drafted by the League of Nations in 1933 but its provisions were limited and it was ratified by only eight states.
36. Although the Universal Declaration of Human Rights was adopted by the United Nations in 1948, it differed from the Geneva Convention on Refugees in that it imposed no legal obligations on states. States were only expected to make a commitment to work towards the eventual realisation of human rights, rather than offer any legal guarantee to uphold them.

CHAPTER 2: FROM DEPENDENCY TO DISPLACEMENT

1. Quoted in John Pilger, ed., *Tell Me No Lies: investigative journalism and its triumphs* (London, Jonathan Cape, 2004), p388.

2. A. Sivanandan, 'Imperialism and disorganic development in the silicon age', in *A Different Hunger: writings on black resistance* (London, Pluto Press, 1982), pp143–61.
3. Claude Alvares, *Decolonizing History: technology and culture in India, China and the West, 1492 to the present day* (Goa, The Other India Press, 1991), pp138–59.
4. Mike Davis, *Late Victorian Holocausts: El Niño famines and the making of the Third World* (London, Verso, 2001), p7.
5. Frantz Fanon, *The Wretched of the Earth* (New York, Grove Press, 1968), p148.
6. Mary Kaldor, *New and Old Wars: organized violence in a global era* (Cambridge, Polity Press, 1999), p8.
7. Susanne Soederberg, *The Politics of the New International Financial Architecture: reimposing neoliberal domination in the global South* (London, Zed Books, 2004), p166.
8. Yao Graham, 'Ghana: the IMF's African success story?', *Race & Class*, vol. 24, no. 3 (Winter 1988).
9. Walden Bello with Shea Cunningham and Bill Rau, *Dark Victory: the United States, structural adjustment and global poverty* (London, Pluto Press, 1994), p63.
10. George Monbiot, *The Age of Consent: a manifesto for a new world order* (London, Flamingo, 2003), p151.
11. Bello, *Dark Victory*, p46.
12. Rudolf Amenga-Etego, 'Ghana's water is not for sale', *Action* (London, World Development Movement, Spring 2005), p14; *Dirty Aid, Dirty Water* (London, World Development Movement, February 2005).
13. Mike Davis, 'Planet of Slums: urban involution and the informal proletariat', *New Left Review*, no. 26 (March–April 2004), p23.
14. In Nigeria, for example, the redirection of funds from healthcare to debt-servicing in the 1980s led to a resurgence of epidemic diseases and diseases of poverty, especially among women. Folasade Iyun, 'The impact of structural adjustment on maternal and child health in Nigeria', in Gloria T. Emeagwali, ed., *Women Pay the Price: structural adjustment in Africa and the Caribbean* (Trenton, NJ, African World Press, 1995).
15. Michel Chossudovsky, *The Globalisation of Poverty: impacts of IMF and World Bank reforms* (London, Zed Books/Third World Network, 1997), p51.
16. Hopeton Dunn, 'Britain cashes in', *Weekly Journal* (9 May 1992), p8.
17. *Rigged Rules and Double Standards: trade globalisation and the fight against poverty* (Oxfam, 2002), p11.
18. *Human Development Report 2003: millennium development goals, a compact among nations to end human poverty* (New York, United Nations Development Programme, 2003), p53; *The State of the World's Children 2002: leadership* (New York, UNICEF, 2002), p6.
19. *States of Unrest III: resistance to IMF and World Bank policies in poor countries* (London, World Development Movement, April 2003).
20. Dilip Hiro, *Iran under the Ayatollahs* (London, Routledge & Kegan Paul, 1987), p36.

21. Thomas Turner, 'Crimes of the West in Democratic Congo: reflections on Belgian acceptance of "moral responsibility" for the death of Lumumba', in Adam Jones, ed., *Genocide, War Crimes and the West: history and complicity* (London, Zed Books, 2004).

22. Mark Curtis, 'Complicity in a Million Deaths', in Pilger, ed., *Tell Me No Lies*, pp509–10.

23. John Pilger, *The New Rulers of the World* (London, Verso, 2003), p23.

24. Jêdrzej George Frynas, Matthia P. Beck and Kamel Mellahi, 'Maintaining corporate dominance after decolonisation: the "first mover advantage" of Shell–BP in Nigeria', *Review of African Political Economy*, vol. 27, no. 85 (Summer 2000), pp407–25.

25. Nick Cohen, *Cruel Britannia* (London, Verso, 2000), p214.

26. 'Defend Nigerian asylum-seekers', *Campaign Against Racism and Fascism*, no. 29 (December 1995/January 1996), p5.

27. 'Safe for profits, not for people', *Campaign Against Racism and Fascism*, no. 30 (February/March 1996), pp6–7.

28. 'Unsettled – but not unsafe', *Campaign Against Racism and Fascism*, no. 30 (February/March 1996), p5.

29. Amnesty International, 'Nigeria ten years on: injustice and violence haunt the oil Delta' (AI Index: AFR 44/022/2005, 3 November 2005).

30. Gregory White and Scott Taylor, 'Well-oiled regimes: oil and uncertain transitions in Algeria and Nigeria', *Review of African Political Economy*, vol. 28, no. 89 (September 2001), pp323–44.

31. A. Sivanandan, *Communities of Resistance: writings on black struggles for socialism* (London, Verso, 1990), p199.

32. Fred Halliday, 'The arc of revolutions: Iran, Afghanistan, South Yemen and Ethiopia', *Race & Class*, vol. 20, no. 4 (Spring 1979), p381.

33. Chossudovsky, *The Globalisation of Poverty*, p102.

34. Mohamed Diriye Abdullahi, 'In the name of the Cold War: how the West aided and abetted the Barre dictatorship of Somalia', in Jones, ed., *Genocide, War Crimes and the West*, p247.

35. Abdullahi, 'In the name of the Cold War', p246.

36. Chris Searle, 'Agony and struggle in northern Somalia', *Race & Class*, vol. 34, no. 2 (October–December 1992).

37. Hermione Harris, *The Somali Community in the UK: what we know and how we know it* (London, Information Centre about Asylum and Refugees in the UK, 2004), p20.

38. Abdullahi, 'In the name of the Cold War', p252.

39. Ken Menkhaus, 'State collapse in Somalia: second thoughts', *Review of African Political Economy*, vol. 30, no. 97 (September 2003).

40. *Statistical Yearbook 2001: refugees, asylum seekers and other persons of concern – trends in displacement, protection and solutions* (Geneva, United Nations High Commissioner for Refugees, 2002), pp119–20.

41. A. Sivanandan, 'Into the waste lands', *New Statesman and Society* (19 June 1992).

42. Sivanandan, *Communities of Resistance*, p228.

43. Sivanandan, *Communities of Resistance*, p246.

44. Frances Webber, *Crimes of Arrival: immigrants and asylum-seekers in the new Europe* (London, Statewatch, 1996), p3.

CHAPTER 3: SEEDS OF SEGREGATION

1. Stokely Carmichael and Charles V. Hamilton, *Black Power: the politics of liberation in America* (New York, Vintage Books, 1967), p44.
2. A. Sivanandan, *From Resistance to Rebellion: Asian and Afro-Caribbean struggles in Britain* (London, Institute of Race Relations, 1986).
3. Frantz Fanon, *Black Skin, White Masks* (London, Pluto Press, 1986).
4. Fanon, *Black Skin, White Masks*, p18.
5. A. Sivanandan, 'The liberation of the black intellectual', in *A Different Hunger: writings on black resistance* (London, Pluto Press, 1982), p87.
6. Fanon, *Black Skin, White Masks*, p30.
7. Carmichael and Hamilton, *Black Power*, p44.
8. A. Sivanandan, 'RAT and the degradation of black struggle', in *Communities of Resistance: writings on black struggles for socialism* (London, Verso, 1990), p79.
9. Anthony Lester, ed., *Essays and Speeches by Roy Jenkins* (London, Collins, 1967), p267.
10. Ruth Levitas, ed., *The Ideology of the New Right* (Cambridge, Polity Press, 1986).
11. Quoted in Verena Stolcke, 'Talking culture: new boundaries, new rhetorics of exclusion in Europe', *Current Anthropology*, vol. 36, no. 1 (February 1995), p3.
12. In 1990, Conservative minister Norman Tebbit argued that non-whites could only be considered British if they supported the English cricket team.
13. Martin Barker, *The New Racism* (London, Junction Books, 1981).
14. Etienne Balibar has called this new racism 'neo-racism', while Verena Stolcke prefers to designate it as a 'cultural fundamentalism'. Etienne Balibar and Immanuel Wallerstein, *Race, Nation, Class: ambiguous identities* (London, Verso, 1991); Stolcke, 'Talking culture'.
15. John Casey, 'One nation: the politics of race', *Salisbury Review*, vol. 1, no. 1 (October 1982), pp23–8.
16. Ray Honeyford, 'Education and race – an alternative view', *Salisbury Review*, vol. 2, no. 2 (January 1984), pp30–2.
17. Quoted in David Docherty, David E. Morrison and Michael Tracey, *Keeping Faith? Channel Four and its audience* (London, John Libbey Books, 1988), p11.
18. Lord Scarman, *The Scarman Report: the Brixton disorders 10–12 April 1981* (Harmondsworth, Penguin, 1981), pp24–5, 28.
19. Department for Education and Science, *Education for All: the report of the committee of inquiry into the education of children from ethnic minority groups* (London, HMSO, 1985); Centre for Contemporary Cultural Studies, *The Empire Strikes Back: race and racism in 70s Britain* (London, Routledge, 1992), p122.
20. Leading criminologist Professor David Smith, of Edinburgh University, for example, argued that family dysfunction explained higher rates of African-Caribbean crime. 'The politics of numbers: police racism and crime figures', *Campaign Against Racism and Fascism*, no. 50 (June/July 1999), p9.

21. Home Office, *Statistics on Race and the Criminal Justice System* (1998).

22. 'Prison boss in race row', *BBC News* (27 March 1998), http://news.bbc.co.uk/1/hi/uk/70534.stm, last accessed 10 September 2006.

23. Lord Swann, *Education for All: the report of the committee of inquiry into the education of children from ethnic minority groups* (London, HMSO, Cmnd 9453, 1985), p5.

24. A. Sivanandan, 'Challenging racism: strategies for the 1980s', in *Communities of Resistance*, pp63–76.

25. In Bradford, for example, the City Council encouraged a Council of Mosques to be constituted in 1981, which provided an alternative voice to represent Muslims in Bradford from the secular Asian Youth Movements that had, till then, played the leading role. The City Council legitimised the mosques as a new class of 'community leaders' through funding and consultation exercises, hoping that they would become allies in a process of absorbing opposition, at the expense of the younger militants. Humayun Ansari, *'The Infidel Within': Muslims in Britain since 1800* (London, Hurst, 2004), p235.

26. A. Sivanandan, address to conference on anti-racist social work, University of Lancaster, 1989.

27. Virinder Kalra, *From Textile Mills to Taxi Ranks: experiences of migration, labour and social change* (Aldershot, Ashgate, 2000).

28. Peter Ratcliffe, *Breaking Down the Barriers: improving Asian access to social rented housing* (Chartered Institute of Housing, 2001), p35.

29. 'Racism in Oldham housing', *Campaign Against Racism and Fascism*, no. 18 (January/February 1994), p15.

30. Herman Ouseley, *Community Pride, not Prejudice: making diversity work in Bradford* (Bradford, Bradford Vision, 2001).

31. 'Education's new ethnocentric order', *Campaign Against Racism and Fascism*, no. 7 (March/April 1992), pp8–9.

32. Terry Eagleton, *The Idea of Culture* (Blackwell, Oxford, 2000), p12.

33. Tariq Modood, 'The end of a hegemony: from political blackness to ethnic pluralism', paper given at Commission for Racial Equality seminar, 29 March 1995.

34. Tariq Modood, *Not Easy Being British: colour, culture and citizenship* (London and Stoke-on-Trent, Runnymede Trust and Trentham Books, 1992), p397.

35. Stuart Hall, 'New ethnicities', in Kobena Mercer, ed., *Black Film/British Cinema*, ICA Documents No. 7 (London, Institute of Contemporary Art, 1988).

36. Homi Bhabha, *The Location of Culture* (London, Routledge, 1994).

37. A. Sivanandan, 'Millwall and after', *Race & Class*, vol. 35, no. 3 (January–March 1994).

38. Commission on British Muslims and Islamophobia, *Islamophobia: issues, challenges and action* (Stoke-on-Trent, Trentham Books, 2004), p30.

39. In 1994, twenty armed racists descended on the Darnall area of Sheffield, threatening to attack Asian children and elderly passers-by, but it was a number of Asians who were arrested by riot police. Over five hundred people packed a meeting at a community centre to demand that the charges against them be dropped. In the Eastwood area of Rotherham,

twenty-one young Asians were arrested during two nights of disturbances in 1994. The events were triggered after a gang of white youths piled out of a van and beat an Asian cab driver at a petrol station with baseball bats. When he ran for help and a group of local Asians came to his defence, it was they who were arrested by the police and charged with public order offences. The following year, in the Manningham area of Bradford, police attempted a heavy-handed and provocative arrest of a group of young Asians, who had complained about a police car running over the foot of one of their group. Two nights of rioting ensued, in which seven hundred people were thought to have participated. 'Defending Darnall', *Campaign Against Racism and Fascism*, no. 21 (July/August 1994), p3; 'Self defence is the only way', *Campaign Against Racism and Fascism*, no. 22 (September/October 1994), p12; 'What sparked the "riots"?', *Campaign Against Racism and Fascism*, no. 27 (August/September 1995).

40. In Oldham, police chief superintendent Eric Hewitt repeatedly claimed to local newspapers that the real problem was Asian racists, who had created 'exclusive areas for themselves' in which whites were driven out by violence. The figures which the police produced to prove their case only showed that Asians had long stopped bothering to report racist incidents, so low was their confidence in the police. This was confirmed in research by Larry Ray (University of Kent), David Smith and Liz Wastell (both University of Sussex). See 'Letters', *Independent* (8 June 2001); Steve Laws, 'Fears growing over plague of racist attacks by Asian gangs', *Oldham Evening Chronicle* (17 March 1998).

CHAPTER 4: WE ARE HERE BECAUSE YOU ARE THERE

1. A. Sivanandan, 'New Circuits of Imperialism', in *Communities of Resistance: writings on black struggles for socialism* (London, Verso, 1990), pp189–90.
2. Karl Polanyi, *The Great Transformation: the political and economic origins of our time* (Beacon Press, Boston, 1957).
3. Philip Bobbitt, *The Shield of Achilles: war, peace and the course of history* (London, Penguin, 2002), p229.
4. Karl Marx called these workers a 'reserve army of labour'. Karl Marx, *Capital: a critical analysis of capitalist production* (London, George Allen & Unwin, 1938), pp642–55.
5. Douglas Massey, 'Economic development and international migration in comparative perspective', *Population and Development Review*, vol. 14, no. 2 (1988), p385.
6. Mike Davis, 'Planet of slums: urban involution and the informal proletariat', *New Left Review*, no. 26 (March–April 2004), p28.
7. E. P. Thompson, *The Making of the English Working Class* (London, Pelican, 1968), p469.
8. Larry Elliot and Dan Atkinson, *The Age of Insecurity* (London, Verso, 1999), p76.
9. Virinder Kalra, *From Textile Mills to Taxi Ranks: experiences of migration, labour and social change* (Aldershot, Ashgate, 2000).

10. Swasti Mitter, *Common Fate, Common Bond: women in the global economy* (London, Pluto Press, 1986), p123.
11. Corporate Watch, *What's Wrong With Supermarkets?* (2004).
12. The gang-master system, which had its roots in the fields of East Anglia and Lincolnshire in the nineteenth century, when it was used to bring women and child labourers into the seasonal agricultural economy, was designed to extract the maximum amount of labour from workers during the short time in which they were needed. Marx, *Capital*, p714.
13. Don Pollard, *Gangmaster System in Sussex* (Rural, Agricultural and Allied Workers' Trade Group, Transport and General Workers Union, 2000); *Gone West: Ukrainians at work in the UK* (Trades Union Congress, 2004).
14. Bridget Anderson, *Doing the Dirty Work* (London, Zed Books, 2000), p87.
15. Anderson, *Doing the Dirty Work*, p113.
16. Kalayaan, *Migrant Workers' Rights: the passport issue* (2003).
17. Personal account presented at Kalayaan public meeting, London, 30 July 2003.
18. The numbers of migrants who are legally resident but work in violation of the conditions of their residence is likely to be higher than the number of migrant workers who are illegally resident. Bridget Anderson, Martin Ruhs, Ben Rogaly and Sarah Spencer, *Fair Enough? Central and East European migrants in low wage employment in the UK* (Joseph Rowntree Foundation, 2006). The term 'semi-compliance' has been introduced to describe these migrant workers. Bridget Anderson and Martin Ruhs, *Semi-compliance in the Migrant Labour Market*, Working Paper No. 30 (Centre on Migration Policy and Society, University of Oxford, 2006).
19. Yara Evans, Joanna Herbert, Kavita Datta, Jon May, Cathy McIlwaine and Jane Wills, *Making the City Work: low paid employment in London* (Queen Mary, University of London, November 2005).
20. Citizens Advice, *Nowhere to Turn* (2004).
21. John Berger and Jean Mohr, *A Seventh Man: the story of a migrant worker in Europe* (Harmondsworth, Penguin, 1975), p64.
22. The name has been changed to preserve anonymity.
23. Laura Smith, 'Migrants' cash outstrips aid flow', *Guardian* (17 November 2005), p28.
24. Asian Development Bank, *Enhancing the Efficiency of Overseas Filipino Workers' Remittances* (2004), p18.
25. 'Philippine health care system swept by a new wave of migration', *Third World Resurgence*, no. 163/164 (2004), p31.
26. Natasha Grzincic, 'Modern heroes, modern slaves', *Red Pepper* (April 2004), p22.
27. 'Cashing in on asylum', Richard Payne, in *Mediactive*, no. 4 (2005), p57.
28. Peter Stalker, *No-Nonsense Guide to Migration* (London, Verso, 2001), p21.
29. The year in which the highest number of asylum claims have been received to date is 2002, when 85,865 claims for asylum were submitted. Of these, around 10 per cent were recognised as refugees by Home Office caseworkers and 16 per cent won on appeal. A further 24 per cent, many of them Iraqis fleeing Saddam Hussein, were deemed to be in substantial

danger if deported and granted 'exceptional leave to remain'. Some 15 per cent were rejected on 'non-compliance' grounds, which meant that the asylum application was rejected simply because the paperwork was not filled in correctly or on time. There was no way of knowing whether these claims were valid or not. Lastly, one can assume that many valid asylum claims would have been rejected even after the appeals process, owing to widely recognised biases in the entire system. What these figures suggest is that asylum seekers were, more often than not, fleeing from genuinely life-threatening situations. *Asylum Statistics: 4th Quarter 2002* (Home Office, March 2003), pp14, 20.

30. Stephen Castles, Heaven Crawley and Sean Loughna, *States of Conflict: causes and patterns of forced migration to the EU and policy responses* (London, Institute of Public Policy Research, 2003), p. iii.
31. Tony Blair, speech to the Confederation of British Industry, 27 April 2004, http://www.number-10.gov.uk/output/Page5708.asp, last accessed 19 March 2006.
32. Blair, speech to the Confederation of British Industry.
33. The Commonwealth Immigrants Act 1968.
34. Blair, speech to the Confederation of British Industry.
35. *Refugees Benefit from Home Office Funding*, Home Office Press Release, 20 October 2005.
36. *Statistical Yearbook 2001: refugees, asylum seekers and other persons of concern – trends in displacement, protection and solutions* (Geneva, UNHCR, 2002), p91.
37. Jack Straw, speech to the European Conference on Asylum, Lisbon, 16 June 2000, quoted in Lydia Morris, *The Control of Rights: the rights of workers and asylum seekers under managed migration* (Joint Council for the Welfare of Immigrants, 2004), p13.
38. Frances Webber, *Crimes of Arrival: immigrants and asylum-seekers in the new Europe* (London, Statewatch, 1996).
39. Webber, *Crimes of Arrival*, p3.
40. Liz Fekete, 'Death at the border – who is to blame?', *European Race Bulletin*, no. 44 (July 2003), pp2–4; Andrew Bradstock and Arlington Trotman, eds, *Asylum Voices: experiences of people seeking asylum in the United Kingdom* (Churches Together in Britain and Ireland), p18.
41. John Morrison, '"The dark-side of globalisation": the criminalisation of refugees', *Race & Class*, vol. 43, no. 1 (July–September 2001).
42. Diane Taylor and Hugh Muir, 'Asylum seekers jailed for having no passport', *Guardian* (18 March 2005), p2.
43. Liz Fekete, 'Monitoring Maritime Border Controls', *European Race Bulletin*, no. 45/46 (Autumn 2003/Winter 2004), pp2–4.
44. Fekete, 'Death at the border – who is to blame?', p2.
45. Harmit Athwal, *Death Trap: the human cost of the war on asylum* (Institute of Race Relations, 2004), p2.

CHAPTER 5: ASYLUM AND THE WELFARE STATE

1. Jeremy Hardy, *Jeremy Hardy Speaks to the Nation* (London, Methuen, 1993), p5.

2. Peter Mandelson, 'The new conservative enemy', *Independent* (13 September 1999).

3. Anne Gray, 'New Labour – new labour discipline', *Capital and Class*, no. 65 (Summer 1998), pp1–8; Chris Grover, '"New Labour", welfare reform and the reserve army of labour', *Capital and Class*, no. 79 (Spring 2003), pp17–23.

4. Tony Blair, 'Values and the power of community', speech given at Tübingen University, Germany (30 June 2000).

5. Blair, 'Values and the power of community'.

6. David Blunkett, *Active Citizens, Strong Communities: progressing civil renewal* (Home Office, 11 December 2003), p4.

7. Steve Cohen, *No One is Illegal: asylum and immigration control past and present* (Stoke-on-Trent, Trentham Books, 2003), p104.

8. 'No to passport checks', *Campaign Against Racism and Fascism*, no. 14 (May/June 1993), pp6–7.

9. A. Sivanandan, 'Editorial', in 'Europe: variations on a theme of racism', *Race & Class*, vol. 32, no. 3 (January–March 1991), p v.

10. 'From ill treatment to no treatment', *Campaign Against Racism and Fascism*, no. 27 (August/September 1995), pp7–8.

11. 'Burn the Race Card', *Campaign Against Racism and Fascism*, no. 5 (November/December 1991).

12. *Fairer, Faster and Firmer: a modern approach to immigration and asylum* (Home Office, 1998), p39.

13. *Understanding the Decision-Making of Asylum Seekers* (Home Office, Research Study 243, July 2002).

14. *Another Country: implementing dispersal under the Immigration and Asylum Act 1999* (London, Audit Commission, 2000), p9.

15. 'Racial violence: taking stock', *Campaign Against Racism and Fascism*, no. 10 (September/October 1992), p3.

16. Human Rights Watch / Helsinki, *Racist Violence in the United Kingdom* (New York, 1997), pp47–9.

17. Human Rights Watch / Helsinki, *Racist Violence in the United Kingdom*, pp36–7.

18. 'Deportations: more violence, more deaths', *Campaign Against Racism and Fascism*, no. 56 (August/September 2000), p5.

19. In June 1996, the Court of Appeal ruled that the policy of withdrawing benefits from 'in country' asylum seekers and rejected asylum seekers, who might still appeal, was unlawful. But this judgment was overturned by the 1996 Asylum and Immigration Act. In October 1996, the High Court ruled that, in spite of the Act, local authorities would, under the 1948 National Assistance Act, have a duty to look after asylum seekers whom central government had rendered destitute and homeless. 'Lilley's Pride: Britain's Shame', *Campaign Against Racism and Fascism*, no. 33 (August/September 1996), p11; 'Asylum seekers caught by the Act', *Campaign Against Racism and Fascism*, no. 35 (December 1996/January 1997), pp4–6.

20. 'We want to wash dross down drain', *Dover Express* (1 October 1998).

21. Nicky Winstanley-Torode, '"The Gypsy Invasion"': from state persecution to media denigration?' (unpublished Master's thesis, September 1998), pp9 and 31.
22. Winstanley-Torode, '"The Gypsy Invasion"', p19.
23. Winstanley-Torode, '"The Gypsy Invasion"', p52.
24. Winstanley-Torode, '"The Gypsy Invasion"', p32.
25. 'No safety for Roma', *Campaign Against Racism and Fascism*, no. 41 (December 1997/January 1998), pp4–5.
26. 'Stop this bogus tabloid nationalism', *Campaign Against Racism and Fascism*, no. 55 (April/May 2000), p5.
27. Andrea Busfield and Neil Syson, 'Hard day on the scrounge', *Sun* (9 March 2000).
28. 'Stop this bogus tabloid nationalism', p5.
29. *Daily Express* (20 January 2004).
30. Ian Hancock, *We are the Romani people* (Hatfield, University of Hertfordshire Press, 2002), p48.
31. Isabel Fonseca, *Bury Me Standing: the Gypsies and their journey* (New York, Vintage, 1995), p143.
32. Saleh Mamon, 'Britain "fast-tracks" Roma back to discrimination', *IRR News* (1 April 2003), http://www.irr.org.uk/2003/april/ak000004.html, last accessed 13 January 2006.
33. 'Romani women subject to forced sterilization in Slovakia', Press Release (New York, Center for Reproductive Rights, 28 January 2003).
34. 'No asylum for Czech and Slovak Roma', *European Race Bulletin*, no. 27 (May 1998), p29.
35. 'Try and imagine this', *Inexile* (February 1999), pp8–9.
36. David Jones and Steve Doughty, 'The good life on asylum alley', *Daily Mail* (6 October 1998).
37. Personal correspondence, 12 November 1998.
38. Personal correspondence, 23 October 1998.
39. *Government Reply to the Third Report from the Home Affairs Committee Session 1984–85, HC 72-I, Refugees and Asylum, with Special Reference to the Vietnamese* (London, HMSO, Cmnd. 9626, 1985), p10.
40. Gaby Hinsliff, 'Asylum help "may worsen the crisis"', *Daily Mail* (25 August 1999).
41. *Fairer, Faster and Firmer*, p39.
42. *Dossier of Racial Attacks on Dispersed Asylum Seekers in Glasgow, April 2000–February 2001* (Glasgow Asylum Rights Campaign, March 2001).
43. Monica Hingorani, 'A right to life: the story of Ramin Khaleghi', *Race & Class*, vol. 32, no. 2 (October–December 2001), pp128–31.
44. Harmit Athwal, *Death Trap: the human cost of the war on asylum* (Institute of Race Relations, 2004).
45. Daniel Foggo and Tony Freinberg, 'Racial tensions halt dispersal of asylum seekers around UK', *Daily Telegraph* (14 November 2004).
46. *Human Rights Audit 2000: UK foreign and asylum policy* (Amnesty International UK, 2000), p53.
47. *Today*, BBC Radio 4 (24 April 2002).
48. *Hansard*, Column 353 (24 April 2002).
49. David Goodhart, 'Too diverse?', *Prospect* (February 2004).

CHAPTER 6: THE DIALECTICS OF TERROR

1. Tony Blair, Speech to Labour Party conference, October 2001, http://politics.guardian.co.uk/labourconference2001/story/0,1220,561988,00.html, last accessed 1 October 2006.
2. Quoted in William K. Tabb, 'The Face of Empire', *Monthly Review*, vol. 54, no. 6 (November 2002).
3. Linda Melvern, *A People Betrayed: the role of the West in Rwanda's genocide* (London, Zed Books, 2000).
4. Project for the New American Century, *Rebuilding America's Defenses: strategy, forces and resources for a new century* (2000), p14.
5. Office Of The Deputy Under Secretary Of Defense, *Department Of Defense Base Structure Report* (2003).
6. Robert Cooper, 'The post-modern state', in Mark Leonard, ed., *Re-ordering the World: the long-term implications of 11 September* (London, Foreign Policy Centre, 2002).
7. Raja Anwar, *The Tragedy of Afghanistan: a first-hand account* (London, Verso, 1988), p36.
8. Anwar, *The Tragedy of Afghanistan*, pp84–109.
9. John K. Cooley, *Unholy Wars: Afghanistan, America and international terrorism* (London, Pluto Press, 2000), p19.
10. Cooley, *Unholy Wars*, p62.
11. Nafeez Mosaddeq Ahmed, *The War on Truth: 9/11, disinformation and the anatomy of terrorism* (Moreton-in-Marsh, Arris Books, 2005), pp8–9.
12. Adnan A. Musallam, *From Secularism to Jihad: Sayyid Qutb and the foundations of radical Islamism* (Westport, Praeger, 2005), pp180–2; Richard Bonney, *Jihad: from Qur'an to bin Laden* (Basingstoke, Palgrave Macmillan, 2004), pp215–23.
13. Abdel Bari Atwan, *The Secret History of al-Qa'ida* (London, Saqi Books, 2006), p73.
14. Eqbal Ahmad, edited by Carollee Bengelsdorf, Margaret Cerullo and Yogesh Chandrani, *The Selected Writings of Eqbal Ahmad* (New York, Columbia University Press, 2006), p518.
15. Ahmad, *The Selected Writings*, p511.
16. *Statistical Yearbook 2001: Refugees, asylum seekers and other persons of concern – trends in displacement, protection and solutions* (Geneva, UNHCR, 2002), pp119–20.
17. *Human Rights Audit 2000: UK Foreign and Asylum Policy* (Amnesty International UK, 2000), p47.
18. *Asylum Statistics* (Home Office, June 2000), p6.
19. Bruce Lawrence, ed., *Messages to the World: the statements of Osama Bin Laden* (London, Verso, 2005), p73.
20. Atwan, *The Secret History of al-Qa'ida*, pp79, 205.
21. Atwan, *The Secret History of al-Qa'ida*, p40; Tariq Ali, *Rough Music: Blair, bombs, Baghdad, London, terror* (London, Verso, 2005), pp47–8; Jason Burke, *Al-Qaeda: the true story of radical Islam* (London, Penguin Books, 2004), p25.
22. David Cameron MP, then shadow education minister, speech to the Foreign Policy Centre, London, 24 August 2005.

23. Scilla Elworthy and Gabrielle Rifkind, *Hearts and Minds: human security approaches to political violence* (London, Demos, 2005), p29.
24. See, for example, Robert Spencer's jihadwatch.org.
25. Robert Pape, *Dying to Win: the strategic logic of suicide terrorism* (New York, Random House, 2005).
26. House of Commons Intelligence and Security Committee, *Iraqi Weapons of Mass Destruction – Intelligence and Assessments* (September 2003), p34.
27. 'London bomber: text in full', *BBC News* (1 September 2005), http://news.bbc.co.uk/1/hi/uk/4206800.stm, last accessed 9 June 2006.
28. Tony Blair, speech to Labour Party national conference, 16 July 2005, http://news.bbc.co.uk/1/hi/uk/4689363.stm, last accessed 9 June 2006.
29. Tony Blair, foreign policy speech, London, 21 March 2006, http://www.number10.gov.uk/output/Page9224.asp, last accessed 9 June 2006.
30. Tony Blair, speech to the Los Angeles World Affairs Council, 1 August 2006, http://www.number10.gov.uk/output/Page9948.asp, last accessed 1 October 2006.
31. Blair, foreign policy speech.
32. Anthony Browne, 'Fundamentally, we're useful idiots', *Times* (1 August 2005); Melanie Phillips, 'This lethal moral madness', *Daily Mail* (14 July 2005), p15; Richard Littlejohn, *Sun* (15 July 2005), p11.
33. Johnny Burnett and Dave Whyte, 'Embedded expertise and the new terrorism', *Journal for Crime, Conflict and the Media*, vol. 1, no. 4 (2005), p13.
34. Burnett and Whyte, 'Embedded expertise and the new terrorism', p14.
35. Blair, speech to the Los Angeles World Affairs Council.
36. Fares al-Braizat, 'Muslims and democracy: an empirical critique of Fukuyama's culturalist approach', paper, Department of Politics and International Relations, University of Kent at Canterbury, pp8–9.
37. David Leigh and Rob Evans, 'Third of MoD arms sale unit works for Saudis', *Guardian* (9 March 2005).
38. Al-Braizat, 'Muslims and democracy'; Mark Tessler, 'Do Islamic orientations influence attitudes toward democracy in the Arab world? Evidence from Egypt, Jordan, Morocco and Algeria'; both papers available from http://www.worldvaluessurvey.org, last accessed 7 October 2006.
39. Eqbal Ahmad, *Confronting Empire: interviews with David Barsamian* (London, Pluto Press, 2000), p95.
40. 'The *Sun* says', *Sun* (8 July 2005), p7.
41. Joint Committee on Human Rights, *Counter-Terrorism Policy and Human Rights: Terrorism Bill and related matters; third report of session 2005–06* (London, House of Commons, December 2005), p13.
42. Jason Burke and Imtiaz Gul, 'The drone, the CIA and a botched attempt to kill bin Laden's deputy', *Guardian* (15 January 2006).
43. Burke, *Al-Qaeda*, pp15–19.
44. Burke, *Al-Qaeda*, p16.
45. *Listen to the Refugee's Story: how UK foreign investment creates refugees and asylum seekers* (Ilisu Dam Campaign, Corner House and Peace in Kurdistan, 2003), p53.
46. Richard Norton-Taylor, 'UK to boost arms sales to Pakistan', *Guardian* (21 May 2005), p18.

47. Selig S. Harrison, 'Pakistan's Baluch insurgency', *Le Monde Diplomatique, English Edition* (October 2006), p10.
48. Eliza Manningham-Buller, *Statement to House of Lords* (20 September 2005).
49. Human Rights Watch, *In the Name of Counter-Terrorism: human rights abuses worldwide* (25 March 2003), p12.
50. Naomi Klein, 'The rise of disaster capitalism', *The Nation* (2 May 2005).
51. Jason Bennetto, 'Go home and rebuild, Blunkett tells young asylum-seekers', *Independent* (19 September 2002).
52. Nick Paton Walsh, 'The envoy who knew too much', *Guardian* (15 July 2004).
53. Human Rights Watch, *In the Name of Counter-Terrorism*, p24.
54. Richard Norton-Taylor, 'UK trained Uzbek troops weeks before massacre', *Guardian* (30 June 2005), p2.
55. Human Rights Watch, 'Uzbekistan: massive crackdown documented', Press Release (20 September 2005).
56. Craig Murray, 'Hazel Blears made a claim to MPs I know to be false', *Guardian* (19 October 2005).
57. Nick Paton Walsh, 'US sidles up to well-oiled autocracy', *Guardian* (2 July 2004).
58. Human Rights Watch, *In the Name of Counter-Terrorism*, p13.
59. Anders Lustgarten, 'Why campaigners oppose the pipeline', *Observer* (1 December 2002), http://observer.guardian.co.uk/comment/story/0,,850999,00.html, last accessed 5 October 2006.
60. Michael Gillard, Ignacio Gomez and Melissa Jones, 'BP hands "tarred in pipeline dirty war"', *Guardian* (17 October 1998); Robert Verkaik, 'Farmers "terrified out of their homes" to sue BP for £15m', *Independent* (18 June 2005).
61. Arifa Akbar, 'Deported Colombian is shot after losing plea to stay in Britain', *Independent* (16 April 2004).
62. Ahmed, *The War on Truth*, pp113–17.
63. Lisa Anderson, 'Rogue Libya's long road', *Middle East Report*, no. 241 (Winter 2006), pp42–7.
64. Fahad Ansari, *British Anti-Terrorism: a modern day witch-hunt* (London, Islamic Human Rights Commission, October 2005), p13.
65. 'European Commission technical mission to Libya: exporting Fortress Europe', *Statewatch*, vol. 15, no. 2 (March–April 2005), p21; 'EU/Libya: Full steam ahead, without pausing to think', *Statewatch News Online* (June 2005).
66. Gilles Kepel, *Jihad: the trail of political Islam* (London, I. B. Tauris, 2002), p159.
67. Fouzi Slisli, 'The western media and the Algerian crisis', *Race & Class*, vol. 41, no. 3 (January–March 2000), p53.
68. Robert Fisk, *The Great War for Civilisation: the conquest of the Middle East* (London, Fourth Estate, 2005), pp710–19. A number of journalists, including Fisk, have documented evidence of collusion between the 'terrorists' and the Algerian security services.
69. Salima Mellah and Jean-Baptiste Rivoire, 'El Para, the Maghreb's Bin Laden', *Le Monde Diplomatique, English Edition* (February 2005), pp6–7.

CHAPTER 7: THE HALABJA GENERATION

1. Quoted in Susan Meiselas, *Kurdistan: in the shadow of history* (New York, Random House, 1997), p90.
2. Gary Bell, 'Return from refuge: the government's returns policy', *inExile*, no. 33 (September 2004), pp12–13.
3. Letter from Bail Circle, 10 December 2004.
4. *Control of Immigration: statistics United Kingdom* (Home Office, Cm 5684, 2001), p62.
5. Human Rights Watch, *Genocide in Iraq: the Anfal campaign against the Kurds* (1993).
6. Human Rights Watch, *Claims in Conflict: reversing ethnic cleansing in Northern Iraq* (2004), p9.
7. Human Rights Watch, *Genocide in Iraq*.
8. Soran Karim, 23, an asylum seeker from Iraq who had lost his parents and a brother in the chemical attack on Halabja, died on 7 July 2003 when the minibus he was in collided with a train on a level crossing in Worcestershire. The minibus was carrying migrant agricultural workers and was being driven by another Iraqi, Adnan Kadir Karim, who admitted not being able to read English signs. Harmit Athwal, *Death Trap: the human cost of the war on asylum* (Institute of Race Relations, 2004), p11.
9. Athwal, *Death Trap*, p12.
10. 'Asylum seeker died of hypothermia', *BBC News* (26 April 2005), http://news.bbc.co.uk/go/pr/fr/-/1/hi/england/west_midlands/4486949.stm, last accessed 5 October 2006.
11. Greg Muttitt, *Crude Designs: the rip-off of Iraq's oil wealth* (PLATFORM with Global Policy Forum, Institute for Policy Studies, New Economics Foundation, Oil Change International and War on Want, November 2005); Iraq Occupation Focus, *Newsletter*, no. 17 (9 April 2005).
12. Haifa Zangana, 'So much for illusions', *Guardian* (7 March 2005).
13. Press Release, US Committee for Refugees and Immigrants, 14 June 2006; available at: http://www.refugees.org/newsroomsub.aspx?id=1622, last accessed 1 October 2006.
14. *Asylum Statistics* (Home Office, July 2000); *Asylum Statistics* (Home Office, February 2001).
15. Vikram Dodd, 'Secret u-turn to send Kurds back', *Guardian* (25 April 2001).
16. Tony Blair, speech at Labour Party Local Government, Women and Youth conference, Glasgow, 15 February 2003, http://www.labour.org.uk/news/tbglasgow, last accessed 17 August 2004.
17. Interview with Tony Blair, *Newsnight*, BBC (7 February 2003), http://news.bbc.co.uk/1/hi/programmes/newsnight/2745155.stm, last accessed 4 October 2006.
18. Interview with Tony Blair, *Breakfast with Frost*, BBC (19 February 2003), http://news.bbc.co.uk/1/hi/uk_politics/2695787.stm, last accessed 4 October 2006.
19. Interview with Tony Blair, *Breakfast with Frost*.
20. Tony Blair, speech at Labour Party Local Government, Women and Youth conference.

21. Meiselas, *Kurdistan*, p64.
22. Research Unit for Political Economy, *Behind the Invasion of Iraq* (New York, Monthly Review Press, 2003), p22.
23. Meiselas, *Kurdistan*, p64.
24. Haifa Zangana and Sami Ramadani, 'Resistance and sectarianism in Iraq', *International Socialist*, no. 109 (Winter 2006), pp57–68.
25. Hanna Batatu, *The Old Social Classes and the Revolutionary Movements of Iraq: a study of Iraq's old landed and commercial classes and of its Communists, Baathists and Free Officers* (Princeton, NJ, Princeton University Press, 1978), p959.
26. Andrew Cockburn and Patrick Cockburn, *Saddam Hussein: an American obsession* (London, Verso, 2002), p74; Michel Despratx and Barry Lando, 'Iraq: crimes and collusions', *Monde Diplomatique, English Edition* (November 2004), pp1–2; Batatu, *The Old Social Classes and the Revolutionary Movements of Iraq*, pp985–6.
27. John K. Cooley, *An Alliance Against Babylon: the US, Israel and Iraq* (London, Pluto Press, 2005), pp98–9.
28. Mark Curtis, 'How Britain helped Saddam into power', *Red Pepper* (November 2004), p19.
29. Fred Halliday, *Nation and Religion in the Middle East* (London, Saqi Books, 2000), p115.
30. Sinjari Hussain, 'Notes on the Kurdish struggle', *Race & Class*, vol. 27, no. 3 (Winter 1986), p92.
31. Eric Herring, 'The No Fly Zones in Iraq: the myth of a humanitarian intervention', *Cambridge Review of International Affairs*, vol. 14, no. 3 (January 2002).
32. Dilip Hiro, *The Longest War* (London, Paladin, 1990), pp162, 217. Cockburn and Cockburn, *Saddam Hussein*, p35.
33. Hiro, *The Longest War*, pp224–6; Cockburn and Cockburn, *Saddam Hussein*, p81.
34. National Security Archive, *Iraqgate: Saddam Hussein, US policy and the prelude to the Persian Gulf War, 1980–1994*, http://nsarchive.chadwyck.com/igintro.htm, last accessed 8 August 2005.
35. Hiro, *The Longest War*, p1.
36. US Senate Committee on Banking, Housing and Urban Affairs, *US Chemical and Biological Exports to Iraq and Their Possible Impact on the Health Consequences of the Persian Gulf War* (1994), http://www.chronicillnet.org/PGWS/tuite/chembio.html, last accessed 1 October 2006.
37. National Security Archive, *Iraqgate*.
38. Despratx and Lando, 'Iraq', p2.
39. Hussain, 'Notes on the Kurdish struggle', p91.
40. Herring, 'The No Fly Zones in Iraq'.
41. 'Pawns in a deadly game', *Campaign Against Racism and Fascism*, no. 42 (February/March 1998), pp12–13.
42. Eric Herring, 'Between Iraq and a hard place: a critique of the British government's case for UN economic sanctions', *Review of International Studies*, no. 28 (2002).
43. Herring, 'The No Fly Zones in Iraq'.

44. Kerim Yildiz, *The Kurds in Iraq: the past, present and future* (London, Pluto Press, 2004), p74.
45. Herring, 'Between Iraq and a hard place', p39.
46. 'No welcome for Iraqis', *Campaign Against Racism and Fascism*, no. 70 (Spring 2003), p3.
47. 'How the tabloids harass refugees', *Campaign Against Racism and Fascism*, no. 61 (April/May 2001), p12.
48. Article 19, *What's the Story? Media representation of refugees and asylum seekers in the UK* (November 2003), p47.
49. Athwal, *Death Trap*.
50. 'Hull faces asylum pull-out', *Law Gazette* (15 April 2004).
51. 'Call for action on city's 200 homeless asylum seekers', *Hull Daily Mail* (27 October 2004).
52. 'A victory against racial violence', *Hull Daily Mail* (8 June 2004).
53. 'Street battle confirms city's worst fears', *Yorkshire Post* (27 July 2003).

CHAPTER 8: INTEGRATIONISM: THE POLITICS OF ANTI-MUSLIM RACISM

1. Edward Said, *Covering Islam: how the media and the experts determine how we see the rest of the world* (London, Vintage, 1997), pp xxxv–xxxvi.
2. Gordon Brown, speech to Fabian Society, 14 January 2006, http://www.fabian-society.org.uk/press_office/news_latest_all.asp?pressid=520, last accessed 6 October 2006.
3. David Goodhart, 'Discomfort of strangers', *Guardian* (24 February 2004), p25.
4. Alice Miles, 'Four pathetic young bombers', *The Times* (13 July 2005), p19.
5. Boris Johnson, 'This is a turning point: we have to fly the flag for Britishness again', *Daily Telegraph* (14 July 2005), p28.
6. Melanie Phillips, 'This lethal moral madness', *Daily Mail* (14 July 2005), p15.
7. Anthony Browne, *The Retreat of Reason: political correctness and the corruption of public debate in modern Britain* (London, Civitas, 2006), p xiii.
8. Hugo Young, 'A corrosive national danger in our multicultural model', *Guardian* (6 November 2001).
9. Anthony Lester, ed., *Essays and speeches by Roy Jenkins* (London, Collins, 1967), p267.
10. In early 2004, Trevor Phillips had been strongly critical of David Goodhart's critique of diversity but, within a few months, he was airing similar views himself.
11. Trevor Phillips, speech to the Manchester Council for Community Relations, 22 September 2005.
12. A Mori survey published in January 2004 found that 41 per cent of whites did not want an Asian or black Briton as a neighbour, compared to 26 per cent of those from ethnic minorities who wanted races to live separately. Similarly, a survey of school students in Burnley and Blackburn in 2006 found that Asian Muslim and white non-Muslim

students shared similar views on issues of free speech, national loyalty and self-reliance but students from a school with a predominantly white intake had much higher levels of intolerance towards people of different faith and ethnicity and a widespread belief in racial superiority, compared to students from a school with a mixed intake or students from a school with a predominantly Asian Muslim intake. Vikram Dodd, 'Four out of 10 whites do not want black neighbour, poll shows', *Guardian* (19 January 2004); Andrew Holden, *The Burnley Project: evaluating the contribution of interfaith dialogue to community cohesion, interim report* (University of Lancaster, 2006).

13. Jytte Klausen and Alan Wolfe, 'Other people', *Prospect* (December 2000).
14. Nasreen Suleaman, 'Koran and Country: biography of a bomber', BBC Radio 4, 8–8.30pm (17 November 2005).
15. David Goodhart, 'Too diverse?', *Prospect* (February 2004).
16. John Pilger, *Stealing a Nation*, ITV1, 11pm (6 October 2004).
17. Miranda Lewis, *Asylum: understanding public attitudes* (London, Institute of Public Policy Research, 2005).
18. David Cameron MP, then shadow education minister, speech to the Foreign Policy Centre, London, 24 August 2005. He returned to these themes in his 2006 party conference speech, http://news.bbc.co.uk/1/hi/uk_politics/5407714.stm, last accessed 7 October 2006.
19. Said, *Covering Islam*, p li.
20. Rod Liddle, 'Immigration is a timebomb', Channel 4, 9pm (10 March 2005); Niall Ferguson, 'If they pass the "cricket test", how do we stop the suicide bombers?', *Telegraph* (17 July 2005); Niall Ferguson, 'Tomorrow's world war today', *Los Angeles Times* (16 January 2006); Niall Ferguson, 'The widening Atlantic', *Atlantic Monthly* (January/February 2005), p43.
21. Olivier Roy, *Globalised Islam: the search for a new ummah* (London, Hurst, 2004), p124.
22. Christian Delacampagne, 'Racism and the West: from praxis to logos', in David Theo Goldberg, ed., *Anatomy of Racism* (University of Minnesota Press, Minneapolis, 1990).
23. Paul Statham, 'State policies, political discourse and "white" public opinion on ethnic relations and immigration in Britain: pushing the borders of "extremity"?' Democracy and the New Extremist Challenge in Europe, Joint Sessions of Workshops (European Consortium for Political Research, Grenoble, April 2001).
24. Islamic Human Rights Commission, *The Hidden Victims of September 11: the backlash against Muslims in the UK* (2002).
25. BBC News, 'Hate crimes soar after bombings' (4 August 2005), http://news.bbc.co.uk/1/hi/england/london/4740015.stm, last accessed 1 November 2005.
26. Figures supplied by Harmit Athwal, Institute of Race Relations, 27 April 2006.
27. *Secure Borders, Safe Haven: integration with diversity in modern Britain* (Home Office, CM 5387, 2002).
28. *Secure Borders, Safe Haven*, p3.

29. 'Major Building Blocks of Immigration Reform', Home Office press release (31 March 2003).

30. Lester, ed., *Essays and speeches by Roy Jenkins*, p267.

31. Colin Brown, 'If we want social cohesion we need a sense of identity', interview with David Blunkett, *Independent on Sunday* (9 December 2001), p4; David Blunkett, 'It's not about cricket tests', *Guardian* (14 December 2001).

32. House of Commons, *Hansard* (17 July 2001), Column 8WH.

33. *Secure Borders, Safe Haven*, p18.

34. Arifa Akbar, 'Blunkett: British Asians should speak English at home', *Independent* (16 September 2002), p7.

35. Sir William Macpherson, chair, *The Stephen Lawrence Inquiry* (Home Office, CM 4262, 1999).

36. Stephen Glover, 'The institutional hysteria dies down', *Spectator* (13 March 1999), pp10–11.

37. 'Blunkett dumps institutional racism', *Guardian* (14 January 2003).

38. 'School anti-racism undermined', *Campaign Against Racism and Fascism*, no. 50 (June/July 1999), p11.

39. Doreen Lawrence, speech at the United Against Racism conference, 22 February 2003, London, organised by the National Assembly Against Racism.

40. House of Commons Home Affairs Committee, *Asylum Removals*, HC 654-I (May 2003), p5.

41. *The End of Parallel Lives? The report of the community cohesion panel* (July 2004), p15.

42. Robert Putnam, 'Diversity, equality and social capital', lecture at Institute of Public Policy Research, London (12 January 2005); Peter Hallberg and Joshua Lund, 'The business of apocalypse: Robert Putnam and diversity', *Race & Class*, vol. 46, no. 4 (April–June 2005), pp53–67.

43. Keighley International Friendship Council, *Developing Closer Racial Harmony Within the Keighley Community* (1965).

44. David Goodhart, *Progressive Nationalism: citizenship and the left* (London, Demos, 2006), p53.

45. A recent influential statement of this position is Geoff Dench, Kate Gavron and Michael Young, *The New East End: kinship, race and conflict* (London, Profile, 2006).

46. Paul Foot, *Immigration and Race in British Politics* (Harmondsworth, Penguin, 1965), p186.

47. When Labour passed its 1968 Commonwealth Immigrants Act, which sought to prevent British citizens of Asian origin from coming to Britain from Kenya, it was defended at the time by Richard Crossman, diarist and cabinet minister in Harold Wilson's government, on the grounds that such measures 'had taken the poison out of politics' and that, had they not been passed, 'Powellism would become the philosophy of the Birmingham area'. A month after writing this diary entry, with the new controls just imposed, Powell delivered his 'rivers of blood' speech. Rather than quelling fears, the 1968 Act had legitimised them. Richard Crossman, *The Diaries of a Cabinet Minster, Vol. Two* (London, Hamish Hamilton and Jonathan Cape, 1976), p689.

48. Peter John, Helen Margetts, David Rowland and Stuart Weir, *The British National Party: the roots of its appeal* (Democratic Audit, Human Rights Centre, University of Essex, 2006).

49. Tony Blair, speech to the Los Angeles World Affairs Council, 1 August 2006, http://www.number10.gov.uk/output/Page9948.asp, last accessed 1 October 2006.

50. An equal exchange between different cultural horizons is a requirement of democratic political communication in a culturally diverse society. This does not imply cultural relativism, either in the sense that different cultures ought to be regarded as equally valid or in the sense that different cultures are incommensurable.

51. Tania Branigan, 'British-born dual nationals could lose citizenship in bill's sanctions', *Guardian* (2 December 2005), p13.

52. Life in the United Kingdom Advisory Group, *Life in the United Kingdom: a journey to citizenship* (Home Office, 2004), p32.

53. See, for example, Caroline Elkins, *Britain's Gulag: the brutal end of empire in Kenya* (London, Jonathan Cape, 2005).

54. Philip Webster, 'Brown calls for an end to guilt over the Empire', *The Times* (15 March 2005), p2.

55. Liz Fekete, 'Enlightened fundamentalism? Immigration, feminism and the Right', *Race & Class*, vol. 48, no. 2 (October–December 2006), pp1–22.

56. Sylvia Walby, *The Cost of Domestic Violence* (Women & Equality Unit, 2004), p30.

57. Amrit Wilson, *Dreams, Questions, Struggles: South Asian women in Britain* (London, Pluto Press, 2006), p64.

58. Hannana Siddiqui, '"It was written in her kismet": forced marriage', in *From HomeBreakers to Jailbreakers: Southall Black Sisters*, edited by Rahila Gupta (London, Zed Books, 2003), p78.

59. Amartya Sen, 'Culture and human rights', in *Development as Freedom* (Oxford, Oxford University Press, 1999).

60. 'Young Muslims and extremism', Foreign and Commonwealth Office and Home Office Paper, 2004, leaked to the *Sunday Times*, July 2005, http://www.timesonline.co.uk/printFriendly/0,,1-523-1688261-523,00.html, last accessed 27 September 2005.

CHAPTER 9: MIGRATION AND THE MARKET-STATE

1. John Steinbeck, *The Grapes of Wrath* (London, Arrow Books, 1998), pp331–2.

2. Charles Leadbeater, *Living on Thin Air: the new economy* (London, Penguin, 2000), p141.

3. Jonathan Freedland, *Bring Home the Revolution: the case for a British republic* (London, Fourth Estate, 2000), p141.

4. Sarah Spencer, ed., *Strangers and Citizens: a positive approach to migrants and refugees* (London, Institute of Public Policy Research/Rivers Oram Press, 1994), p344.

5. Office of National Statistics, *Control of Immigration: statistics, United Kingdom, 2002* (2003), p22.

6. Stephen Glover et al., *Migration: an economic and social analysis*, RDS Occasional Paper No. 67 (Home Office, 2001), p38.
7. *Secure Borders, Safe Haven: integration with diversity in modern Britain* (Home Office, CM 5387, 2002).
8. *Secure Borders, Safe Haven*, p48.
9. *Secure Borders, Safe Haven*, p38.
10. Lydia Morris, *The Control of Rights: the rights of workers and asylum seekers under managed migration*, Immigration Rights Project discussion paper (Joint Council for the Welfare of Immigrants, 2004).
11. *A Points-Based System: making migration work for Britain* (Home Office, March 2006).
12. James Clarke and John Salt, 'Work permits and foreign labour in the UK: a statistical review', *Labour Market Trends* (Office of National Statistics, November 2003), p573.
13. Clarke and Salt, 'Work permits and foreign labour in the UK'.
14. Office of National Statistics, *Control of Immigration*, p18. A British Council study found that foreign students contributed £3 billion annually to the economy in fees and living expenses. Tony Halpin and Christine Buckley, 'Forget Oil – Overseas Students Bring in the Money', *The Times* (21 April 2004), p29.
15. Patrick Hennessy, 'Blair calls for quotas on immigrants from "New Commonwealth"', *Sunday Telegraph* (6 June 2004), p10.
16. Don Pollard, *Gangmaster System in Sussex* (Rural, Agricultural and Allied Workers' Trade Group, Transport and General Workers Union, 2000).
17. *Gone West: Ukrainians at work in the UK* (Trades Union Congress, 2004), p15.
18. Glover et al., *Migration*.
19. Andrew Taylor, 'Poles lead surge in migrant workers', *Financial Times* (22 July 2006), p4.
20. Yara Evans, Joanna Herbert, Kavita Datta, Jon May, Cathy McIlwaine and Jane Wills, *Making the City Work: low paid employment in London* (Queen Mary, University of London, November 2005), pp4–5.
21. *Fair, Effective, Transparent and Trusted: rebuilding confidence in our immigration system* (Home Office, July 2006), p8.
22. House of Commons, *Hansard*, Written Answers (13 September 2004), Column 1408W.
23. Illegal Working Taskforce, *Regulatory Impact Assessment for Immigration, Asylum and Nationality Bill* (June 2005).

CHAPTER 10: HERE TO STAY

1. Quoted in Liza Schuster, 'Asylum and the lessons of history', *Race & Class*, vol. 44, no. 2 (October–December 2002), p48.
2. Interview with author, London, 16 November 2004.
3. Jubilee Action, *Kids Behind Bars, Why We Must Act: a global report into children in prison* (2005).
4. National Coalition of Anti-Deportation Campaigns, *News Service* (25 April 2005).

5. Theodore Trefon, Saskia Van Hoyweghen and Stefan Smis, 'State failure in the Congo: perceptions and realities', *Review of African Political Economy*, vol. 29, no. 93/94 (September/December 2002), p386.

6. Colette Braeckman, 'Congo's abandoned miners', *Le Monde Diplomatique, English Edition* (July 2006), p8.

7. Trefon, Van Hoyweghen and Smis, 'State failure in the Congo', p383.

8. René Lemarchand, 'The tunnel at the end of the light', *Review of African Political Economy*, vol. 29, no. 93/94 (September/December 2002), p394.

9. Ingrid Samset, 'Conflict of interests or interests of conflict? Diamonds and war in the DRC', *Review of African Political Economy*, vol. 29, no. 93/94 (September/December 2002), p469.

10. 'The Congo's transition is failing: crisis in the Kivus', *Africa Report*, no. 91 (30 March 2005, International Crisis Group), p1.

11. Kate Holt and Sarah Hughes, 'Sex and the UN: when peacemakers become predators', *Independent* (11 January 2005).

12. All Party Parliamentary Group on the Great Lakes Region, *The OECD Guidelines for Multinational Enterprises and the DRC* (House of Commons, February 2005), p8.

13. Oxfam, *Foreign Territory: the internationalisation of EU asylum policy* (2005).

14. Jeevan Vasagar, 'Afghan deportees tied up and forced on to planes', *Guardian* (30 April 2003).

15. Liz Fekete, *The Deportation Machine: Europe, asylum and human rights* (Institute of Race Relations, 2005), p27.

16. National Coalition of Anti-Deportation Campaigns, 'Home Office removes Zimbabweans to what Foreign Office say is a human rights "crisis"', *News Service* (27 January 2005).

17. Gary Jones, 'Intruder II', *Daily Mirror* (8 December 2003), p4.

18. 'Asylum Undercover', BBC1, 9pm (2 March 2005).

19. Charlotte Granville-Chapman, Ellie Smith and Neil Moloney, *Harm on Removal: Excessive force against failed asylum seekers* (London, Medical Foundation for the Care of Victims of Torture, 2004).

20. Anne Owers, *Report on an Announced Inspection of Haslar Immigration Removal Centre, 9–14 May 2005* (London, Her Majesty's Inspectorate of Prisons, 2005), p5.

21. *Asylum Statistics: 2nd Quarter 2006* (Home Office, 2006), pp2, 32; Madeleine Watson and Philip Danzelman, *Asylum Statistics United Kingdom 1997* (Home Office, 1998), pp1, 11.

22. *Prison Privatisation Report International* (No. 58, Public Services International Research Unit, University of Greenwich, October 2003); 'Security giant website allegations', *Copenhagen Post* (19 September 2002).

23. Sophie Goodchild and Steve Bloomfield, 'Secret quotas target children for deportation', *Independent* (14 September 2003).

24. Nigel Morris, 'More than 2,000 children of asylum-seekers detained', *Independent* (28 March 2006), p10.

25. Bail for Immigration Detainees, 'Detention of families in the UK: an update' (May 2004); House of Lords, *Hansard* (27 April 2004), Columns 706–7.

26. Diane Taylor and Hugh Muir, 'Restraint of asylum young criticised', *Guardian* (17 January 2005).
27. Press Release, The Monitoring Group (18 March 2005).
28. British Association of Social Workers, *Briefing on the Asylum and Immigration (Treatment of Claimants, etc.) Bill* (18 December 2003).
29. Interviewed by Andrew Neil on *The Daily Politics*, BBC2, 12pm (26 October 2005).
30. Diane Taylor, 'Kurdish girl wins battle to stay in Britain', *Guardian* (2 April 2005).
31. David Blunkett, House of Commons, *Hansard* (24 April 2002), Column 353.
32. *Today*, BBC Radio 4 (24 April 2002).
33. Select Committee on Education and Skills, *Minutes of Evidence*, Examination of Witnesses (9 February 2005), Q533.

CHAPTER 11: THE NEW LEVIATHAN

1. Thomas Hobbes, *Leviathan* (Cambridge, Cambridge University Press, 1996), p120.
2. The name has been changed to preserve anonymity.
3. Hobbes, *Leviathan*, pp120–1.
4. John Stuart Mill, *On Liberty and Other Writings*, edited by Stefan Collini (Cambridge, Cambridge University Press, 1989), p8.
5. *Section 95 Statistics on Race and the Criminal Justice System 2003* (Home Office, 2004); *Section 95 Statistics on Race and the Criminal Justice System 2004* (Home Office, 2005).
6. 'UK: Stop & search: ethnic injustice continues unabated', *Statewatch*, vol. 15, no. 1 (2005), p15.
7. *Section 95 Statistics on Race and the Criminal Justice System 2003*.
8. Oral evidence by Sir John Quinton, Metropolitan Police Authority, to House of Commons Home Affairs Committee (8 July 2004).
9. Lord Carlile of Berriew QC, *Report on the Operation in 2005 of the Terrorism Act 2000* (May 2006), p28.
10. Home Office, http://www.homeoffice.gov.uk/security/terrorism-and-the-law/terrorism-act, last accessed 10 September 2006.
11. Figures supplied by Harmit Athwal, Institute of Race Relations, 1 December 2005.
12. Case details supplied by Harmit Athwal, Institute of Race Relations, 17 March 2005.
13. Gareth Peirce, 'Internment: the truth behind the "war on terror"', Liberty lecture, 15 December 2003, London School of Economics.
14. Liz Fekete, 'Anti-Muslim racism and the European security state', *Race & Class*, vol. 46, no. 1 (July 2004).
15. Joint Committee on Human Rights, *Counter-Terrorism Policy and Human Rights: draft Prevention of Terrorism Act 2005 (continuance in force of sections 1 to 9) order 2006*, Twelfth Report of Session 2005–06, HL paper 122, HC 915, p16.

16. Frances Webber, 'The Human Rights Act: a weapon against racism?', *Race & Class*, vol. 43, no. 2 (October–December 2001), p82; John Upton, 'In the streets of Londonistan', *London Review of Books* (22 January 2004), p7.

17. Upton, 'In the streets of Londonistan', p7.

18. Peirce, 'Internment'.

19. Peirce, 'Internment'.

20. Peirce, 'Internment'.

21. House of Commons Written Ministerial Statements, *Hansard* (12 June 2006), Column 48WS.

22. 'UK: The Prevention of Terrorism Act 2005', *Statewatch*, vol. 15, no. 1 (January–February 2005), pp21–2.

23. Joint Committee on Human Rights, *Counter-Terrorism Policy and Human Rights*, p24.

24. Eliza Manningham-Buller, *Statement to House of Lords* (20 September 2005).

25. Stephen Grey, 'America's gulag', *New Statesman* (17 May 2004), pp22–5.

26. In 1978, UK military and security services were found by the European Court of Human Rights to have practised 'cruel, inhuman and degrading treatment' against terrorist suspects in Northern Ireland. During the 1950s, British colonial authorities attempted to suppress the Mau Mau rebellion by establishing a vast system of detention camps and prison villages in Kenya in which a million and a half people were held. Interrogations known as 'screenings' involved beatings and torture with whips and electric shocks. Tens of thousands, perhaps hundreds of thousands, of these detainees were killed. Yet the episode has largely been erased from Britain's collective memory and the phrase 'Mau Mau' retains the connotation of African savagery that was imparted to it at the time. Caroline Elkins, *Britain's Gulag: the brutal end of empire in Kenya* (London, Jonathan Cape, 2005); Human Rights Watch, *Dangerous Ambivalence: UK policy on torture since 9/11* (November 2006).

27. Home Office, 'Tackling terrorism – behaviours unacceptable in the UK', Press Release (24 August 2005).

28. Tania Branigan, 'British-born dual nationals could lose citizenship in bill's sanctions', *Guardian* (2 December 2005), p13.

29. United Nations Security Council, *Security Council meeting of world leaders calls for legal prohibition of terrorist incitement, enhanced steps to prevent armed conflict, resolutions 1624 (2005), 1625 (2005) adopted unanimously* (14 September 2005), http://www.un.org/News/Press/docs/2005/sc8496.doc.htm, last accessed 1 October 2006.

CHAPTER 12: COMMUNITY: THEIRS AND OURS

1. Shirin Ebadi, *Iran Awakening: from prison to peace prize: one woman's struggle at the crossroads of history* (New York, Random House, 2006), pp215–16. The original quote refers specifically to Iranians.

2. Olivier Roy, *Globalised Islam: the search for a new ummah* (London, Hurst, 2004); Amrit Wilson, *Dreams, Questions, Struggles: South Asian women in Britain* (London, Pluto Press, 2006), pp55, 69.

3. The Jamaat-i Islami is an Islamist political organisation that was established by Abul a'la Maududi in colonial India in 1941. Its ideology of an Islamic state has never won more than minority support in elections in Pakistan or Bangladesh but Maududi's writings have had a strong influence on Islamist politics across the world.

4. Chetan Bhatt, *Hindu Nationalism: origins, ideologies and modern myths* (Oxford, Berg, 2001).

5. Parita Mukta and Chetan Bhatt, eds, 'Hindutva movements in the West: resurgent Hinduism and the politics of diaspora', *Ethnic and Racial Studies*, vol. 23, no. 3 (May 2000).

6. Awaaz-South Asia Watch, *In Bad Faith? British charity and Hindu extremism* (2004).

7. Some argue that the ultimate aim of campaigns against the immigration system should be the total abolition of border controls. But even the most ardent supporters of a 'no borders' position accept that there are occasions when a society, if not a state, is entitled to limit free movement (of colonial settlers, for example). Their objection is to state-controlled borders, rather than to all blocks on free movement, because they believe that state-controlled borders will necessarily involve nationalism, which they tend to equate with racism. The argument is, therefore, not so much about the validity of borders as the validity of states policing them. Steve Cohen, in his *No One is Illegal*, correctly draws out the logic of such a position, which is that the abolition of border controls 'would require the end of the state'. This position is either based on anarchism or on a belief that the state will wither away in the transition to socialism. Those who do not share those starting points will be less persuaded of an absolute rejection of all state-controlled borders and will want to distinguish between racist state borders and the possibility of a state that differentiates between citizens and foreign nationals in a non-racist way (recognition of national differences need not imply chauvinism), while also guaranteeing a core of basic rights for foreign nationals that embody a sense of universal human dignity. Steve Cohen, *No One is Illegal* (Stoke-on-Trent, Trentham Books, 2003), pp264–5.

8. http://www.livingwage.org.uk, last accessed 5 July 2006.

9. Rajeev Dhavan, 'The road to Xanadu: India's quest for secularism', in K. N. Panikkar, ed., *The Concerned Indian's Guide to Communalism* (New Delhi, Viking, 1999).

10. A. Sivanandan, speech to the 'Racism, Liberty and the War on Terror' conference, London, 16 September 2006.

Index